Utopian Drama

Methuen Drama Engage offers original reflections about key practitioners, movements and genres in the fields of modern theatre and performance. Each volume in the series seeks to challenge mainstream critical thought through original and interdisciplinary perspectives on the body of work under examination. By questioning existing critical paradigms, it is hoped that each volume will open up fresh approaches and suggest avenues for further exploration.

Series Editors
Mark Taylor-Batty, University of Leeds, UK
Enoch Brater, University of Michigan, USA

Titles

Crisis, Representation and Resilience: Perspectives on Contemporary British Theatre
Edited by Clare Wallace, Clara Escoda, Enric Monforte and
José Ramón Prado-Pérez
ISBN 978-1-3501-8085-7

Brecht and Post-1990s British Drama
Anja Hartl
ISBN 978-1-3501-7278-4

Performing Arousal: Precarious Bodies and Frames of Representation
Edited by Julie Listengarten and Yana Meerzon
ISBN 978-1-3501-5563-3

A Companion to British-Jewish Theatre Since the 1950s
Edited by Jeanette R. Malkin, Eckart Voigts and Sarah Jane Ablett
ISBN 9781-3501-3596-3

Mediatized Dramaturgy: The Evolution of Plays in the Media Age
Seda Ilter
ISBN 978-1-3500-3115-9

Harold Pinter: Stages, Networks, Collaborations
Edited by Basil Chiasson and Catriona Fallow
ISBN 978-1-3501-3362-4

Drag Histories, Herstories and Hairstories: Drag in a Changing Scene Volume 2
Edited by Mark Edward and Stephen Farrier
ISBN 978-1-3501-0436-5

Contemporary Drag Practices and Performers: Drag in a Changing Scene Volume 1
Edited by Mark Edward and Stephen Farrier
ISBN 978-1-3500-8294-6

The Schaubühne Berlin under Thomas Ostermeier: Reinventing Realism
Edited by Peter M. Boenisch
ISBN 9781-3501-6579-3

Performing the Unstageable: Success, Imagination, Failure
Karen Quigley
ISBN 978-1-3500-5545-2

Drama and Digital Arts Cultures
David Cameron, Michael Anderson and Rebecca Wotzko
ISBN 978-1-472-59219-4

Social and Political Theatre in 21st-Century Britain: Staging Crisis
Vicky Angelaki
ISBN 978-1-474-21316-5

Watching War on the Twenty-First-Century Stage: Spectacles of Conflict
Clare Finburgh
ISBN 978-1-472-59866-0

Fiery Temporalities in Theatre and Performance: The Initiation of History
Maurya Wickstrom
ISBN 978-1-4742-8169-0

For a complete listing, please visit https://www.bloomsbury.com/series/methuen-drama-engage/

Utopian Drama

In Search of a Genre

Siân Adiseshiah

Series Editors

Enoch Brater and Mark Taylor-Batty

methuen | drama

LONDON · NEW YORK · OXFORD · NEW DELHI · SYDNEY

METHUEN DRAMA
Bloomsbury Publishing Plc
50 Bedford Square, London, WC1B 3DP, UK
1385 Broadway, New York, NY 10018, USA
29 Earlsfort Terrace, Dublin 2, Ireland

BLOOMSBURY, METHUEN DRAMA and the Methuen Drama logo
are trademarks of Bloomsbury Publishing Plc

First published in Great Britain 2023
This paperback edition published 2024

Copyright © Siân Adiseshiah, 2023, 2024

Siân Adiseshiah has asserted her right under the Copyright, Designs and
Patents Act, 1988, to be identified as author of this work.

For legal purposes the Acknowledgements on p. x constitute an extension
of this copyright page.

Series design by Louise Dugdale
Cover image © Laura Tate / Alamy

All rights reserved. No part of this publication may be reproduced or transmitted
in any form or by any means, electronic or mechanical, including photocopying,
recording, or any information storage or retrieval system, without prior
permission in writing from the publishers.

Bloomsbury Publishing Plc does not have any control over, or responsibility for,
any third-party websites referred to or in this book. All internet addresses given
in this book were correct at the time of going to press. The author and publisher
regret any inconvenience caused if addresses have changed or sites have
ceased to exist, but can accept no responsibility for any such changes.

A catalogue record for this book is available from the British Library.

Library of Congress Cataloging-in-Publication Data
Names: Adiseshiah, Sian Helen, author.
Title: Utopian drama : in search of a genre / Siân Adiseshiah.
Description: London ; New York : Methuen Drama, 2022. |
Series: Methuen drama engage | Includes bibliographical references and index.
Identifiers: LCCN 2022014180 (print) | LCCN 2022014181 (ebook) |
ISBN 9781474295796 (hardback) | ISBN 9781350349315 (paperback) |
ISBN 9781474295802 (epub) | ISBN 9781474295819 (ebook)
Subjects: LCSH: Utopian plays. | Drama–History and criticism. |
Imaginary places in literature.
Classification: LCC PN1650.U86 A35 2022 (print) |
LCC PN1650.U86 (ebook) | DDC 809.2–dc21
LC record available at https://lccn.loc.gov/2022014180
LC ebook record available at https://lccn.loc.gov/2022014181

ISBN: HB: 978-1-4742-9579-6
PB: 978-1-3503-4931-5
ePDF: 978-1-4742-9581-9
eBook: 978-1-4742-9580-2

Series: Methuen Drama Engage

Typeset by RefineCatch Limited, Bungay, Suffolk

To find out more about our authors and books visit www.bloomsbury.com
and sign up for our newsletters.

For my academic friends Erin Bell, Jacqueline Bolton, Ruth Charnock, Amy Culley, Martin Eve, Rupert Hildyard, Paul Jenner, Louise LePage, Christopher Marlow, and Darren Webb whose friendship and solidarity keep me going in academia

Also, for Charlie and Xanthe (naturally)

Contents

Acknowledgements	x
Introduction: dramaturgies of hope	1
1 Utopia, genre, drama	11
2 Genealogical beginnings: Old Comedy, longing, and laughter	31
3 Temporary utopias of female community	65
4 The enhanced utopian subject	99
5 Utopia and the triumph of ordinary life	129
6 Utopian conversations	159
Epilogue	185
Bibliography	191
Index	213

Acknowledgements

I started contemplating this book around a decade ago. Many scholars, students, librarians, administrative staff, and friends have contributed to my thinking. *Utopian Drama* would not have been completed without two periods of research leave generously granted by the University of Lincoln, where I worked until 2018. There I ran an MA option, 'Writing Utopia and Dystopia', where I was able to explore utopian ideas with excellent postgraduate students over several years. At Loughborough University, where I have worked since, I teach a third-year undergraduate module, 'Better Worlds? Utopian and Dystopian Texts and Contexts', which again, has given me the opportunity to think through multiple ideas explored in the book with highly engaged students. I have also benefited hugely from many fruitful conversations with my wonderful doctoral researchers. I am grateful to have been supported intellectually, emotionally, and practically by an excellent community of academics and students at both Loughborough and Lincoln universities.

Former commissioning editor of Methuen Drama's Engage series, Mark Dudgeon, was present at a paper I delivered on utopian drama at the International Federation of Theatre Research conference in Barcelona in 2015. His enthusiasm and encouragement were decisive in my decision to develop my research on utopian plays into a book project for Methuen Drama, and to expand the historical parameters of the study to include classical Greek theatre. Anna Brewer, who took over Mark's role, has been highly supportive and patient, as the book took quite a bit longer to complete than originally anticipated. I am also grateful to the series editors, Enoch Brater and Mark Taylor-Batty, for their astute and constructive reviews of the book's chapters and the overall manuscript.

My participation in scholarly communities – particularly the Utopian Studies Society, the International Federation of Theatre Research, the Theatre and Performance Research Association, Contemporary Drama in English, and the British Association for Contemporary Literary Studies – has helped enormously in the development of ideas for this book. I have had fruitful conversations with and been supported by numerous scholars, including David Amigoni, Vicky Angelaki, Mireia Aragay, Simon Barker, Erin Bell, Anne-Marie Beller, Katie Beswick, Jacqueline Bolton, Paola Botham, Ruth Charnock, Barbara Cooke, Jennifer Cooke, Amy Culley, Fred Dalmasso, Laurence Davis, Ben Davies, Cristina Delgado-García, Andrew Dix, John Drakakis, Jacqueline

Dutton, Caroline Edwards, Clara Escoda, Clare Finburgh Delijani, Marissia Fragkou, Nick Freeman, Catie Gill, Lynette Goddard, Sam Haddow, Rebecca Hillman, Nicholas Holden, Nadine Holdsworth, Clare Hutton, Maggie Inchley, Brian Jarvis, Chris Megson, Enric Monforte, Martin Middeke, Tom Moylan, Claire O'Callaghan, Adam O'Meara, Mark O'Thomas, Sarah Parker, Nicole Pohl, Alan Read, Sara Read, Catherine Rees, Stephen Regan, Trish Reid, Steve Rice, Lyman Tower Sargent, Graham Saunders, Jonathon Shears, Adam Stock, Darko Suvin, Liz Tomlin, Merle Tönnies, Eckart Voigts, Clare Wallace, Renée Ward, Claire Warden, Tim Waterman, Patricia Waugh, Darren Webb, and Mike Wilson. Thank you to Mojisola Adebayo, who generously shared with me a rehearsal video of *STARS*; to Howard Brenton for granting me a fulsome interview; and to Andy Smith for kindly sharing his work, exchanging ideas, and helping me to sustain my faith in the project. I am especially grateful to Martin Eve, Rupert Hildyard, Elaine Hobby, Paul Jenner, Louise LePage, and Christopher Marlow for reading chapter drafts, and to David Bell with whom I have had many helpful exchanges.

Thank you to my family Kam, Gary, and Havana, and to old comrades and cherished friends Anna Currado, Paul Newnham, Gelly Sinnott, Pete Orton, and to Liz, Shad, Rosa, and Leon Shadforth-Groucutt. This has often felt an impossible project and I would not have been able to finish the book without my anwyliaid Charlie and Xanthe.

Introduction: dramaturgies of hope

In an interview about Red Ladder's adaptation of the novel *The Damned United* (2006) for the stage, its author David Peace responded to the question '[w]hat do you think theatre can do that novels can't?' with the following answer:

> [t]he origins and traditions of storytelling are oral and communal. The novel, written by the individual for the individual, has broken with and nigh-on destroyed that tradition; it is a very isolated and limited art form. The theatre [...] is its very antithesis, and illuminates the possibilities for something more; something communal, something shared. A different way of living.[1]

Theatre moves beyond the private interiority of the novel and speaks directly with audiences in social settings. Theatre has, as playwright Mojisola Adebayo observes, 'a unique power and possibility because it is the art of art forms. All art forms can be part of theatre (music, animation, light, sound, digital arts, circus, literature, dance, poetry, painting, puppetry, sculpture, ritual, film and so on)'.[2] The social dimension of theatre – affectively charged, collective encounters with stories and experiences – makes it a form potentially befitting for staging alternative visions of human life, its organization, and practices. Theatre's particular mix of the sensual, emotional, philosophical, and political, of embodied performances of the hopes and fears of its audience, in an encounter at once baldly public and tenderly intimate, makes it an art form – in theory at least – especially suited to exploring utopian longing and imagining alternative worlds. The collaborative effort of all those involved in the making of theatre (actors, directors, technicians, stage managers, makeup artists, costume directors, marketing, and front of house) offers the potential for a practical rehearsal of a social model of the kind of working together

---

[1] David Peace, 'David Peace: Why I'm Letting Red Ladder Stage *The Damned United*', Interview by Chris Wiegand, *Guardian* (22 October 2014), http://www.theguardian.com/stage/2014/oct/22/david-peace-red-ladder-stage-the-damned-united-brian-clough-theatre

[2] Mojisola Adebayo, Interview, in *Theatre in Times of Crisis: 20 Scenes for the Stage in Troubled Times*, ed. Dom O'Hanlon (London: Bloomsbury Methuen, 2020), 4.

which underpins utopian processes of alternative worldmaking. The ephemerality of utopia (utopia means 'nowhere') maps onto the impermanence of performance. The stage – with its hosting and reshaping of a myriad of stories from different historical moments and contexts – is inflected with a similar transformational capacity of the good place/no-place of utopia. Given this, theatre should be the exemplary form for utopia.

These ideas were the starting point for writing *Utopian Drama*. For many years, I have focused on the utopian potential of drama and the political effects of utopian desire in modern and contemporary theatre.[3] I remain struck by the near absence of attention to drama within the field of Utopian Studies and equally to the neglect of utopian drama within Theatre Studies. I found it surprising when starting this project that there were so few journal articles or book chapters on utopian drama, and not a single book – except for Dragan Klaić's *The Plot of the Future: Utopia and Dystopia in Modern Drama* published in 1991. However, Klaić's study – as the title indicates – attends to (male-authored) utopias *and dystopias*. In fact, dystopian plays occupy most of the book's attention.

Utopian Drama: In Search of a Genre is therefore the first book dedicated to the study of exclusively utopian plays. Motivated by the absence of sustained attention to utopias in dramatic form, my book – as its subtitle signals – seeks to understand why there has been only a smattering of genuinely utopian plays. It proposes that this is beginning to change in the contemporary period. The book is an analysis of the production of work in key historical mo(ve)ments – ancient Greece, early modern, modernism, and the later twentieth and twenty-first centuries. It examines examples of utopian drama from a wide historical span as a way of analysing continuities and discontinuities in themes and conventions over time. As well as attending to the plays' interactions with their various sociopolitical contexts, the book asks what is to be gained by considering utopian plays from different historical periods together. Except for the examples from Greek theatre, the plays analysed here were all published in English and emerge from England, Scotland, Ireland, and the USA. Over forty plays are discussed as utopian, from which eighteen are analysed as utopias and form the object of extended scrutiny.

[3] This interest is present in most of my work. Select examples are: 'Utopian Space in Caryl Churchill's History Plays: *Light Shining in Buckinghamshire* and *Vinegar Tom*', *Utopian Studies* 16.1 (Spring 2005): 3–26; '"We Said We Wouldn't Look Back": Utopia and the Backward Glance in Dorothy Reynolds and Julian Slade's *Salad Days*', *Studies in Musical Theatre* 5.2 (2011): 149–61; '"I just die for some authority!" Barriers to Utopia in Howard Brenton's *Greenland*', *Comparative Drama* 46.1 (Spring 2012): 41–55; 'The Utopian Potential of Aging and Longevity in Bernard Shaw's *Back to Methuselah*', *Age, Culture, Humanities: An Interdisciplinary Journal* 4 (May 2019): https://ageculturehumanities.org/WP/the-utopian-potential-of-ageing-and-longevity-in-bernard-shaws-back-to-methuselah-1921/

This book additionally takes account of the broader literary context for utopian drama. It considers how utopian plays compare with the prose tradition of utopia. Utopian prose narratives are commonly understood to be synonymous with fictional utopias. Hermeneutic frameworks for understanding literary utopias assume the object of scrutiny is the prose utopia. The intellectual scaffolding for utopian literary studies has developed on the basis of prose narrative as its object of study. The field of Utopian Studies is oriented by circumscriptive definitions of utopia that presuppose prose narrative as its fictional application. Interpretative formulations based on generic, thematic, and stylistic conventions of utopian prose underpin methodological approaches to reading utopias and form the field's regulatory parameters. *Utopian Drama* examines the generic, thematic, and stylistic specificities of utopian plays and considers how utopian intellectual frameworks might be affected if we take utopian drama seriously.

Equally the book attempts to make a case within the field of Theatre Studies for the utopian potential of drama. The common claim that drama is not a good form for utopia has prevented the field from developing its own theories and methodologies for making sense of utopian theatre. We need to appreciate the existing transhistorical repertoire of utopian plays and recognize the idiosyncratic advantages of theatre in combining a plurality of sign systems and facilitating a live encounter – experienced intellectually, affectively, and collectively. If we do this, we can begin to celebrate the potential of theatre's capacity to provide an alternative to, what Marc Augé describes as, 'the idea or image of a world without history or future, a world that has arrived, a finished world whose space is closing in on itself for good'.[4] The shared experience of theatre and its foregrounding of human subjects, social relationality, role playing, and power dynamics make possible a distinctively generative experimentation with the utopian imagination.

While utopia has been neglected within Theatre Studies, dystopian drama has had considerably more traction, particularly recently.[5] At its best,

---

[4] Marc Augé, *The Future* (London: Verso, 2015), 42.
[5] There has been a striking increase in contemporary dystopian plays. This prompted a workshop organized by Universität Bielefeld called 'Dystopian/Utopian Theatre in Britain after 2000 and its Political Spaces' (March 2021). This increase is also reflected in Laura Di Simoni's PhD thesis 'Staging the Dark Times: Contemporary Dystopian Theatre in the UK 2000–2019' (Nottingham, 2021), as well as the following publications: Trish Reid, 'The Dystopian Near-future in Contemporary British Drama', *Journal of Contemporary Drama in English* 7.1 (2019): 72–88; Eckart Voigts and Merle Tönnies, 'Posthuman Dystopia: Animal Surrealism and Permanent Crisis in Contemporary British Theatre', *Journal of Contemporary Drama in English* 8.2 (2020): 295–312; and Merle Tönnies, 'The Immobility of Power in British Political Theatre after 2000: Absurdist Dystopias', *Journal of Contemporary Drama in English* 5.1 (2017): 156–72.

dystopian critique defamiliarizes well-worn narratives of the evils of the prevailing system, presenting them afresh, this in turn interrupting feelings of political fatigue and impotence, and functioning as cognitive and affective agitation. Utopian desire for society to be fundamentally different permeates the logic of the most politically acerbic dystopias. However, dystopian cultural production – novels, films, TV, drama – is now everywhere. Fredric Jameson observes 'a marked diminution in the production of new utopias over the last decades (along with an overwhelming increase in all manner of conceivable dystopias, most of which look monotonously alike)'.[6] Mark Bould suggests that as we 'already inhabit the worst of all possible worlds – the one that actually exists – [...] perhaps there is no critique left that dystopia can effect'.[7] Jill Lepore claims dystopia has become 'a fiction of submission [...] of helplessness and hopelessness'.[8] Each of these criticisms holds mainstream fiction and film as its primary targets, their mass commercial appeal an essential factor in their commodification and limp politics. Dystopian drama, a staple of subsidized theatre venues associated with new writing, is, perhaps, less determined by this logic, and there are multiple examples of contemporary work that retain dystopian criticality.[9]

Nevertheless, we need utopia too. As Darren Webb writes, '[u]topian visions liberate the imagination as to the possibilities for change and help to both generate and shape dreams, yearnings and desires'.[10] Utopia interrupts ideological constraints. It encourages us, as Augé observes, 'to pay no attention to the myriad arguments that may be marshalled against it, short of simply regarding them [...] as utterances of the [...] the prevailing system'.[11] Utopia stubbornly refuses social reality and its ideological reproduction, negating the anti-utopian consciousness of common sense. In Thomas More's *Utopia* (1516), Raphael Hythloday, the traveller who returns from the island of Utopia, responds to the scepticism of More (who appears as a character in the

---

[6] Fredric Jameson, 'An American Utopia', in *An American Utopia: Dual Power and the Universal Army*, ed. Slavoj Žižek (London: Verso Books, 2016), 1–96, 1.

[7] Mark Bould, 'Dulltopia: On the Dystopian Impulses of Slow Cinema', *Boston Review* (22 January 2018), https://bostonreview.net/literature-culture-arts-society/mark-bould-dulltopia

[8] Jill Lepore, 'A Golden Age for Dystopian Fiction: What to make of our new literature of radical pessimism', https://www.newyorker.com/magazine/2017/06/05/a-golden-age-for-dystopian-fiction 29 March 2017.

[9] I would include the following as among examples of dystopian plays that sustain a critique of the prevailing system and implicate utopian hope as an essential politics: Caryl Churchill's *Far Away* (2000) and *Escaped Alone* (2016), debbie tucker green's *hang* (2015), Edward Bond's *The Chair Plays* (2012), and Stef Smith's, *Human Animals* (2016).

[10] Darren Webb, 'Critical Pedagogy, Utopia and Political (Dis)Engagement, *Power and Education* 5 (3): 280–90, 286.

[11] Augé, *The Future*, 93.

book) by observing '[y]ou're bound to take that view, for you simply can't imagine what it would be like'.[12] Anti-utopianism conditions language, discourse, ways of knowing and understanding, so that utopian ways of thinking appear as eccentric, absurd, embarrassing, or didactic.

Hence this book's purpose is not motivated solely by an intellectual interest in examining an uncharted area of Theatre Studies and Utopian Studies, but equally by a desire to contribute to a growing number of works – across multiple areas and disciplines – that refuse the anti-utopianism of our times. Transition Town movement founder, Rob Hopkins, claims in his new book that there is a crisis of the imagination resulting from both the macro politics of neoliberalism and more specifically from the narrow, regimented, assessment-driven schooling that reduces opportunities for creativity, play, and imaginative co-production: 'the deeper we get into a crisis such as climate change, the harder it becomes to imagine a way out'.[13] Another example is philosopher, Kate Soper's recent book, *Post-Growth Living: For an Alternative Hedonism*, which hopes to enable a 'new political imaginary' by making the case for the social benefits of anti-growth forms of consumption, opening up 'forms of happiness that people might be able to enjoy were they to opt for an alternative economic order'.[14] Lynne Segal's book *Radical Happiness: Moments of Collective Joy* joins these hopeful voices in its argument for the political potential of happiness, joy, connectedness, and hope, as she rebalances Affect Studies' fascination with negative affects (shame, guilt, trauma, loss, self-hate) and opposes the assumption that positive affect is 'more trivial, less stirring, interesting or memorable than the tragic, and closer to what is seen as dull and coercive normality'.[15]

Hope understood in these works is not naïve optimism but a political position, a praxis combining political commitment with faith in the *potential* of collectivism. Segal refers to 'the exhilarating joy of resistance itself, the sense of shared agency expressed in helping to build any alternative, autonomous spaces, for as long as they might last'.[16] Shared alternative spaces, creativity, play, and co-production – elements constitutive of utopian practice – also proximate the means and methods of theatre and performance. The historic containment of utopian hope in the private space of the novel may explain the awkwardness of presenting embodied utopian visions in public

[12] Thomas More, *Utopia*, trans. Paul Turner (London: Penguin, 2003), 45.
[13] Rob Hopkins, *From What Is to What If: Unleashing the Power of Imagination to Create the Future We Want* (London: Chelsea Green Publishing, 2019), 9.
[14] Kate Soper, *Post-Growth Living: For an Alternative Hedonism* (London: Verso, 2020), 67; 66–7.
[15] Lynne Segal, *Radical Happiness: Moments of Collective Joy* (London: Verso, 2017), 30.
[16] Ibid., 206.

collective spaces, but in multiple ways theatre is the aesthetic form most like utopia. It is a space of social interaction, an opportunity to experiment with subjectivity and social relationality in physical, material, psychological, affective, and performative ways. Theatre is spatially grounded, space part of its presentation, an encounter resonant of the no-place of utopia – a placeless space, ephemeral, social, creative, imaginative – and a forum for dialogue, conversation, and social exchange.

A handful of books within Theatre Studies articulate interests similar to those of *Utopian Drama*. Klaić's *The Plot of the Future*, as mentioned, foregrounds mostly dystopian male-authored drama, paying particular attention to Eastern European playwrights. The book has, as he notes, a 'predictive perspective, which goes from the present toward the future'.[17] Utopias and dystopias are understood in temporal terms, his examples being plays whose setting is the future. My book focuses exclusively on utopian drama from mostly Anglophone countries, and it does not limit its scope to utopian plays that dramatize the future. Some of the plays' utopias are set in the future, some move across different temporalities (including the past), and others are located spatially. *Utopian Drama* also examines work by women and Black playwrights.

Other interventions worth noting are Joanne Tompkins' *Theatre's Heterotopias: Performance and the Cultural Politics of Space* (2014) and Cathy Turner's *Dramaturgy and Architecture: Theatre, Utopia and the Built Environment* (2015). Tompkins examines space (architectural, narrative, imaginative, and imaginary) and the Foucauldian concept of the heterotopia in the context of theatre and performance. Tompkins uses the heterotopia as a lens through which to explore performance space as a way of understanding particular theatrical experiences and contexts. Her case studies include site-specific performances, productions from the National Theatre of Scotland and Shakespeare's Globe, and multimedia performance. Also focused on performance space, Turner's study examines the architectural features of dramaturgy, and considers ways in which theatre and performance have appraised everyday spaces, reflected utopian desires, and made suggestions for the future. Turner explores the history of site-specific postdramatic theatre, finding its influences in the work of the Russian Constructivists, Bauhaus artists, and Situationists, and discusses theatre in British Garden Cities.

Jill Dolan's *Utopia in Performance* (2005) and José Esteban Muñoz's *Cruising Utopia: The Then and There of Queer Futurity* (2009) offer investments in utopian hope similar to my own, but both differ in scope,

---

[17] Dragan Klaić, *The Plot of the Future: Utopia and Dystopia in Modern Drama* (Ann Arbor, MI: University of Michigan Press, 1991), 7.

thematics, and methodology. Dolan analyses a diverse selection of contemporary performances that produce affects facilitative of a utopian form of spectatorship. Her interest is in the potential of performance to prompt utopian feeling in audiences, 'a hopeful feeling of what the world might be like if every moment of our lives were as emotionally voluminous, generous, aesthetically striking, and intersubjectively intense'.[18] She makes a powerful argument for the potential of select performances to inspire a collective form of hope for a better future. Muñoz's study responds to the critique of reproductive futurism dominant within queer studies (as exemplified by Lee Edelman's *No Future: Queer Theory and the Death Drive* [2004]) with a retheorization of queer as utopian: his opening lines are '[q]ueerness is not yet here. Queerness is an ideality. Put another way, we are not yet queer'.[19] He analyses a selection of aesthetic works from different historical moments that range across writing, theatre, performance, film, dance, and nightlife, and include acts of political protest and public sex. Drawing on ideas of queer temporality in conversation with a Blochian notion of critical hope, Muñoz traces the possibility of a queer collectivity.

Central to the approach of *Utopian Drama* is a focus on ways in which utopia is rendered distinctively in drama. This involves consideration of the specificity of drama as both form and practice, as well as a comparative discussion of prose utopias where this sheds light on the particularity of the plays in question. I establish generic and thematic links among examples of utopian theatre across key historical moments of dramatic production and consider the advantages and disadvantages of constructing a genealogy of utopian drama. In particular, I reflect on the implications of the genres within which dramatic utopias emerge, and consider the consequences of examining this body of work together. The book's scrutiny of generic development takes account of the historical contingency of genre, appraising the political character and function of utopian drama with reference to the socio-historical conditions within which it arises. The book endeavours to bring fresh attention to overlooked plays and reposition utopian drama in new contexts, producing original readings, transhistorical links, and as a result, formulating a new basis upon which further research into utopian drama can be generated.

Equally important is the book's engagement with utopian theory. *Utopian Drama* works within and between a variety of conceptualizations of utopia (as process, method, and system) to think through the implications of

---

[18] Jill Dolan, *Utopia in Performance: Finding Hope at the Theater* (Ann Arbor, MI: University of Michigan Press, 2005), 5.
[19] José Esteban Muñoz, *Cruising Utopia: The Then and There of Queer Futurity* (New York and London: New York University Press, 2019, revised edition), 1.

dramatizing utopia in a range of forms and styles. As part of this, the book establishes the ways in which utopian drama has functioned as political theatre. It assesses the political significance of utopian drama, paying particular attention to the ways in which the plays selected for analysis articulate different forms of political desire, political agency, and political transgression. The book considers for utopian drama, the tendency of utopian aesthetics to defamiliarize the non-utopian world, thus making visible the dysfunctions, inequalities, and injustices of the social context within which the utopian work is produced. I also contextualize historically the utopian aesthetics at work in the case studies offering an analysis of how utopian drama emerges from and responds to a particular set of socio-historical circumstances. In this way, the book's focus on genre, genre development and genre mutation, is inflected with a sensitivity to the socio-historical contexts within which this narrative occurs. As such, the intertwining of genre, socio-historical conditions, and the political, forms an interconnecting interplay across the chapters.

Utopian Drama's extensive historical timespan and wide variety of work thus coheres around a consistent interest in utopian concepts and themes, generic considerations, and an assessment of the political content and context of each utopian play. There is not (yet) a recognized tradition, genre, category, or grouping of utopian drama, but there are multiple plays that imagine full utopias in dramatic form. This book aims to capture this fascinating body of work and to establish utopian drama as a helpful descriptor of a collection of plays that dramatize utopia. Chapter 1 provides an introductory overview of utopian themes and concepts, where they have a bearing on a discussion of drama. It engages with definitional debates in Utopian Studies scholarship and provides coverage of some key theoretical areas of utopian thinking, especially where these relate to a discussion of drama and performance. It pays particular attention to the formal distinctiveness of drama (*contra* prose narrative) in terms of its facilitation of utopian worlds. The chapter also seeks to understand the generic inheritances of utopian drama, and how the difference in generic identity of utopian plays (compared with prose narrative) impacts on the development of utopian drama across the centuries. It also considers the implications of utopian drama's distinctive deployment of temporality, use of fantasy, fate, and the supernatural, as well as individual and collective forms of identity and political agency.

The earliest example of utopia in the European theatrical tradition is the Old Comedy of Aristophanes, particularly *The Birds* (414 BCE) and *The Assemblywomen or Women Seize the Reins* (391 BCE), and these – along with other fragments of Old Comic plays (including Crates' *Wild Beasts* and Metagenes' *Thurio-Persians*) – are the subjects of Chapter 2. Against the common view that More's prose fiction is the first fictional utopia, I suggest that *The Birds* is in fact the first full, surviving fictional utopia we know of in Western literature. The chapter discusses utopian thinking in this period with specific attention to Homer's *The Odyssey* and *Iliad*, Hesiod's *Works and Days*, Plato's *The Republic* and *Laws*, and Aristotle's *Politics*. In these works, utopia is often expressed either in terms of rational planning or satisfaction of the senses. Significantly for this book, these usually discrete utopian modes appear in utopian drama as intertwined. The chapter also offers an extended consideration of characteristics of Old Comedy, its suitability as a form for utopian expression, and the implications of its neglect within scholarly accounts of utopianism.

The book then moves to the next significant time of utopian cultural production – the early modern period. Margaret Cavendish wrote a trilogy of utopian plays almost 150 years after More's *Utopia*: *The Female Academy* (1662), *Bell in Campo* (1662) and *The Convent of Pleasure* (1668), and these form the subject of Chapter 3. This chapter contextualizes Cavendish's work with reference to the flourishing of early modern utopias (including those by Tomasso Campanella, Francis Bacon, and Francis Godwin) and plays with utopian themes, such as Shakespeare's *The Tempest* (1611) and Aphra Behn's *The Emperor of the Moon* (1687). Women's community, feminine sociability, the affective relations of friendship and the communal sharing of good food, pleasant music, and dancing (all privileged in Cavendish's trilogy but especially so in *The Convent of Pleasure*), offer a cheering antidote to the more cerebral and ascetic society imagined by More, and foreshadow the importance of utopian sensuality and sensibility in twentieth-century critical feminist utopias. Like Aristophanes' utopian worlds, Cavendish's utopias are proximate to the here and now of the non-utopian present. They are presented as heterotopic, liminal spaces of countercultural community. Individual will, effort, and agency are prized in Cavendish's plays, but equally so are female community, an aggregation of minds and bodies in the pursuit of pleasure, liberty, independence, and enlightenment.

Chapter 4 focuses on George Bernard Shaw's utopian plays: *Back to Methuselah* (1921), *The Simpleton of the Unexpected Isles* (1934) and *Farfetched Fables* (1950), the first and last of these offering full utopias in dramatic form. Again, as with other utopian plays discussed in this book, they draw on the prose tradition focused on More but move creatively beyond that frame, particularly in their mixing of science fiction (sf) and fantasy, and human will and theological thinking. The potential of human agency – present in Aristophanes and Cavendish – re-emerges in Shaw's plays in the form of an enhanced human. His plays offer extended scrutiny of human potential to make and sustain a new utopian society, this enabled through extreme longevity, which is made possible by Creative Evolution, a theory to which Shaw subscribed. Shaw's utopias smash temporal boundaries. In a utopian vision of epic proportions, his plays look both backwards to mythical origins and into the future, far beyond current horizons.

Howard Brenton's trilogy of utopian plays *Sore Throats* (1978), *Bloody Poetry* (1984) and *Greenland* (1988) form the subject of Chapter 5. In contrast to Shaw's superhumans, Brenton's utopians are unremarkable. They enjoy simple forms of living: an unhurried and gentle approach to life. These are rare examples of utopian plays (or any form of utopian literature) during the Thatcher years. *Greenland* is in part an *homage* to William Morris's utopian novel *News from Nowhere* (1890), but it is equally inspired by the anarcho-libertarian forms of socialism of the 1960s counterculture. Indeed, the ideas of the Situationist International and Guy Debord's *The Society of the Spectacle* (1967) in particular, provide a lens through which Brenton's vision of utopian life beyond the capitalist spectacle – the triumph of ordinary life – is effectively illuminated.

Chapter 6 reflects on the prevalence of dystopian and post-apocalyptic cultural production in the contemporary period, and seeks out examples of utopian drama amidst the domination of an aesthetics of despair. Utopian plays across history have been sporadic and exceptional, awkward, and self-conscious, but in the present moment, I suggest, this might be changing. I examine work by Claire MacDonald, Cesi Davidson, and Mojisola Adebayo as examples of utopian drama, and as theatre that combines postdramatic aesthetics with a reworking of the Morean literary utopia. More's dialogic structure is reframed in contemporary work: the socio-structural format of the conversation becomes the primary means for creating utopian drama. This theatre ceases trying to depict utopian worlds, instead crafting political conversations that work hard to discover ways of keeping alternative futures as genuinely possible.

Utopian Drama examines an eclectic range of work across a vast period of history. Its Epilogue offers some provisional synthesis of the various strands of thinking by reflecting on the continuities and discontinuities of utopian traits and generic characteristics over time. It draws out some of the thematic preoccupations of utopian plays across the centuries, and considers the implications of drama's distinctive handling of them. The book aims to offer useful thinking about the presence of utopia, utopianism, and hope in drama across time. It also intends to put pressure on current frameworks for understanding fictional utopias. I hope the book contributes new critical perspectives for engaging with utopian plays, which will enable further development of work on utopian drama both from the past and the future.

1

Utopia, genre, drama

Introduction

Why is it that utopia has been so richly imagined in prose narrative but appears not to have been in drama? A tradition of utopian narrative has taken root in literary fiction and developed over six centuries as a recognizable form, but in the theatre, utopia is scarcely acknowledged – despite, I would propose, the first utopias appearing fully formed in drama (in Classical Greek comedy) – slightly earlier than the often-cited first example in discursive prose, Plato's *Republic*. One answer might be that if utopia is the 'not yet' of a better world, a world beyond existing socio-economic, discursive, and psychological borders, a world surpassing ideological delimitation, how could it take the form of embodied presence on stage, and yet, simultaneously, articulate such other-worldly promise? The 'cognitive estrangement' Darko Suvin considers essential to science fictional attempts to precipitate a fresh politicized attention to the familiar is, perhaps, easier to render in the more abstract semiotics of writing, than in embodied performance (although strikingly, Suvin's concept is substantially indebted to Bertolt Brecht's *Verfremdungseffekt*).[1]

A second answer might relate to the essentially demonstrable and descriptive character of the utopian form as developed in prose at least up until the twentieth century. Utopian narrative fiction, particularly in its classic form, includes extensive description of the utopian society. The description is expressed through a dialogic exchange: it usually takes the form of a visitor to utopia, who returns to the non-utopian world, and recounts to other characters and the reader an outline of the utopia's economic, political, and social structures; or, it takes the form of a dialogue between the utopian citizen and the visitor to utopia, from which details of the utopian society are gradually revealed. Long, detailed descriptions in prose of the workings of the utopian society are not easily translatable into dramatic performance. A third, related, answer emerges from common

---

[1] Darko Suvin, *Metamorphosis of Science Fiction: On the Poetics and History of a Literary Genre* (New Haven and London: Yale University Press, 1979).

assumptions about what makes good drama and what characterizes a utopia. Dragan Klaić cites an often-repeated claim that 'Utopia is, by its very nature, without conflict – a state of stasis, harmony, and balance. These are not ingredients for exciting theatre, which is always based on conflict, opposition, and contradiction, or at least tension'.[2] I do not follow Klaić's definition of utopia or drama and will return to interrogate his claim, and other aspects of this challenge, more fully, later in this chapter, but his perspective – a familiar view – helps explain the historic neglect of the utopian form within mainstream drama and its institutions.

I explore these key questions in this chapter by providing an introductory overview of some of the central themes within the field of Utopian Studies, especially where these have a bearing on drama. In particular, this involves engaging with thorny definitional debates on what constitutes a utopia: how is utopia defined? What is its content, form, and function? I pursue the question of genre by establishing the generic contexts of literary and dramatic utopias, and by asking, within which generic classifications have prose fictional and dramatic utopias emerged? Why might examination of the generic specificities of prose fictional and dramatic utopias be relevant for understanding what is at stake in searching for a genre of utopian drama? A primary aim for this chapter is to establish the central concepts, themes, and approaches for the rest of this book.

Utopia

The short, much overused word – utopia – has spawned a complicated but generative and ongoing debate on its meaning. Is it an ideal or real place? Can it refer to an actual community living a better life on the edges, or in the interstices, of existing society? Or is utopia a nowhere, a no-place? Is it an impossible dream or fantasy? Does the pursuit of utopian ideas inevitably result in an oppressive society?[3] Should the focus be less on content and form, and more on function? If so, is utopia's significance its power to inspire fundamental change, rather than provide a blueprint of a predetermined new world? Should it be defined more loosely as the expression of desire for a better world? Must its fictional application be narrative prose? Could it take the form of philosophy, architecture, painting, sculpture, film, music, poetry, or indeed drama?

---

[2] Dragan Klaić, 'Utopia Sustained', *Theater* 26.1–2 (1995): 60–9, 61.
[3] See Karl Popper, *The Open Society and Its Enemies*, rev. edn (Princeton, NJ: Princeton University Press, 1950); John Gray, *Black Mass: Apocalypse, Religion and the Death of Utopia* (London: Allen Lane, 2007).

This dizzying range of questions emerge partly from an ambiguity contained within the origins of the word, utopia, coined by Thomas More in his work *Utopia* (1516). More's coinage combines *topos* – Greek for 'place' – and *ou* – Greek for 'no'. He adds a further linguistic element by using the Latin spelling *u*. The sound 'u' puns the first syllable of the Greek word *eutopia*, which means 'the good place'. Hence, the slippage of translation combined with the no-place/good place pun, has famously captured a curious oscillation of meaning that frames the development of a rich landscape of utopian depictions and a dynamic body of utopian thought. The semantic shift within and between concepts of the good and theories of place (or placelessness) arising from utopia's etymological context, have expanded its capacity to speak to what seems to be a human propensity to desire a better world and widened the range of articulations of this desire.

This debate is only partly meaningful by way of reference to the etymology of the word utopia for it must also be understood as explicitly political terrain. Utopian envisioning of a fundamentally different, and better, society is simultaneously a radical negation of the prevailing system. Utopian refusal of, rather than negotiation with, the status quo is unacceptable to both proponents of capitalism and capitalism's detractors whose critique is limited to negotiation and modification of its most harmful effects. The post-capitalist imaginary has suffered an unfortunate alignment with the oppressive regimes operative under the Soviet bloc in the mid- to late twentieth century, and the association of those regimes with utopianism continues to condition conceptualizations of utopia. Conflation of total systemic change with totalitarian oppression remains a currency – even within the field of Utopian Studies. The fall of the Berlin Wall, the rise of the new Right and the ascendancy of neoliberalism in the late twentieth and twenty-first centuries form the context for utopia's retreat into hiding with appearances limited to micro-utopian moments, dystopian critique, or, more recently in rehabilitated, appropriated forms that demonstrate no serious systemic threat.[4] Nevertheless, as suggested in my introduction, there has, in recent years, been a number of high-profile counterhegemonic interventions that insist on a radically transformative politics. Subversive possibilities of utopia continue to motivate anti-capitalist thinking and politics.

---

[4] For an extended discussion of this, see Laurence Davis, ed., 'The Domestication of Utopia', Special Issue, *Mediazoni* 27 (2020), http://www.mediazioni.sitlec.unibo.it/index.php/no-27-2020/120-dossier-the-domestication-of-utopia/401-introduction-special-issue-on-the-domestication-of-utopia.html For an example of a recent book that identifies small glimpses of utopian possibility in otherwise realist literary fiction of the twenty-first century, see Caroline Edwards, *Utopia and the Contemporary British Novel* (Cambridge: Cambridge University Press, 2019).

Like Darren Webb, I value the political potential of the 'holistic utopia' with the 'potent pedagogical effects' of 'defamiliarising the familiar, familiarising the strange, liberating the imagination from the constraints of common sense, throwing up new solutions to pressing contemporary problems, generating new patterns of desire, and catalysing change'.[5] I also support a more expansive understanding of the literary utopia than is commonly the case. *Utopian Drama* presses at the edges of definitional boundaries circumscribed by mainstream utopian scholarship. For example, utopian scholar Krishan Kumar claims:

> Utopia [...] is first and foremost a work of imaginative fiction in which, unlike other such works, the central subject is the good society. This distinguishes it at the same time from other treatments of the good society, whether in myths of a Golden Age, beliefs in a coming millennium, or philosophical speculation on the ideal city. Fictive elements no doubt have their part to play in these modes but in none of them is narrative fiction, as in the utopia, the defining form.[6]

Kumar restricts utopia to a particular aesthetic form, to 'narrative fiction', and places further limits by proposing that it first appears 'at a certain point in history, within a certain intellectual and cultural tradition'.[7] He means More's *Utopia*, which he sees as 'different from anything that had appeared before in the classical or Christian world' and 'different from anything we find in the non-Western world'.[8] Fátima Vieira's boundaries are looser: she recognizes 'the literary form as just one of the possible manifestations of utopian thought', and acknowledges that 'More did not invent utopianism, which has at its core the desire for a better life'.[9] She appreciates the utopian significance of the cultural production of ancient Greece, the myth of the Golden Age, Christian narratives of the afterlife, and the medieval myth of the Land of Cockaigne, but ultimately prioritizes More's *Utopia* as in some way foundational: 'More's concept of utopia [...] differs from all the previous

---

[5] Darren Webb, 'Critical Pedagogy, Utopia and Political (Dis)Engagement', *Power and Education* 5.3 (2013): 280–90, 286.
[6] Krishan Kumar, *Utopianism* (Milton Keynes: Open University Press, 1991), 27.
[7] Ibid.
[8] Ibid., 33; Fredric Jameson also considers utopias to be 'by-products of Western modernity', *Archaeologies of the Future: The Desire Called Utopia and Other Science Fictions* (London: Verso, 2005), 11. David Harvey recognizes the significance of Plato for More, and notes that Homer's *Odyssey* has 'many of the characteristics later alluded to by More'. *Spaces of Hope* (Edinburgh: Edinburgh University Press, 2000), 156.
[9] Fátima Vieira, 'The Concept of Utopia', in *The Cambridge Companion to Utopian Literature*, ed. Gregory Claeys (Cambridge: Cambridge University Press, 2010), 3–27; 7; 6.

crystallizations of the utopian desire; these can in fact be seen as prefigurations, as they lack the tension between the affirmation of a possibility and the negation of its fulfilment'.[10] Lucy Sargisson takes issue with limiting utopia by form ('Utopias are expressed in many forms') and treating More's *Utopia* as the model; in fact she refers to the medieval Land of Cockaigne's subversive qualities, its '(playful?) engagement in contemporary political debates' as 'one lasting feature of utopianism that can actually be considered a "utopian convention" or ingredient of utopian expression'.[11]

In a much-cited essay within utopian scholarship, 'The Three Faces of Utopianism Revisited', Lyman Tower Sargent establishes elastic designatory terms: for example, utopian literature is a subset of utopia, not its definition. Yet he defines utopia as 'a non-existent society described in considerable detail and normally located in time and space'.[12] That Sargent makes detailed description a defining quality has the effect of limiting the literary utopia to prose fiction rather than allowing for dramatic or poetic forms.[13] J. Max Patrick also prioritizes the descriptive mode in his definition: '[a] utopia should describe in a variety of aspects and with some consistency an imaginary state or society which is regarded as better, in some respects at least, than the one in which its author lives'.[14] Expectation of detailed description of the utopian world is not uncommon. Yet detailed description appears not to be consistently insisted upon, even by Sargent. A decade after 'The Three Faces of Utopianism Revisited', in 'What is Utopia?', Sargent modifies his definition: 'there are two central aspects of a utopia, both of which must be there. First, the society described must not exist; second, the author must in some way evaluate that society'.[15] The writerly practice of description in this later definition – while still present in modified form – is no longer such a priority. However, the introduction of author evaluation has significant implications.

Sargent himself recognizes the complications of introducing authorial intention into the definitional apparatus. Besides the question of the

---

[10] Ibid., 6.
[11] Lucy Sargisson, *Contemporary Feminist Utopianism* (London: Routledge, 1996), 13; 18.
[12] Lyman Tower Sargent, 'The Three Faces of Utopianism Revisited', *Utopian Studies* 5 (1994): 1–37, 9.
[13] Although Sargent includes some plays in his online bibliography of utopia, 'Utopian Literature in English: An Annotated Bibliography From 1516 to the Present' http://openpublishing.psu.edu/utopia/
[14] J. Max Patrick, 'Introduction', in 'Utopias and Dystopias, 1500–1750', comp. R. W. Gibson and J. Max Patrick, Section IX of *St. Thomas More: A Preliminary Bibliography of His Works and of Moreana to the Year 1750*, comp. R. W. Gibson (New Haven, CT: Yale University Press, 1961), 293.
[15] Sargent, 'What is a Utopia?', *Morus: Utopia e Renascimento*: 2 (2005): 153–60, 157.

intentional fallacy, utopian literature, as Sargisson has noted, often contains playfulness. There is a deliberate troubling of the earnest register of the utopian narrative with comic conceits. In More's *Utopia* the Greek surname of the visitor to Utopia, Raphael Hythloday, translates as a 'dispenser of nonsense', whilst his first name evokes the Archangel in the Book of Tobit and patron saint of travellers. The river Anydrus means 'not water', and the title of a chief magistrate Ademus translates as 'not people'. In his introduction to *Utopia*, Paul Turner adds 'joker' to More's roles of saint, martyr, and political thinker, which in turn enables More to pursue 'his apparent habit of dodging about behind a smoke-screen of humour'.[16] The difficulty of establishing authorial intention in utopian literature also extends to the more consequential issue – at least for the significance of utopia's ideological effects – which is its reception. While there is a consensus on the broad political outlooks of some utopian texts (such as the industrial state socialism of Edward Bellamy's *Looking Backward* [1888] or the pastoral communism of William Morris's *News from Nowhere* [1890] – perhaps in these cases because dystopia had, as Kumar says, split from utopian fiction and developed its own subgenre[17]), there is not a consensus over the political messages of others. More's *Utopia* is a case in point, and novels such as Aldous Huxley's *Brave New World* (1932) and B. F. Skinner's *Walden Two* (1948) have been interpreted in opposite ways to the stated intentions of their authors (the former interpreted incorrectly as a utopia, the latter as dystopia). While these apparent misreadings may be rare, utopian texts – like all genres of literature – have generated much discussion and debate on hermeneutical issues: for example, is Charlotte Perkins Gilman's *Herland* (1915) an ahead-of-its-time radical critique of the social construction of gender, or an essentialist alignment of female personhood with maternal feeling? It is probably both, and an ambiguity of political meaning adds richness to the reading experience and the development of utopian thinking.

Marxist geographer David Harvey identifies a dialectic at the heart of fictional utopias, which involves the simultaneous construction of a socially harmonious stable society made possible by some form of authority and order, at the same time as the utopia expressing and being expressive of 'imaginative free play'.[18] Indeed it is this authoritarian aspect of utopias that has led to a common perspective among critics of utopia that utopian schematizing inevitably leads to totalitarianism. This prompts Harvey's

---

[16] Paul Turner, 'Introduction', in Thomas More, *Utopia* (London: Penguin, 2003), xi–xxiv; xiv.
[17] Kumar, *Utopianism*, 26.
[18] Harvey, *Spaces of Hope*, 163.

speculation that in constructing real utopias (as opposed to fictional ones), '[p]erhaps Utopia can never be realized without destroying itself'.[19] However, in fictional form, a dialectical effect becomes a generative possibility. As Jameson states, what is important is not 'judgment on the individual work in question so much as [...] its capacity to generate new ones, Utopian visions that include those of the past, and modify or correct them'.[20] So the process and function of utopian imaginative art is important in this formulation: the act of producing social alternatives incites further imaginative acts, and in the process, keeps the possibility of engaging with new and different ways of living alive.

Similarly, Ruth Levitas insists that 'utopia cannot be understood as a political blueprint'.[21] Indeed, challenging the idea of utopia as blueprint is commonly espoused in utopian scholarship. As part of this espousal, a familiar narrative within the field of Utopian Studies (exemplified by Tom Moylan) converges around the view that the literary characteristics of classic utopian fiction, from More to Morris – including extensive description of the utopian world; the construction of a static, hermetically-sealed society; and the expression of a single, confident vision of a non-conflicted good place – were rethought and revised in post-1960s 'critical' utopian fiction.[22] Ursula Le Guin's *The Dispossessed* (1974) was subtitled 'an ambiguous utopia' and in that novel, Urras, Le Guin's anarchist-inspired utopian world, is simultaneously a place of scarcity and not immune from conflict. In Marge Piercy's *Woman on the Edge of Time* (1976) the visitor to utopia, Connie Ramos, moves in and out of a more permeable utopian space, influencing as well as being influenced by the utopian society of Mattapoisett. Joanna Russ's *The Female Man* (1975) presents utopia as contingent and precarious through brief experimental snippets of comic narrative rather than long descriptive passages. In these critical utopias, utopia is not a static, totalizing blueprint but an exploratory and self-critical, although still hope-bearing, experimental fiction. Levitas observes that '[i]n the critical utopia, the traveller is both more developed as a character and more central to the action of the novel; the active human subject is emphasised both in the structure of the novel and in the process of transformations from old society to new, and both worlds are backgrounds to the development of character and plot'.[23] It is significant that the critical

---

[19] Ibid., 167.
[20] Jameson, *Archaeologies of the Future*, xv.
[21] Ruth Levitas, 'Preface to the Student Edition', *The Concept of Utopia* (Oxford: Peter Lang, 2011), ix–xv, xiv.
[22] Tom Moylan, *Demand the Impossible: Science Fiction and the Utopian Imagination*, ed. Raffaella Baccolini (Oxford: Peter Lang, 2014).
[23] Levitas, *The Concept of Utopia*, 198.

utopia's incorporation of conflict, provisionality, and contingency into its fictional space – combined with a much greater attention to character, agency, and plot – makes it more compatible with the mechanisms of drama, a point to which I will return towards the end of this chapter.

Yet this account of the development of utopian fiction – from blueprint utopias to open-ended, deconstructive narratives – overstates (a little at least) the stagnant, earnest, and totalizing characteristics of the former. After all, More's *Utopia*, as I have said, employs satirical, deconstructive aspects. Other utopian novels demonstrate similar qualities: for example, H. G. Wells' *A Modern Utopia* (1905) anticipates Le Guin's work in its departure from what Wells calls 'perfect and static States' to a 'kinetic' utopia and Morris' *News from Nowhere* employs comic conceits (the obsolete Houses of Parliament in his utopia are used as a manure store).[24] While there is stasis, long passages of description, and a sincere utopian register in classic utopian fiction less suited to drama, there are also playful, deconstructive, satirical, and self-reflexive features. Hence, while utopian narrative fiction has always recognized the difficulty of being taken seriously in arguing sincerely for readerly consideration of a radically different society in fictional form and has shown this recognition in a limited inclusion of comic conceits, moments of irony, and self-reflective jokes, these latter elements have become much more pervasive features as the utopian novel has developed. Russ's *The Female Man* exemplifies this with its comic utopian character Janet Evason who has violent outbursts, a penchant for big bottoms, and is considered unremarkable by her fellow utopians (Janet was sent from the utopian society of Whileaway to earth because her utopian comrades could easily spare her).[25] What is striking about utopian drama is that this comic aspect has not been limited to the margins of the form or only emerged in the recent period, but has instead formed its central aesthetic mode from its inception in Greek Old Comedy through to contemporary work.

Genre

As I have said, utopia's home in the arts is conventionally located in prose fiction, starting with what is often considered the foundational text, More's *Utopia*. A literary prose tradition of utopianism is traced from More, through Francis Bacon and Tommaso Campanella and peaks in the late nineteenth century with the trilogy of utopian classics: Edward Bellamy's *Looking*

---

[24] H. G. Wells, *A Modern Utopia* (London: Penguin, 2005), 11.
[25] Joanna Russ, *The Female Man* (New York: Bantam Books, 1975), 34.

Backward, William Morris's *New from Nowhere*, and H. G. Wells' *A Modern Utopia*. Dystopias dominate the early to mid-twentieth century with Yevgeny Zamyatin's *We* (1921), Aldous Huxley's *Brave New World*, Katharine Burdekin's *Swastika Night* (1937), and culminate in George Orwell's *Nineteen Eighty-Four* (1949). The 1970s revival in utopian fiction – in the form of the critical utopia – included the depiction of dynamic feminist utopian spaces that were more provisional, unstable, and in process than had been imagined in previous utopian fictions. Contemporary utopian and dystopian fiction of the late twentieth and twenty-first centuries resides predominantly in the genre of science fiction – for example in the work of Kim Stanley Robinson, Margaret Atwood, and Brian Aldiss, and in the twenty-first century explosion of young adult speculative fiction. The genealogical development of the genre of utopian fiction is well established and has served effectively as a contextual framework for appreciating contributions of individual utopian novels.

However, the novel's ubiquity in scholarly discussion of the literary utopia has had the unfortunate effect of obscuring other literary and cultural forms, along with neglect of the cross-fertilization that emerged from the novel's relationship with other forms. Jameson reflects this tendency in his observation that a distinction of utopian fiction is self-conscious dialogue identifiable across the canon of utopian prose narratives: 'what uniquely characterizes this genre is its explicit intertextuality: few other literary forms have so brazenly affirmed themselves as argument and counterargument'.[26] An exclusive focus on the diachronic development of the utopian novel at the expense of its encounter with other forms has been reinforced by theorists of the novel, such as Mikhail Bakhtin, who argues that the novel 'gets on poorly with other genres', and that other genres, such as dramatic naturalism, take on a novelization of style.[27] Whilst developments in the novel undoubtedly impacted the progress of drama, this was not without reciprocation. Not enough attention has been paid to influences in the other direction: for example, the comic and satirical are undoubtedly important elements of utopian fiction, and these are influences from Old Comic drama, I would suggest.

To engage substantially with the literary utopia's relationship with the complications of generic categorization would be a different book: fundamentally I am concerned here with identifying prominent and explicit examples of utopian drama in the Western dramatic tradition, ascertaining their political-historical significance as utopian texts, and evaluating them together as a genre. Given my preference for a broader definition, some

---

[26] Jameson, *Archaeologies of the Future*, 2.
[27] Mikhail Bakhtin, 'Epic and Novel: Toward a Methodology for the Study of the Novel', *Modern Genre Theory*, ed. David Duff (Essex: Longman, 2000), 71.

clarification of the way I am thinking about genre should prove useful. Aristotle's tripartite generic division of epic, lyric, and drama, whilst reframed more commonly in modernity as the three distinct *forms* (rather than genres) of poetry, fiction, and drama, is still relevant here, particularly as I reframe utopias in this book as first emerging fully formed in drama rather than in epic. Post-Aristotelian rethinking of genre as 'types' of text that exist mostly within, but sometimes across, the three forms of literature to include such common 'kinds' as tragedy, comedy, satire, lyric, novel, biography, and the essay, provides a further complication for placing the literary utopia. Utopia emerges in two apparently discrete traditions: in comic, satirical drama in ancient Greece, and in prose fiction in sixteenth-century Europe (but with an indebtedness to Plato's *Republic*). Utopian prose narrative additionally cross-hatches from travel writing, political treatise, and epistolary writing. Scholarly positioning of prose as the original home of the literary utopia in Western Europe has meant a disregard of the early Old Comic utopian dramas as, somehow, not properly utopian. It has also meant a neglect of influence across forms.

If, as I am proposing in this book, utopia first emerges fully formed in classical Greek comedy, it is instructive to note what is significant about utopian drama's affinity with comedy. Whilst travel writing/philosophical treatise/epistolary/essay/realist novel (all present in utopian prose fiction) combine to facilitate an earnest, rhetorical register, one equipped to demonstrate to the reader the advantages of the strange new utopian society, comedy might be an unstable medium for such a didactic message. This is not to suggest that comedy is inherently subversive; classical, neoclassical, and modern and contemporary comedy have often performed the function of social and political reconciliation. Yet, there are self-aware, deconstructive, troublesome, tricksy, humorous features in comedy that press against this ideological function, particularly, though not exclusively, in Attic comedy. Ian C. Storey observes that while '[t]ragedy always preserves the dramatic illusion, comedy does all it can to remind the spectators that they are spectators'.[28] That utopian drama uses a comic form of address creates a mode of attention open to criticality, festivity, revelry, buffoonery, or romance, which is different from that produced by the more serious reading position set up by utopian prose. Utopian prose provides a compensatory realism, an attempt at plausibility to make up for the profound differences of the utopian scheme, whereas utopian drama dwells in the radical instability of the comic, often making no attempt whatsoever to convince spectators that the utopian representation is real.

---

[28] Ian C. Storey, *Fragments of Old Comedy* Vol.1 (Cambridge, MA: Harvard University Press, 2011), 51.

The radical instability of comic drama undermines its utopian articulation at the same time as making this articulation possible. In other words, the romantic, comedic, and self-reflexive characteristics of comedy lend themselves to the mediation of the apparent outlandishness of utopian ideas; yet the frivolity of the mediation threatens the earnestness of the utopian vision. There are, however, some qualities of comedy that seem more straightforwardly suited to expressing utopian ideas. In contrast to classical tragedies, which represented already existing stories, histories, myths, and legends, Greek comedy created new stories and characters. The imperative on playwrights to imagine new characters, scenarios, and stories simultaneously created opportunities to propose radically alternative worlds. While the temporality of tragedy maps on to the time of the past, the time of comedy concerns itself with the present and future. The utopian imagination invests in the futurity of the not-yet of a better world, even if, at times in Old Comedy, it borrows from myths of the past, or, of the golden age, to find symbols, images, and languages to express desires for different futures.

Beyond the discussion of comedy as a form, generic investigation becomes increasingly complicated. For instance, written in the late 1950s, but still influential in genre theory today, Northrop Frye's *Anatomy of Criticism* adapts Aristotelean genre theory to propose a series of modes (mythic, romance, high mimetic, low mimetic, ironic). For Frye, in the romance mode 'ordinary laws of nature are slightly suspended' and the protagonist is modestly superior to others and to the environment;[29] in the high mimetic mode the protagonist's powers are superior to other people but not to the environment; in the low mimetic mode, the protagonist is neither superior nor inferior to the everyperson: 'the hero is one of us'; in the ironic mode the protagonist is inferior to the everyperson and the audience oversees scenes of absurdity.[30] Prose fictional utopias tend to use both romance and low mimetic modes; for example utopian citizens – the utopian hosts in particular – are often represented as slightly superior to the non-utopian visitor (and reader) and while many pre-1960s prose utopias work hard to maintain realistic modes of representation, in some works, the 'ordinary laws of nature are slightly suspended' as part of evoking the superiority of the utopian world. For example, in Wells' *A Modern Utopia* the visitors arrive in the utopian world by way of some mysterious portal in the Alps ('And behold! In the twinkling of an eye we are in that other world!').[31] At the same time, utopian

---

[29] Northrop Frye, *Anatomy of Criticism: Four Essays* (Princeton, NJ: Princeton University Press, 1959), 33.
[30] Ibid., 34.
[31] H. G. Wells, *A Modern Utopia* (London: Penguin, 2005), 16.

prose contains features of the low mimetic mode: the protagonist is usually the visitor to utopia – for example, Julian West in Bellamy's *Looking Backward* – who is an everyperson aligned with the reader and placed in a dialogic exchange with utopian ideas.

Utopian drama in contrast is rendered through several of Frye's modes: romance, high and low mimetic, and ironic. There are multiple scenes of absurdity, buffoonery, and irony in Aristophanes' *The Birds* and *The Assemblywomen* and Margaret Cavendish's utopian plays, and there are humans both significantly superior and inferior to the everyperson in Bernard Shaw's utopian drama. While this disruption of generic categorization may work to expose the limitations of taxonomies, classifications nevertheless shape our reception of art. As John Frow asserts, '[g]enres define a set of expectations that guide our engagement with texts; these expectations are structured as cues which frame a text in particular ways and which may take a particular material form'.[32] That utopian drama emerges through a mix of several modes – and without a clear hierarchy of modal priority – has meant utopian plays have not been well understood.

In a further complication, utopia is considered by some dominant voices in the field (such as Suvin, Kumar, and Jameson) to be a subgenre of science fiction. They observe sf as emerging later, but consider it, retrospectively, to encompass utopia, which in turn is considered to emerge in 1516 with More's *Utopia*.[33] In this view, sf is a product of modernity, beginning either in 1895 with Wells' *The Time Machine* or further back in 1818 with Mary Shelley's *Frankenstein*. Positioning utopia as a subgenre of sf thus places double limits on utopia as both confined to the generic constraints of sf and, effectively, to the modern period, thus ruling out pre-Morean utopias in general, and, for the interests of this book, Attic Comedy in particular.[34] Yet, there is by no means a critical consensus on locating utopia as a subgenre of sf or conflating sf/utopia with the modern period: more recent work locates the emergence of science fiction in a much earlier period of time – and, in some cases, as far back as ancient Greece.[35]

---

[32] John Frow, *Genre* (London: Routledge, 2015), 133.
[33] See Suvin, *Metamorphoses of Science Fiction*, 61; Jameson, *Archaeologies of the Future*, xiv.
[34] Even Sargent, who defines utopia more flexibly, in effect establishes More's *Utopia* as the first utopia in his *Utopian Literature in English: An Annotated Bibliography from 1516 to the Present*. The bibliography 'attempts to be the definitive bibliography for utopian literature in the English language', http://openpublishing.psu.edu/utopia/home
[35] See Charlotte Runcie, 'Is This the First Ever Sci-fi Novel?' *The Telegraph* (7 November 2013), http://www.telegraph.co.uk/culture/books/10432784/Is-this-the-first-ever-sci-fi-novel.html; and Susan Gray and Christos Callow Jr., 'Past and Future of Science Fiction Theatre', *Foundation* 117 (Spring 2014): 60–9.

Attributing utopias to the genre of sf has simultaneously meant excluding utopias that prioritize fantasy from the utopian canon. Jameson claims that 'the scientific pretensions of SF lend the Utopian genre an epistemological gravity that any kinship with generic fantasy is bound to undermine and seriously unravel: associations with Plato or Marx are more dignified credentials for the Utopian text than fantastic trips to the moon in Lucian or Cyrano'.[36] Both Lucian and Cyrano de Bergerac's moon voyages have been discussed as early examples of science fiction,[37] but a more significant problem with this framing is its exclusion of generic fantasy from the category of utopia. The rationale for this is that, unlike fantasy, sf provides utopia with credibility. The scientific materialism of sf apparently lends plausibility to utopian representation, which the supernatural and ahistorical characteristics of fantasy do not. Yet, as China Miéville's challenge to the sf/fantasy binary makes clear, this proposition often means impossible technological propositions are deemed part of a (plausible) utopian future, whilst fantastical beasts or supernatural powers are rejected as ridiculous fantasy.[38] Jameson's dismissal of fantasy as a premodern genre, a genre expressive of supernatural, ahistorical tendencies is a *tout court* position that does not appreciate the diverse applications of fantasy nor the fragility and frequent boundary crossing of the sf/fantasy binary in both utopian and non-utopian fiction. Irene Eynat-Confino considers '[t]he use of the fantastic in theatre' as performing a politically generative role; she sees it as 'a conscious attempt to apprehend complexity in all its perplexing contradictions' and that 'by dissolving the commonly accepted boundaries between the possible and the impossible, the natural and the supernatural, and between the human and nonhuman, the fantastic offers an apprehension of experiential reality that has been pared down by reigning ideologies'.[39] Recognizing the heterogeneity of fantasy – including its utopian potential – is important for my purposes as several of the utopian plays discussed in this book use fantasy as a generative means to think beyond the familiar.

---

[36] Jameson, *Archaeologies of the Future*, 57.
[37] See Arthur B. Evans (ed.) *Vintage Visions: Essays on Early Science Fictions* (Middletown, CT: Wesleyan University Press, 2014).
[38] China Miéville, 'Afterword: Cognition as Ideology: A Dialectic of SF Theory', in *Marxism and Science Fiction*, ed. Mark Bould and China Miéville (London: Pluto Press, 2009), 231–48. Similarly, Gregory Claeys insists that for a dystopia to be a proper dystopia, the negative societal aspects must be 'feasible' and by this he means that 'no extraordinary or utterly unrealistic features dominate the narrative'. Claeys, 'The Origins of Dystopia: Wells, Huxley and Orwell', in *The Cambridge Companion to Utopian Literature*, ed. Claeys (Cambridge: Cambridge University Press, 2010), 109.
[39] Irene Eynat-Confino, *On the Uses of the Fantastic in Modern Theatre: Cocteau, Oedipus, and the Monster* (New York: Palgrave Macmillan, 2008), 150.

Disqualifying utopian worlds that embrace fantasy aligns with a tendency within the field of Utopian Studies to privilege 'city utopias' or 'utopias of human contrivance' authored by writers such as More, Campanella, Bacon, Bellamy, Morris, Wells, and Gilman over and above 'body utopias' or 'utopias of sensual gratification' or 'utopias of escape' to use Sargent's terms.[40] Sargent uses the label 'body utopias' to describe utopias before More, those rooted in pre-modernity: for example, religious beginnings and after-lives, golden age myths in Hesiod, some Greek and Roman myths (the Isles of the Blessed), festivals and carnivals, and the medieval Land of Cockaigne. Body utopias offer 'simplicity, unity, security, immortality or an easy death, unity with God or the gods, abundance without labor, and no enmity between homo sapiens and the other animals'.[41] Lewis Mumford discusses Plato's *Republic* as the foundational example of the city utopia, or, to use Mumford's term 'utopias of reconstruction' (in contrast to 'utopias of escape'); he emphasizes Plato's 'horror of laxity and easy living' and claims: '[t]he fragrance that permeates his picture of the good life is not the heavy fragrance of rose-petals and incense falling upon languorous couches: it is the fragrance of the morning grass, and the scent of crushed mint or marjoram beneath the feet'.[42] This Platonic antipathy towards sensual gratification continues in various anti-hedonistic permutations through many city utopias that come after. The greatest pleasures of More's utopians are enjoyed through the pursuit of education, (unalienated) work is one of the supreme gratifications for Morris' utopians, and motherhood is the ideal state for Gilman's Herlanders.

In contrast, utopian drama has embraced the pleasures of the body utopia. The earliest utopias of Old Comedy are utopias of abundance. In the work of Metagenes and Pherecrates, fish self-barbeque and then hurl their deliciously chargrilled bodies into the mouths of hungry humans, an expression of a hedonistic desire for a bountiful nature, where bodily cravings are instantly satiated without labour or effort. While it is notable that this is a pre-Christian representation, there is nevertheless marked enjoyment of fine silks, perfumes, foods, music, and dancing in Margaret Cavendish's 1668 play, *The Convent of Pleasure*, which in turn, is in stark contrast to the more ascetic preference for plain smocks, extracurricular educational lectures, and eight o'clock bedtimes in More's *Utopia*. The presence of bodies on stage in drama and the live interaction with audiences seems particularly well-suited to registering physical and sensual desires, haptic encounters with material objects or other

---

[40] See Sargent, *Utopianism: A Very Short Introduction* (Oxford: Oxford University Press, 2010), 12; Sargent, 'The Three Faces of Utopianism Revisited', 10.
[41] Sargent, 'The Three Faces of Utopianism Revisited', 10.
[42] Lewis Mumford, *The Story of Utopias* (Gloucester, MA: Peter Smith, 1959), 38.

humans, consumption of food and drink, and auditory experiences of song and music. Indeed, drama's origins in public ritual, festivity, and commemoration make it peculiarly attuned to the celebratory or pageant aspects of the body utopia.

Something the body utopia and comic drama have in common is a registration of human ties with the non-human animal world. In classic utopian fiction mostly concerned with imagining city utopias, there is a dependence on a non-animalistic conception of the human, a concept of humanity distinguished by reason and an ability to remake the world according to will. These utopias validate a particular idea of human nature, one peculiarly divorced from animalistic associations of the fleshly body, physical desire, predatory behaviour, or violent sociality. In contrast, there are several examples of Old Comic plays that dramatize peaceful inter-species relations. Plays by Aristophanes that focus on animal worlds include *The Wasps*, *The Frogs*, and his utopian play discussed in Chapter 2, *The Birds*, which imagines humans and birds collaborating to create a new utopian community in the sky. While animals do not feature centrally in later utopian drama, the non-human natural world – or 'nature' – is far more integrated into utopian life: for example, the utopian Ancients in Shaw's *Back to Methuselah* wander over mountains rather than enclose themselves in urban centres and Brenton's Greenlanders live a low-tech life, close to nature.

While most of the utopian plays discussed in this book exploit the affective possibilities of live bodily interaction, they also register new political structures, and as such, provide an interweaving of features of both the body and city utopia. Human agency is considered by utopian scholars to be a defining element of the fictional utopia, and body utopias are therefore less important, or at least less politically radical, because nature, the gods, or the supernatural provide the good life without human intervention. A distinctive characteristic of utopian drama is its expression of both these elements: human action in bringing about new structures and human desire to be sensually or fancifully satisfied, sometimes without exertion. So, in Aristophanes and Shaw, preoccupation with human will and political organization combine with talking birds, a utopia in the sky, incredible leaps in age, and disembodiment. Cavendish is interested in both sensual gratification, feminist community, and women's empowerment. Brenton stages a libertarian anarcho-communist political economy with a superstructure of free love, telepathic communication, and zen football (a game with two teams but only one goal). Adebayo combines space travel with feminist sexual fantasy and electronic dance music, casting an octogenarian Black woman as the central protagonist.

A further limitation of the body/city binary for utopian drama is the association of the body utopia with the past or golden age, and the city utopia with futuristic projection. In some Old Comic dramas myth, the past, and the golden age emerge as imaginaries onto which utopian longing for new futures are projected. Shaw looks both backwards to beginnings, to the genesis of human society (as narrated in the Bible) as well as substantially forwards, to thousands of years beyond Shaw's own moment. Both these examples are not well served by the body/city binary, which devitalizes the former's power by underestimating the potential force of using both the past and fantasy as utopian figurations. Susan Gray and Christos Callow describe sf theatre as 'a theatre of absolute freedom, hovering somewhere between the coherence of realism and the non-sense of absurdism'.[43] This description equally applies to utopian drama, which often experiments with both sf and fantasy, body and city, golden age, and futuristic features as part of its utopian vision. Utopian plays help us to recognize the contribution of fantastical thinking to serious political speculation and vice versa.

Drama

Utopian texts – both fictional and philosophical – have expressed a longstanding ambivalence and, on occasion hostility, towards theatre. Famously Plato excluded poets from his ideal city state because he considered dramatic representations of life to be perversions of truth, which troubled the relationship between ethics and epistemology. Poetry – including dramatic mimesis – was for Plato not an expression of truth but an imitation of the appearance of character, action, and context. Socrates claims in *The Republic*, 'all the poets from Homer downwards have no grasp of truth but merely produce a superficial likeness of any subject they treat'.[44] Plato asks what Homer really knows about military strategy that equips him sufficiently to represent the Trojan Wars truthfully. Yet, a good poet – through skilled artistry – will persuade ignorant audiences of the truth of the representation despite that representation's distance from real events. Plato also expressed concern about dramatists' tendency to portray 'recalcitrant' aspects of character at the expense of 'deliberation' and 'reason' regardless of what was truthful or morally desirable.[45] Socrates' verdict in *The Republic* was to 'refuse to admit [the poet] to a properly run state, because he wakens and encourages

---

[43] Susan Gray and Christos Callow Jr., 'Past and Future of Science Fiction Theatre', 64.
[44] Plato, *The Republic* (London: Penguin, 1987), 367.
[45] Ibid., 373.

and strengthens the lower elements in the mind to the detriment of reason, which is like giving power and political control to the worst elements in a state and ruining the better elements'.[46]

Suspicion of theatre lingers in much of the utopian fiction of the modern period. Francis Bacon's utopian society of *New Atlantis* (1627) excludes theatre ('we do hate all impostures and lies') and instead allows 'houses of deceit of the senses' with 'false apparitions, impostures, and illusions'.[47] This perversion of reality is acceptable to Bacon as it does not pretend to articulate truth; instead, it makes clear in its very name that all the representations contained therein are false. Theatre is completely ignored in many other utopias. An exception is the sensual utopianism of Charles Fourier, whose interest in liberating the passions as an essential accompaniment to eliminating poverty and socializing labour makes his utopianism an unusual interweaving of the characteristics of both body and city utopia.[48] This tendency to omit theatre from utopias also extends to other literary and artistic forms: note, for example, the cultural devaluing of texts and reading in Morris's *News from Nowhere* and the textless society of Brenton's *Greenland*.

The general omission of theatre from fictional utopias may mark a Platonic suspicion of drama, theatre, and performance, but it might simultaneously demonstrate John Sullivan's view that 'theater thrives on the issues, malfunctions, and complex moral and ethical contradictions of a very dystopian world. All a utopian world would need is entertainment'.[49] That the best works of art thrive on unhappiness, injustice, and hardship is a familiar trope. Nigel Spivey argues that the concept of the tortured artist, and the close association of great art and the experience of pain are demonstrable alignments through much of human history.[50] Much has been said about the close correlation between anguish and poetry,[51] while tragedy – at least in a loosely deployed sense of the dramatic representation of suffering, disaster, and death – continues to dominate on our theatre stages and to be held in high esteem. Indeed, as noted in the Introduction, our contemporary moment – of environmental crises, economic and social precarity, and a global health pandemic – has spawned numerous plays that richly reply to this dystopian

---

[46] Ibid.
[47] Francis Bacon, *The New Atlantis* (Seattle, WA: Amazon Publishing, 2017), 45.
[48] Charles Fourier, *The Theory of the Four Movements*, ed. Gareth Stedman Jones and Ian Patterson (Cambridge: Cambridge University Press, 1996), 158.
[49] John Sullivan, 'Utopia Forum', *Theater* 26.1–2 (1995): 182–9, 182.
[50] Nivel Spivey, *Enduring Creation: Art, Pain, and Fortitude* (Oakland, CA: University of California Press, 2001).
[51] See Mutlu Konuk Blasing, *Lyric Poetry: The Pain and Pleasure of Words* (Princeton, NJ: Princeton University Press, 2006); Mary Ebbott, 'Tell Me How it Hurts: An Intersection of Poetry and Pain in the *Iliad*', *New England Review* 37.2 (2016): 31–47.

predicament. It is plausible that a future utopian world – un- or at least less-troubled and pained – would result in a very different form of artistic expression.

In a special issue on utopias of the Duke University Press journal *Theater*, some of its focus was on what theatre would be like in a future utopian society. Anna Deavere Smith imagines that '[t]he utopian theater would long for flesh, blood, and breathing. It would be hopelessly old-fashioned in a technical world, hopelessly interested in presence, hopelessly interested in modes of communication requiring human beings to be in the same room at the same time'.[52] While Smith envisages a high-tech utopian society to which utopian theatre would respond (critically, it seems), Cheryl Faver speculates that '[t]heater in a utopian future [...] could make subjectivity less abstract and more accessible to others. [...] Interactive media might empower audiences, inspiring them to rethink their individual lives'.[53] For Tom Sellar, '[t]he utopian theater should embrace its ability to dissemble, should specialize in it, manufacture it, and ship it out into the world at large'.[54] Theatre has a place, it seems, in a future utopian society and is imagined in diverse ways.

What theatre would look like in a utopian future is, of course, unknowable. Theatre's representation of utopias in this world is *Utopian Drama*'s concern. Explanations for why theatre is only rarely included in fictional utopias – such as Sullivan's – have also been marshalled in support of the familiar view that drama is not, apparently, a good form for the representation of utopia. The rationale for this position is that drama is generated by conflict, contradiction, opposition, or tension, whereas utopias – which are supposed to be peaceful and harmonious (according to Klaić) are not.[55] Anne Bogart develops further Klaić's idea that conflict is a defining element of theatre, and harmony of utopia: 'I believe the basic tenet of the theater is to resist. As the idea of utopia usually means there's no resistance, I would then resist utopia. The theater is dialectic, and the notion of a utopian theater, to me, is antithetical to the notion of theater.'[56] The peaceful, congruent, contented societies of typical utopias seem not to be well served by a form that is dependent on tension and that follows through a single action – in Aristotle's sense – from beginning to end, or that has fulfilled the expectations of Freytag's pyramid (exposition, rising action, climax, falling action, denouement).[57]

---

[52] Anna Deavere Smith, 'A System of Lights', *Theater* 26.1–2 (1995): 50–2; 50–1.
[53] Cheryl Faver, 'Refracted, Distracted, and Hopeful', *Theater* 26.1–2 (1995): 139–55, 139.
[54] Tom Sellar, 'A Philosophy Which Knows Its Stage', *Theater* 26.1–2 (1995): 83–8, 87.
[55] Dragan Klaić, 'Utopia Sustained', *Theater*, 26.1–2 (1995): 60–9, 61.
[56] Anne Bogart, 'Utopia Forum', *Theater* 26.1–2 (1995): 182–9, 182.
[57] Gustav Freytag, *Freytag's Technique of the Drama: An Exposition of Dramatic Composition and Art* (Hawthorne, CA: Hardpress Publishing, 2012).

However, this perspective does not appreciate the full potential of the form of drama nor the diverse expressions of utopia. It overlooks dramatic expressions that are not plot- or action-driven (for example medieval pageants, the early modern masque, twentieth-century existential theatre, or postdramatic theatre). This view also undervalues the complexity of the utopian genre, including its self-reflexive relationship with opposition, tension, and conflict. Erika Munk writes:

> Utopias are not necessarily built on social stasis, nor do they imply the end of crime, sorrow, vice, and folly. Their immobility has been greatly exaggerated, despite the tidiness (at best) and maniacal control (at worst) that characterize them. Even the plans for utopia's oldest island cities – walled, gated, symmetrical, hierarchical – acknowledge that order would always have to be maintained rather than trusted to flourish spontaneously.[58]

Munk registers the presence of resistance within utopian fictions. The occurrence of dissent in utopias – either rendered formally by the two-part format or by the inclusion of sceptical characters – has been an essential means by which utopias encourage a particular form of reading (or spectatorial) practice. Indeed, the dialectic is a crucial element of many utopian texts: the reader or spectator experiences a transformative encounter by way of a dialectical oscillation between inscriptions, descriptions, or performances of the non-utopian world or the use of a sceptical, dissenting character and the difficult to imagine otherness of the new utopian society.

Munk and Sellar ask, '[a]re possible utopias represented best by theater design and architecture, or through actors' bodies, or in a text, or by the company's ways of relating to each other and the audience? Is a powerful aesthetic experience itself a foreshadowing of utopia?'[59] The idea of a powerfully affective aesthetic experience is harnessed by Jill Dolan in her book *Utopia in Performance: Finding Hope at the Theater*, as mentioned in the Introduction. Dolan makes the case for the utopian potential of theatre to reside in the ways in which some performances 'inspire moments in which audiences feel themselves allied with each other, and with a broader, more capacious sense of a public, in which social discourse articulates the possible, rather than the insurmountable obstacles to human potential'.[60] For Dolan,

---

[58] Erika Munk, 'Exiled From Nowhere', *Theater* 26.1–2 (1995): 101–12, 104.
[59] Erika Munk and Tom Sellar, 'Up Front: An Invitation to Utopia', *Theater* 26.1–2 (1995): 5–6, 6.
[60] Jill Dolan, *Utopia in Performance: Finding Hope at the Theater* (Ann Arbor, MI: University of Michigan Press, 2005), 2.

the content of the representation is important, but more crucial is the intersubjective encounter, an encounter affirming a solidaristic engagement with the hopeful anticipation of a better future.

This feeling of utopia – so peculiarly potent as an affect circulating among groups of people at a performance – is compellingly claimed by Dolan as something that can be experienced, occasionally, at the theatre. But what about dramatic representations of utopian societies? On thinking about utopia as nowhere, Paul Schmidt claims this core meaning of utopia denies 'the most essential thing we know about theater: that it can exist only in a known location, in a particular time and place, where an audience is confronted *in its own language* with images that both justify and call into question its sense of itself'.[61] The material presence of theatre makes this especially so, but Schmidt's charge is more generally applicable: the utopian novel endeavours to describe a world outside of its experience in the language of its experience. Schmidt's claim overlooks the affinities between utopia and theatre: the ephemerality of performance; its partial existence on the page; its movement from venue to venue; its inherent impermanence. Theatre has a utopian nomadic quality in that, as Klaić claims, 'it postulates the freedom to create and communicate without physical or cultural boundaries'.[62] As a philosophical riposte to Schmidt, Erik Ehn argues that what 'distinguishes theater is not rhythm, speech, or melody – it is the present. The present doesn't exist, utopia doesn't exist, theater doesn't exist – but they are.'[63] Despite the charges against drama as an appropriate form for utopia, there are strong arguments for the shared interests of, and affinities between, drama, theatre, and performance, and utopia and its fictional possibilities.

---

[61] Paul Schmidt, 'Observations on Ideal Stage Languages', *Theater* 26.1–2 (1995): 162–4, 162.
[62] Klaić, 'Utopia Sustained', 66.
[63] Erik Ehn, 'Translations and Fragments From the New Panic Compound in Damascus, Kansas', *Theater* 26.1–2 (1995): 126–38, 127.

2

Genealogical beginnings: Old Comedy, longing, and laughter

Introduction

In this chapter, I analyse surviving plays and play fragments from the genre of so-called Old Comedy as examples of early utopian dramas. A handful of scholars of classical literature have discussed the utopian features of these plays, but surprisingly, there has been almost no attention to them from within the field of Utopian Studies. The reasons for this are discussed in more detail in the next section of this chapter, but relate to the criteria used to define literary utopias. As I outlined in Chapter 1, for some influential Utopian Studies scholars, the utopian literary tradition begins with More's *Utopia* in 1516, with earlier utopias identified instead as golden age, or pastoral, *fantasies*, and Plato's *Republic* regarded as philosophical speculation. Contrary to this view, this chapter establishes the utopias of Old Comedy not just as genuine literary utopias, but as the earliest examples of the literary utopia in the Western tradition. I also examine the peculiarities of the genre of Old Comedy, the impact of this genre on the utopian aesthetics and politics of the dramas, and the contemporary resonance of Old Comic utopianism.

There are scholarly impediments worth noting, such as the enormous gaps in primary evidence, which seem to generate a more than usually contested critical ground in relation to the nature, meaning, and political significance of Old Comedy. It is also difficult to attain a clear understanding of the ways in which Old Comedy signified to its contemporaries in the late fifth century BCE. Stephen Halliwell observes, '[in] Greek, the expression τὸ γελοῖον, "the laughable" or "the ridiculous", is often practically synonymous with "comedy", *kômôidia*, itself'.[1] Old Comedy involved crude, sexual, and scatological jokes, buffoonery, lampooning of known civic figures, and fantastical narratives. Yet, Old Comedy was simultaneously overtly political and had serious messages to deliver. For Ian Ruffell, '[t]his paradox goes to

---

[1] Stephen Halliwell, 'Laughter', in *The Cambridge Companion to Greek Comedy*, ed. Martin Revermann (Cambridge: Cambridge University Press, 2014), 189.

the heart of comic utopias, being often both aspirational and satirical'.[2] This paradoxical feature has led to much interpretive contestation, this further compounded by the frequent appearance of metatheatricality in Old Comedy. C. W. Marshall observes that 'Athenian comedy was always metatheatrical, and found new ways of demonstrating its debts and awareness of other theatrical genres and the process of theatre itself'.[3] That utopian worlds were mediated through this complicated, self-aware genre further compounds the problem of interpretation. An additional impediment is the full supersession of the genre by a quite different form of comedy (New Comedy, most associated with Menander) by the mid-fourth century BCE. Hence, to understand better the utopian meanings in Old Comedy, we need to grasp the ways in which utopianism permeated this period, and it is to this that the following section turns.

Classical utopianism

As discussed in Chapter 1, More coined the word 'utopia' in his famous prose narrative. A genre-blurring prose text, *Utopia* makes direct reference to Plato's *Republic* in a poem that forms its prologue. In doing so, it positions itself as improving on the original utopia:

> NOPLACIA was once my name,
> That is, a place where no one goes.
> Plato's *Republic* now I claim
> To match, or beat at its own game;
> For that was just a myth in prose,
> But what he wrote of, I became,
> Of men, wealth, laws a solid frame,
> A place where every wise man goes:
> GOPLACIA is now my name.[4]

More transforms Plato's hypothetical 'noplacia' (utopia) into a 'goplacia' (eutopia or the 'good place') and in doing so claims his 'good place' as superior. *Utopia* proclaims itself as not a 'myth in prose', but a fully activated, animated, and embodied place, which the wise seek out. Krishan Kumar argues against

---

[2] Ian Ruffell, 'Utopianism', in *The Cambridge Companion to Greek Comedy*, 212.
[3] C.W. Marshall, 'Dramatic Technique and Athenian Comedy', in *The Cambridge Companion to Greek Comedy*, 145.
[4] Thomas More, *Utopia*, trans. Paul Turner (London: Penguin, 2003), 5.

locating classical Greece as the beginning of the Western utopia. His argument is that even *The Republic*, which Kumar admits comes close to his definition of a utopia ('the presentation of an ideal society in all the detail of its private and public life'), is not a 'true utopia': it is instead 'a portrayal of the principles of the ideal state, not an exemplification of those principles in action, in concrete institutions and ways of life'.[5] In line with Kumar (as *The Republic* is philosophical speculation, not an exemplification, of the good society), Fátima Vieira prefers to categorize it alongside other early utopias such as Saint Augustine's *The City of God*, where the utopian world is relocated to the afterlife, and call them 'prefigurations of utopia'.[6] Yet, for More, *The Republic* is a utopia, and one that offers a model, against which he develops his distinctive utopian world, at once dissimilar to, and overlapping with many of the same concerns as, *The Republic*.[7]

A primary example of this overlapping is the detailed description of the city state or the *polis*. Plato's outline of the state is less motivated by a desire to develop an ideal state and more inspired by his project of exploring the concept of justice, and in particular to construct a context, within which it is possible to delineate the just 'man'. Plato shares with More an exploration of a proto-Communistic approach to property, a rethinking of the family, and a partial undoing of patriarchal structures. Another quality in common is the identification of certain appetites of the senses, or, as Patrick Parrinder describes it, 'the craving for passion and longing for incident',[8] as potentially disruptive or harmful to the maintenance of a productive and just society. As we have seen, Plato famously excluded poets from his ideal state because of the inherent deceptiveness of aesthetic representation.

Plato's *Republic* (c.380 BCE) is very likely to have been influenced by the utopian plays of Aristophanes. However, some scholars argue that Aristophanes was influenced by the ideas of *The Republic*, or Socratic thought more generally, and that *The Republic* actually responded to Aristophanes' satirical take on Socratic philosophy.[9] Holger Thesleff exemplifies this position,

[5] Krishan Kumar, *Utopianism* (Milton Keynes: Open University Press, 1991), 39.
[6] Fátima Vieira, 'The Concept of Utopia', in *The Cambridge Companion to Utopian Literature*, ed. Gregory Claeys (Cambridge: Cambridge University Press, 2010), 6.
[7] See J. H. Hexter, *More's Utopia: The Biography of an Idea* (Princeton, NJ: Princeton University Press, 1952); James Steintrager, 'Plato and More's *Utopia*', *Social Research* 36.3 (1969): 357–72.
[8] Patrick Parrinder, 'Utopia and Romance', in *The Cambridge Companion to Utopian Literature*, 156.
[9] See Helene P. Foley, 'The "Female Intruder" Reconsidered: Women in Aristophanes' *Lysistrata* and *Ecclesiazusae*', *Classical Philology* 77.1 (1982): 1–21, 15–16; R. G. Ussher, *Aristophanes: Ecclesiazusae* (Oxford: Oxford University Press, 1986), xvi–xviii; Kenneth S. Rothwell, *Politics and Persuasion in Aristophanes' Ecclesiazusae* (Leiden and New York: E. J. Brill, 1990), 9–10.

providing the following rationale: 'Plato had a distinct political philosophy before 388, long before *The Republic* received its final shape'.[10] The argument is that the ideas of *The Republic* were in circulation quite a while before its publication and Aristophanes responded to them in his plays, particularly in *The Assemblywomen*. However, Peter Nicholls exemplifies a strongly supported position in establishing *The Assemblywomen* as 'probably published not less than twelve years before the *Republic* – 392 BC and 380–370 BC, respectively', which makes it highly unlikely that Aristophanes' play responded to the ideas of *The Republic*.[11] Nicholls' support for the view that *The Republic* was cognizant of the work of Aristophanes is based largely on Plato's references to comedy in *The Republic* and what is assumed to be *The Assemblywomen* in particular.[12] Hence, the overlapping themes of *The Assemblywomen* and the *Republic* have been well established, but more important for this discussion is to ascertain the character of the utopian imagination in antiquity.

John Ferguson locates the earliest example of utopian representation in Homer and claims this passage from *The Odyssey*, most likely to have been written towards the end of the eighth century BCE,[13] as the first utopia in European literature, or at least 'the first surviving Utopia'.[14] The following excerpt relates to Scheria, the island paradise of the Phaeacians:

> Just outside the entrance to the courtyard, surrounded by a wall, lies a large orchard of four acres – pears and pomegranates, apple trees with glossy fruit, sweet figs and luxuriant olives. Their fruit never fails nor runs short, winter and summer alike. It comes at all seasons of the year, and there is never a time when the West Wind's breath is not assisting, here the bud, and there the ripening fruit; so that pear after pear, apple after apple, cluster on cluster of grapes, and fig up on fig are always coming to perfection.[15]

---

[10] Holger Thesleff, 'Platonic Chronology', *Phronesis* 34.1 (1989): 1–26, 11–13. See also Amy L. Bonnette, 'Aristophanes' Feminine Comedies and Socratic Political Science', in *The Political Theory of Aristophanes*, ed. Jeremy J. Mhire and Bryan-Paul Frost (New York: State University of New York Press, 2014), 309–10.

[11] Peter Nichols, 'The Comedy of the Just City: Aristophanes' *Assemblywomen* and Plato's *Republic*', in *The Political Theory of Aristophanes*, 273.

[12] Desmond Lee's edition of *The Republic* includes the following note in Book 5 (Women and the Family): 'Aristophanes in the *Ecclesiazusae* ("Women in Parliament") had already made fun of ideas similar to those which Plato expresses in this section, and Plato probably had him in mind.' (Lee, *The Republic* [London: Penguin, 1987], 171). In this section, Socrates says, 'whether it's asked in joke or in earnest, we must allow people to ask the question, Is the female of the human species naturally capable of taking part in all the occupations of the male, or in none, or in some only?' (Plato, *The Republic*, 171).

[13] E. V. Rieu, Introduction. Homer, *The Odyssey* (London: Penguin, 2003), xi.

[14] John Ferguson, *Utopias of the Classical World* (London: Thames and Hudson, 1975), 14.

[15] Homer, *The Odyssey*, Book 7, trans. E. V. Rieu (London: Penguin, 2003), 87–8.

This expresses a utopian desire for the stimulation of the senses: for effortless and complete satiation, and to be surrounded by an infinitely bountiful nature. Nature is forever generous with suggestions of a broader sexual munificence, and the promise of a leisurely life not curtailed by the drudgery of labour. Ferguson sees this utopian depiction as 'an attempt to peg back society at the monarchical stage and to suppress the power of the barons and oncoming oligarchy'.[16] This is a utopian vision of an idealized, pastoral nature, which forms part of a wider critique of contemporary political conditions. However, although this utopian depiction might appear to be part of a nostalgic, backward glance, Homer connects it to a more modern idea of state-building. We are told the Phaeacians have constructed a 'pleasant town': '[a]s he walked, Odysseus marvelled at the harbours with their trim ships, at the meeting-place of the sea-lords and at their long and lofty walls, surmounted by palisades, presenting a wonderful sight'.[17] This is in marked contrast to Odysseus' visit to the Cyclopes:

> we came to the land of the Cyclopes, a fierce, lawless people who never lift a hand to plant or plough but just leave everything to the immortal gods. All the crops they require spring up unsown and untilled, wheat and barley and vines with generous clusters that swell with the rain from heaven to yield wine. The Cyclopes have no assemblies for the making of laws, not any established legal codes, but live in hollow caverns in the mountain heights, where each man is lawgiver to his own children and women, and nobody has the slightest interest in what his neighbours decide.[18]

Thus, the Cyclopes' neglect of technological and social progress is not presented as utopian primitivism, and clearly Homer is advocating the *polis* of the Phaeacians as the ideal settlement. As Annette Lucia Giesecke observes: '[the Phaeacians] alone practice agriculture and viticulture. They alone build temples for and worship the gods. Theirs is a walled, well-organized, architecturally differentiated city with a just and progressive system of government.'[19]

Another utopian image in *The Odyssey* is the afterlife, the Elysian Fields. We are told that Menelaus will be sent to this paradise, which is 'at the world's end [...] in the land where living is made easy for mankind, where no snow

---

[16] Ferguson, *Utopias of the Classical World*, 15.
[17] Homer, *The Odyssey*, Book 7, 85–6.
[18] Ibid., Book 9, 113.
[19] Annette Lucia Giesecke, 'Homer's Eutopolis: Epic Journeys and the Search for an Ideal Society', *Utopian Studies* 14.2 (2003): 23–40, 33.

falls, no strong winds blow and there is never any rain, but day after day the West Wind's tuneful breeze comes in from the Ocean to refresh people'.[20] A similar idea to the Elysian Fields – the Isles of the Blessed – emerges in Hesiod's *Works and Days* (written, it is speculated, 'in the last third of the eight century BC'[21]):

> There some of them were engulfed by the consummation of death, but to some Zeus the father, son of Kronos, granted a life and home apart from men, and settled them at the ends of the earth. These dwell with carefree heart in the Isles of the Blessed Ones, beside deep-swirling Oceanus: fortunate Heroes, for whom the grain-giving soil bears its honey-sweet fruits thrice a year.[22]

As with *The Odyssey*, spatial separation – a utopian land 'at the ends of the earth' – is an important element of its construction. Anticipating the separation of the island utopia presented in More, the Isles of the Blessed are similarly apart and practically unreachable. In the following excerpt, also from *Works and Days*, temporal rather than spatial separation is the key cause of isolation:

> The race of men that the immortals who dwell on Olympus made first of all was of gold. They were in the time of Kronos, when he was king in heaven; and they lived like gods, with carefree heart, remote from toil and misery. Wretched old age did not affect them either, but with hands and feet ever unchanged they enjoyed themselves in feasting, beyond all ills, and they died as if overcome by sleep. All good things were theirs, and the grain-giving soil bore its fruits of its own accord in unstinted plenty, while they at their leisure harvested their fields in contentment amid abundance.[23]

There is no consensus on whether Homer's or Hesiod's work came first, but this is not important to this discussion. It is noteworthy that while Homer is considered to have had a far greater impact on the Western literary tradition, it is Hesiod's poetry, and this passage in particular, that generated the utopian myth of the golden age, or the 'golden race'. Unaffected by the so-called

---

[20] Homer, *The Odyssey*, book 4, 42.
[21] M. L. West, Introduction to Hesiod, *Theogony* and *Works and Days* (Oxford: Oxford University Press, 1988), vii.
[22] Hesiod, *Works and Days*, in *Theogony* and *Works and Days*, trans. M. L. West, 41–2.
[23] Hesiod, *Works and Days*, 108–118, in *Theogony* and *Works and Days*, 40.

ravages of old age, free from troubles, and unsaddled with the demands of labour, the golden race enjoyed the limitless fruits of a bountiful nature with little exertion, and in blissful contentment. These utopias of the golden age are simple, primitivist, and peaceful, and, as Rhiannon Evans describes: 'just outside of mapped spaces: in the Atlantic (the Islands of the Blessed), to the far north (the Hyperboreans), and in the Indian Ocean (Panchaia)'.[24]

Utopias of natural abundance project a kind of superagency onto a bountiful, generous nature, suggestions of which are present in the Hesiodic excerpts. Nature gives without receiving. It performs on its own the work needed to bring forth the yield. This automatist utopian projection – 'the grain-giving soil bore its fruits of its own accord in unstinted plenty' – is repeatedly developed imaginatively in Old Comedy, and survives into modern versions of utopia, such as the nineteenth century utopian socialist Charles Fourier's utopian vision that as part of a wider set of climate changes, a 'boreal citric acid' in the seas would combine with saline liquid to produce something akin to lemonade.[25] Although this sounds silly, it nevertheless expresses a libidinal desire for what is profoundly lacking in the prevailing society. Ian Ruffell proposes that classical expressions of automatist utopianism are 'a means of articulating popular grievances and popular dissent' and likens them to the ways in which the radical sects, during the 1640s, particularly Gerrard Winstanley and the Diggers, appealed to mythical tales of Norman English identity to inspire revolutionary political and economic change.[26]

Hence, what emerges from this brief overview (and there are several more varieties of classical utopias discussed by Ferguson in *Utopias of the Classical World*) are two identifiable strands of classical utopianism. First is the realistic description of the well-ordered and just city state facilitative of the best way of life, designed by human intelligence and brought about by human will. This is exemplified in Plato's *The Republic* and *Laws*, and, also, partially, in Aristotle's *Politics*.[27] Less concerned with the material manifestation of the state, as Jeffrey Hurwit writes, 'the *polis* consisted not of houses, stone walls, timber, roads, and dockyards, but of men. The city state [...] was an idea, the

---

[24] Rhiannon Evans, *Utopia Antiqua: Readings of the Golden Age and the Decline at Rome* (London: Routledge, 2008), 7.
[25] Charles Fourier, *The Theory of the Four Movements*, ed. Gareth Stedman Jones and Ian Patterson (Cambridge: Cambridge University Press, 1996), 50.
[26] Ian Ruffell, 'The World Turned Upside Down: Utopia And Utopianism In The Fragments Of Old Comedy', in *The Rivals of Aristophanes: Studies in Athenian Old Comedy*, ed. David Harvey and John Wilkins (Duckworth: The Classical Press of Wales, 2000), 480.
[27] For an argument positioning Aristotle as 'an unheralded exponent of utopian thought', see Michael Jackson, 'Designed by Theorists: Aristotle on Utopia', *Utopian Studies* 12.2 (2001): 1–12, 1.

equivalent of a particularly intense communal or corporate spirit.'[28] The second variety of utopia comprised primitivistic, golden age visions, which tended to be peaceful, were set in a permanently fecund natural landscape and usually located in the past or on the edges of mapped space. Unlike in the city state, the exercise of human will was not a requirement for providing an ideal life; human desire was already anticipated in a pastoral fantasy of a super benevolent natural order, aided by the gods, providing everything needed for a fully satiated and contented life. Although in some ways distinct, the Phaeacians, as described by Homer, forge a middle path between these two; their sensibly devised *polis*, agricultural planning, and practice of piety appear to exist in a more than munificent, bountiful, and lush nature.

Greek comedy

The representation of utopia in Greek comedy – or *kômôidia* – and more precisely Old Comedy, inevitably made the utopian encounter a complicated, inconsistent, and paradoxical event, a problematic that becomes clear as this section progresses. *Kômôidia*, dating back at least as far as the sixth century BCE, involved state-sponsored competitions at the festivals of Dionysus and Lenaea in Athens, which also hosted the older forms of tragedy and the satyr play. Old Comedy, most famously exemplified by the fifth-century BCE poets, Cratinus, Eupolis, and Aristophanes, was a flexible form involving fantasy and satire, vulgarity, political comment, parody, playfulness, and a general destabilization of rules and norms. As the only poet with whole surviving plays (eleven in total out of an estimation of approximately forty), Aristophanes has overshadowed the others, but there are surviving papyrus fragments of the plays of Cratinus, Eupolis, and many other poets, which have been compiled, translated, and published in accessible formats.[29] It was conventional for plays to include three (or sometimes four) speaking actors, who played all parts, and a chorus made up of twenty-four citizen performers (noncitizens were allowed to perform at the Lenaia) and for all performers to dress up in extravagant costumes and masks.[30] Other genre features included

---

[28] Jeffrey M. Hurwit, *The Art and Culture of Early Greece 1100–480 B.C.* (Ithaca, NY: Cornell University Press, 1985), 73.
[29] See Ian C. Storey, *Fragments of Old Comedy I: Alcaeus to Diocles* (Cambridge, MA: Harvard University Press), 2011; Ian C. Storey, *Fragments of Old Comedy II: Diopeithes to Pherecrates* (Cambridge, MA: Harvard University Press, 2011); Ian C. Storey, *Fragments of Old Comedy III: Philonicus to Xenophon* (Cambridge, MA: Harvard University Press, 2011).
[30] See C. W. Marshall, 'Dramatic technique and Athenian comedy', in *The Cambridge Companion to Greek Comedy*, 131.

the presence of the *parados* (flamboyant entrance of the chorus), the *agôn* (a witty verbal contest between the main actors), the *parabasis* (the chorus speaking directly to the audience, sometimes as the poet), and the *exodos* (usually an exuberant finale performed by the chorus).

New Comedy, associated primarily with Menander in the fourth century BCE emerges quite differently as a domestic plot-based comedy of manners: less bawdy, more refined, less political, more situational, and using an aesthetic approaching a heightened realism.³¹ In Keith Sidwell's comparison of Aristophanes' last surviving play *Wealth* and Menander's first play *Samia*, he notes the disappearance of the *agôn*, *parabasis* (although Aristophanes had already omitted the *parabasis* in his final plays) and of the active role of the chorus (the chorus is reduced to a decorative function). Instead, there is a five-act, episodic plot structure, which survives and develops into early modern theatre (via Roman adaptations of Menandrian comedy); '[g]one are the fantastic elements [...] and the iambic attacks on political figures. Instead, we have full-blown domestic comedy, with plots that operate in realistic mode, with everyday language, and virtually no reference to the details of current political life [...]'³² There is dispute over whether there was a linear development from Old Comedy through Middle Comedy (itself a contested category) to New Comedy, or whether instead there were two distinct tracks.³³

What is relevant here is that the form most hospitable to utopian aesthetics – Old Comedy – either transforms into, or is replaced by, a form unable to accommodate the imaginative reach of utopian representation. Despite the formal conventions mentioned above, as well as genre expectations relating to poetic composition and metrical verse, Old Comedy was less restrained in relation to representative modes, scope, setting, and character, than both New Comedy and tragedy. As James Redfield states:

> In Old Comedy [...] the hero need not submit to the gods; neither is nature permanent. The species are not separate or stable; a man could be

---

³¹ Out of an estimation of around 100 plays, there is only one whole (bar a few lines) surviving play by Menander – *Dyskolos* – and substantial parts of several others. Nigel Wilson, 'The Transmission of Comic Texts', in *The Cambridge Companion to Greek Comedy*, 424; 427.
³² Keith Sidwell, 'Fourth-century Comedy Before Menander', in *The Cambridge Companion to Greek Comedy*, 67.
³³ While Keith Sidwell – drawing on evidence from Aristotle – argues in favour of 'two separate highways' of comedy ('Fourth-century Comedy Before Menander', 73), others such as Zachary P. Biles emphasize the 'dynamic and evolving' nature of the genre' ('The Rivals of Aristophanes and Menander', in *The Cambridge Companion to Greek Comedy*, 57). Also, see Susan Lape and Alfonso Moreno, who suggest that the division between Old and New Comedy has been overstated and that there are many continuities ('Comedy and the Social Historian', in *The Cambridge Companion to Greek Comedy*, 367).

a wasp or a horse, could converse with frogs or clouds. Amid such universal anarchy, the cultural order must seem absurdly insubstantial. The invasion of culture by nature results in grotesque deformations and a universal lowering; comedy is the enemy of hierarchy. The great instruments are obscenity and scatology, which remind us that we are all naked under our clothes. Individuals are deprived of their dignity – but in the process, mankind in general, embodied in the audience, recovers a sense of power and liberty.[34]

Unlike tragedy – a genre mapped onto the past, which encourages moral reflection on what is already done, what cannot be changed – comedy, with its looser structure, multiple modes, and tendency towards mutability, is drawn temporally as the present or future.

In addition to the loosening of philosophical and formal binds ('[c]ause and effect are suspended, heaven and hell are opened, time and space are erased, events unfold in dreamlike free association'[35]), individual human will constitutes a central component in many Aristophanic dramas. Ordinary individual citizens (commonly middle-aged men, although obviously not in *The Assemblywomen* or *Lysistrata*) bring about extraordinary, far-reaching changes, such as creating a utopia in the sky (*Birds*); individually procuring a peace deal with Sparta (*Acharnians*); instituting a communist utopia with gender equality (*Assemblywomen*); and using a collective sex strike to bring about an end to the Peloponnesian War (*Lysistrata*). Unlike in New Comedy, wherein chance, luck, or fate play the primary role in the dramatic narrative, in Old Comedy, human agency is the predominant precipitator of plot development. As David Konstan states: '[t]he hero or heroine overcomes all obstacles by sheer will and imagination, and in many cases defends the newly won order of things against sceptics and opportunists'.[36] This focus on human agency's role in bringing about change is strikingly different from the utopianism of Plato or More, where lengthy descriptions of the utopian state are prioritized at the expense of attending to how the utopian society was brought into being. What we find in common instead is the presence of sceptics, who also appear in *The Republic* and *Utopia*, giving both of these texts their dialogical character, which continues to be a trait of utopian prose

---

[34] James Redfield, 'Drama and Community: Aristophanes and Some of His Rivals', in *Nothing to do with Dionysos? Athenian Drama in its Social Context*, ed. John J. Winkler and Froma I. Zeitlin (Princeton, NJ: Princeton University Press, 1990), 328.

[35] R. Bracht Branham, *Bakhtin and the Classics* (Evanston, IL: Northwestern University Press, 2002), 328.

[36] David Konstan, 'Defining the Genre', in *The Cambridge Companion to Greek Comedy*, 41.

narrative more generally, and emerges explicitly in the utopian theatre of the twenty-first century (see Chapter 6).

However, despite the apparently radical themes and aesthetics of Old Comedy, several scholars have claimed that the Old Comics were politically conservative and that this conservatism informed the politics of their work.[37] This assumption emerges mainly from observations of the class backgrounds of the poets, as elite aristocrats, and the tendency of Old Comedy to make satirical swipes at democratic politicians, the most famous example being Aristophanes' attack on Cleon, in *Knights*. Susan Lape and Alfonso Moreno observe:

> Although it has of late become unfashionable to say so explicitly, orthodox opinion still considers Aristophanes a 'Cimonian conservative' (roughly an aristocratic imperialist). The opposite view of Aristophanes as a liberal pacifist, though still alive in popular reception, is by contrast in disfavour.[38]

Alan Sommerstein further argues that Aristophanes' choruses and protagonists satirize prosecutors (at times for targeting the rich), critique state payments to citizens, and are critical of the war with Sparta (although not with anyone else): '[a]t the very least, then, Aristophanes supported a raft of policies which were also supported by oligarchs, and which they seemed to believe [...] would never be accepted in a democratically ruled Athens.'[39]

Cognate to this framing of Old Comics as conservative is the discussion of the apparent tension between the seemingly anarchical, popular form of Old Comedy and its civic containment within a state-sponsored structure. How could the state organize, sponsor, and promote a Bakhtinian form of carnival with the subversive undoing of hierarchical arrangements that carnival implies? Yet, the Old Comics certainly exhibited a deployment of the kind of popular grotesque Mikhail Bakhtin identified in medieval carnival.[40] Edith Hall does not see Old Comedy as performing a carnivalesque role, but instead as shaping '*mainstream* opinion' through its self-positioning 'as the authoritative mouthpiece of the community's central, traditional, collective

---

[37] G. E. M. de Ste Croix uses the phrase 'Cimonian conservative' in *The Origins of the Peloponnesian War* (Ithaca, NY: Cornell University Press, 1972), 355–71.
[38] Susan Lape and Alfonso Moreno, 'Comedy and the Social Historian', in *The Cambridge Companion to Greek Comedy*, 339.
[39] Alan Sommerstein, 'The Politics of Greek Comedy', in *The Cambridge Companion to Greek Comedy*, 297.
[40] See M. M. Bakhtin, *Rabelais and His World*, trans. Hélène Iswolsky (Cambridge, MA: MIT Press, 1968).

value system'.[41] R. Bracht Branham argues that the Old Comics 'exploit the implicitly antiauthoritarian character of the grotesque in order to convey undisguised political messages opposed in intent and origin to the selfsame popular class in which the grotesque finds its roots'.[42] For Branham, conservative political messages are articulated through an aesthetics associated with a popular, grassroots form. In this view there is a perceived tension between content and form: traditional political ideologies reflective of the elite class backgrounds of the poets rub up against an unruly and anarchic demotic form. Like Branham, Anthony Edwards claims that Old Comedy did indeed appropriate the anti-authoritarianism of the popular form but employed it for critiquing the authority of the *dêmos* itself.[43] Victoria Wohl adds that '[w]hen comedy, the vehicle of popular laughter, becomes an institutionalized arm of Athens' popular sovereignty, the people itself becomes the target of its oppositional humour'.[44]

However, evidence of Aristophanes' political beliefs is scant, and, as many others have observed, this makes it impossible to know his political views.[45] While Sommerstein identifies elements in Aristophanes' plays that potentially indicate a conservative political leaning, there are many other aspects of his plays that evidence precisely the opposite. As Stephanie Nelson remarks, Aristophanes' comedy 'subverts all the cultural ideals of the Greek polis, celebrating the old, the ugly, and the physical, not to mention lawless individuality'.[46] In fact, within Aristophanes' undiscriminating subversion of the normative, it is equally possible to position his plays as politically in tune with their radical forms. David Kawalko Roselli emphasizes the tendency for Aristophanic protagonists to be 'commoners exhibiting demotic rather than elite sympathies' who 'forthrightly address unequal economic conditions'.[47] Perhaps an appropriate conclusion is to recognize the limitations of mapping

---

[41] Edith Hall, 'Comedy and Athenian Festival Culture', in *The Cambridge Companion to Greek Comedy*, 307.

[42] Branham, ed. *Bakhtin and the Classics*, 39.

[43] Anthony Edwards, 'Historicizing the Popular Grotesque: Bakhtin's *Rabelais and His World* and Attic Old Comedy', in *Bakhtin and the Classics*, 29.

[44] Victoria Wohl, 'Comedy and Athenian Law', in *The Cambridge Companion to Greek Comedy*, 329.

[45] Note too that other scholars position Aristophanes as a progressive: 'No supporter of oligarchic reaction, Aristophanes was doubtless a patriotic democrat; the whole of *Lysistrate* is in fact a celebration of the traditional Athenian democracy'. Jeffrey Henderson, '*Lysistrate*: The Play and its Themes', in *Aristophanes: Essays in Interpretation*, ed. Jeffrey Henderson (Cambridge: Cambridge University Press, 1980), 188.

[46] Stephanie Nelson, 'Aristophanes and the Polis', in *The Political Theory of Aristophanes*, 109.

[47] David Kawalko Roselli, 'Social Class', in *The Cambridge Companion to Greek Comedy*, 247; 246.

Old Comedy's subversion of the normative directly onto contemporary understandings of political partisanship.

As an anti-realist, multi-modal, meta-theatrical form that frequently includes contradiction and paradox, Old Comedy threatens to destabilize singular readings. As indicated in the introduction to this chapter, the verbal form of *kômôida* – *kômôidei* – translates as something like 'satirise' or 'ridicule', although this does not quite capture the expectation that *kômôida* will also deliver a just message.[48] Andreas Willi similarly notes the combination of parody and serious political meaning, and views 'the entertainment function of comic language' as also having 'an overtly didactic purpose'.[49] Ruffell locates the essential paradox of Old Comedy in its 'being often both aspirational and satirical'[50] and Nelson also notes its inducement of 'contrary emotions' and sees as 'unique [...] that comedy makes the contradiction the point'.[51] Stephen Halliwell analyses contradictions involved in the different forms of laughter that Old Comedy inspires; the interweaving of refined and vulgar comedy complicates the subject position of the spectator: '[a] key effect of this counterpoint is to make it difficult, and sometimes futile, to distinguish psychologically between laughing *with* and laughing *at* the characters or behaviour depicted on stage'.[52] This peculiar mix of high and low comedy, satire and fantasy, parody and utopia, lampooning and serious political comment makes judging the role and effect of the utopian elements of the plays complicated.

Some critics consider the utopian aspects of Old Comedy as simply and straightforwardly satirical. Aristophanes, it is argued, could not have entertained seriously the propositions of economic or gender equality, women bringing about peace through collective action, or individual agency capable of generating far-reaching change. Again, assumptions are made from the outset that only a reading assuming a conservative set of intentions is possible: 'it is plainly ridiculous that the gods should actually lose their power (in the same way that it is ridiculous that women should be actually on top, as they are in *Lysistrata* and *Assembly Women*)', claims Martin

---

[48] David Konstan points to a passage in Aristophanes' *Acharnians*, where the chorus defends Aristophanes' comedy as just: 'his plays deliver a just message, albeit in a comic or satirical manner' ('Defining the Genre', in *The Cambridge Companion to Greek Comedy*, 28).
[49] Andreas Willi, 'The Language(s) of Comedy', in *The Cambridge Companion to Greek Comedy*, 181.
[50] Ruffell, 'Utopianism', in *The Cambridge Companion to Greek Comedy*, 212.
[51] Stephanie Nelson, 'Aristophanes and the Polis', in *The Political Theory of Aristophanes*, 122.
[52] Halliwell, 'Laughter', in *The Cambridge Companion to Greek Comedy*, 194.

Revermann.[53] Indeed, Lyman Tower Sargent in *Utopianism: A Very Short Introduction* dedicates one short paragraph to Aristophanes, and names him 'the first great *anti*-utopian' (emphasis added).[54] This seems to be based on Sargent's readings of *The Assemblywomen* and *Wealth*: in the case of the former Sargent assume that the women's utopia fails at the end of the play (it does not) and in the case of *Wealth* that it closes with an unfair economic redistribution (also not the case). However, Sargent does endorse Greek uses of the golden age as legitimately utopian: a brief quotation from the Old Comic, Teleclides is used to illustrate this fantastical version of utopia (in contrast to the more realistic, social utopian schematizing of the Platonic sort).[55] For others, the idea that there may be a genuine utopianism present in the golden-age-inspired scenes of a munificent nature, or the automatist utopian encounters found frequently in fragments of Old Comedy by poets such as Archippus, Crates, Cratinus, Metagenes, Teleclides, and Pherecrates, is not even contemplated. Paola Ceccarelli is fairly typical of this view when she argues that 'the comic poets seem to have *parodied* the theme of primitive life', and that this 'joking [...] accords with the affirmative and stabilizing function of comedy, [...] a genre that was acted out within the institutional space of the polis'.[56] Again, assumptions are made about the context, form, and function of Old Comedy, which has led to the discounting of particular readings before the content of the plays is even considered. It is to the content of Old Comic utopian plays that this chapter now turns.

Aristophanes' contemporaries

Golden age utopian themes are present in the plays of Aristophanes, but they remain as hints only in his surviving work; the motif is much stronger in the fragmentary remains of some of the work of his contemporaries. Due to the fragmentary nature of the evidence, it is currently impossible to propose a confident narrative that does justice to the varieties of utopian expression in these plays and their development over time, but some conclusions are possible. A common feature among the fragments of Old Comedies with

---

[53] Martin Revermann, 'Divinity and religious practice', in *The Cambridge Companion to Greek Comedy*, 285.
[54] Lyman Tower Sargent, *Utopianism: A Very Short Introduction* (Oxford: Oxford University Press, 2010), 18.
[55] Sargent, *Utopianism*, 10. Sargent notes that this form of utopianism is not admitted to the category of utopia by some utopian scholars (*Utopianism*, 12).
[56] Paola Ceccarelli, 'Life Among the Savages and Escape from the City', in *The Rivals of Aristophanes*, 463.

utopian themes is the presence of animals and animal choruses (which of course is repeated in Aristophanes' *Birds* discussed later). Ian Storey connects this to the mythological narratives of golden age utopianism, which held that 'beasts could talk and associated freely and easily with men'.[57] Hence, in Archippus' *Fishes* there are political negotiations to establish peace between Athenians and fish, and in Crates' *Wild Beasts*, the prohibition of meat-eating – '(B) [w]ill there be no meat, according to your formula, none at all for us to eat?'[58] – profoundly revolutionizes inter-species relations of the *polis*. But the common and pervasive utopian feature of the fragments is the repeated vision of a profuse nature providing all the culinary luxuries one could wish for, located variously in the past (Cratinus' *Wealth-Gods*), the future as a paradise found (Crates' *Wild Beasts*), on the edges of mapped space (Metagenes' *Thurio-Persians*), or below the ground (Pherecrates' *Miners*).

The following excerpt is a passage from Metagenes' *Thurio-Persians*:

> The River Crathis carries huge barley loaves, self-kneaded, downstream for us, and the other river [Sybaris] drives a wave of cakes and meats and boiled skates still wriggling along there. The little streams on the far side here teem with roasted squid and sea bream and crawfish, and on this side with sausages and minced meat, over here with minnows, over there with pancakes. Fish slices that barbecue themselves fly from above right into the mouth, others < appear > [sic] at our feet, while wheat rolls drift round about us in a circle.[59]

Here the good life is located in a far-off land: Thurii in Italy, a city built upon the remains of Sybaris, which, as Storey establishes, was associated with opulence, as was Persia – the other reference in the play's title.[60] Not only do sumptuous foods appear to be ubiquitous, but they also offer themselves ready prepared, fully cooked, and into the mouth. This automated utopia relieves the human beneficiary of the effort of both agricultural and domestic labour. Luxury is not only freely available but, even better, it also impresses itself upon the human visitor, who needs to make no effort at all to become fully indulged. In fact, a striking rewriting of control seems to be at play: part of the utopian dream is the relinquishing of individual will in exchange for complete satisfaction of the bodily appetites, a retreat into a kind of proto-

---

[57] Ian C. Storey, *Fragments of Old Comedy I*, 214.
[58] Crates, *Wild Beasts* Fragment 19, in John Wilkins, 'Edible Choruses', in *The Rivals of Aristophanes: Studies in Athenian Old Comedy*, 341.
[59] Metagenes, *Thurio-Persians* Fragment 6, in *Fragments of Old Comedy II*, 361.
[60] Storey, ed. and trans. *Fragments of Old Comedy II*, 359.

Lacanian imaginary, where the pre-symbolic subject exists in an unhistorical state of contentment and fulfilment. In this analogy, nature becomes the all-providing, completely dependable, mother figure.

In Crates' *Wild Beasts*, *automatos* (of its own accord), extends beyond the living natural world:

> (A) So no one will have a slave boy or slave girl, and every old man will have to work on his own for himself?
> (B) Not at all, for I shall make everything self-mobile.
> (A) What advantage will they get from that?
> (B) Why, every utensil will appear when someone calls. 'Table, put yourself in place here, and set all the places on your own. Grain sack, start kneading. Pitcher, start pouring, Where is that cup? Come and rinse yourself out. Barley loaf, up on the table. The cook pot should be ladling out the beets by now. Fish, get a move on. "But I'm not done yet on the other side." Well, flip yourself over and baste yourself in salt and oil.'[61]

Once more, the utopian dream is located in the anticipation, as well as fulfilment, of human desires, this time not only by the non-human natural world, but by human-made objects: tables, pitchers, cups, cook pots, and utensils, all of which become animated, moving and functioning on their own to satisfy human appetites. Although the mechanism by which these objects fulfil their roles is not made visible – or rather is assumed to be fantastical – this automation of tools comically anticipates the highly roboticized worlds of some twentieth-century science fiction.[62]

A second conspicuous feature of this passage is the presence of a sceptical, or at least questioning voice, a feature prevalent in utopian prose from Plato, More, Bellamy, Morris, Wells, and beyond. This dialogic trait, so common to the prose tradition is easily imagined in drama with the physical presence on stage of a second character. The second character (A) in this passage assumes the position of the implied spectator – at once quizzical of and curious about – the utopian world, and through the role of inquirer, they facilitate the explanation of the first character (B), the utopian spokesperson. A striking difference from prose fictional utopias however, is the drama's foregrounding of individual agency in its role in utopian schematizing. Character (B) talks

---

[61] Crates, *Wild Beasts* Fragment 16, in *Fragments of Old Comedy, Volume 1*, 217. All further references are to this edition and appear in the main body of the text.

[62] See, for example, Isaac Asimov, *I, Robot* (New York: Gnome Press, 1950); Arthur C. Clarke, *2001 A Space Odyssey* (London: Hutchinson, 1968); Philip K. Dick, *Do Androids Dream of Electric Sheep?* (New York: Doubleday, 1968); William Gibson, *Neuromancer* (New York: Ace, 1985); and Iain M. Banks, *Excession* (London: Orbit, 1996).

of bringing the utopia into existence: 'I shall make everything self-mobile'. The founding of utopias – usually in the near past in prose utopias – is in the present or the future in some of these Old Comedies.

Informed by the following passage from Crates, Ruffell's discussion of *Wild Beasts*[63] points to two competing strains of utopianism in the play:

> I shall [...] provide hot baths for my people, straight from the sea on columns, just like at the House of Healing, so that it will flow into everyone's bathtubs. The water will say, 'Turn me off now, people,' and immediately will arrive on its own a jar full of scented oil, a sponge, and sandals.
>
> 219

This version imagines a sumptuous scene, luxurious and excessive, which is subtly different from the utopian account discussed above, which focuses, perhaps less extravagantly, on the removal of exertion, labour, and hardship. The play adjudicates between different forms of utopian comfort and seems to hesitate over excessive indulgence. Just as in *The Odyssey*, where Homer identifies the superabundance of nature in Scheria as an expression of the Phaeacians' well-ordered, just state, several Old Comic treatments of utopian automation, including *Wild Beasts*, appear not to support extreme immoderation. Thus, in the fragments, the seemingly incongruent utopian paths of, on the one hand, remaking the social world for the betterment of all and on the other living in idleness with a benevolently munificent nature, at times shadow each other, or even collide, which also happens in Aristophanes' *The Birds*, which will be discussed next.

Aristophanes, *The Birds*

The Birds is Aristophanes' longest surviving play and is understood to have been performed in Athens at the City of Dionysia festival in 414 BCE, at which it won second prize, first prize being awarded to Ameipsias' *The Revellers* (of which there are no surviving lines).[64] The play was performed midway through the Peloponnesian War with Sparta (431–401 BCE), and soon after the start of the Sicilian expedition – an imperialist military campaign, which ended in disaster for Athens in 415 BCE, but which had some successes at the time of *The Birds*. Although there are no explicit references to the war in the play, some

---

[63] Ruffell, 'The world turned upside down', 483.
[64] David Barrett, 'Introductory Note to *The Birds*', in Aristophanes, *The Birds and Other Plays*, trans. David Barrett and Alan H. Sommerstein (London: Penguin, 2003), 149–51.

scholars have argued that the creation of a bird utopia in the sky by the central characters (two Athenians, Peisthetaerus and Euelpides), resembles the expansionist and overreaching colonizing activities of the Athenian military project. The play's central protagonist, Peisthetaerus, is also claimed by William Arrowsmith to be resonant of the Athenian leader (and disciple of Socrates), Alcibiades, the main proponent of the Sicilian expedition. In this reading, the play is a parable that warns Athenians of the impending catastrophe of the imperial mission through a 'fantasy politics, utterly destructive in its effects and implications'.[65] But Arrowsmith's interpretation of *The Birds* is dependent on political conjecture and through a narrowly drawn biographical account of Aristophanes that works in opposition to the comic spirit of the play, a point to which I will return later. First, I will summarize the play.

Peisthetaerus and Euelpides yearn for an alternative way of life far removed from Athens, and desire 'a land without lawsuits, where [they] can settle down and live in peace'.[66] They seek out the Thracian King, turned colourful bird, Tereus the hoopoe,[67] who they hope will be able to inform them of alternative societies he may have discovered while flying beyond familiar lands. Euelpides asks the hoopoe if he can help them find 'a really comfortable city: warm and welcoming, like a soft, warm, fleecy blanket' (158). They want a city 'easier to live in' than Athens and without 'an aristocratic form of government' (158). They want a relaxed life, where the only pressures felt are nice ones – being implored to attend a wedding feast or told off for not paying someone's good-looking son any sexual attention. The hoopoe suggests possibilities, but they fail to meet our protagonists' expectations. The solution, Peisthetaerus suggests, is for him, Euelpides, the hoopoe and the rest of the bird community to '[s]tay in one place and found a city' (161). Although the hoopoe quickly responds positively to the plan, the bird chorus, and chorus leader in particular, are initially suspicious, and threaten to attack Peisthetaerus and Euelpides. Peisthetaerus manages to convince the chorus

---

[65] William Arrowsmith, 'Aristophanes' *Birds*: the Fantasy Politics of Eros', *Arion: A Journal of Humanities and the Classics* 1.1 (1973): 119–67, 155.
[66] Aristophanes, *The Birds*, in *The Birds and Other Plays*, trans. Alan H. Sommerstein and David Barrett (London: Penguin, 2003), 156. All further references are to this edition and appear in the main body of the text.
[67] According to Greek mythology, Tereus raped his wife's sister, Philomela, and cut out her tongue to prevent her from revealing him as perpetrator and held her captive, pretending she was dead. But Philomela, through sewing letters in a tapestry, exposed him as the culprit and sent the tapestry to her sister, Procne, who in revenge killed Tereus' (and her) son, Itys, and served him up in a pie to Tereus – a story that is adapted by Shakespeare in *Titus Andronicus*. The Gods turned Tereus into a hoopoe, Procne into a nightingale, and Philomela into a swallow. Both Sophocles and Philocles wrote plays focused on Tereus, although neither survive. The hoopoe in *The Birds* mentions the 'Tragedy of Tereus, by Sophocles' and 'the play by Philocles' (Aristophanes, *The Birds*, 159; 164).

of his good intentions by persuading the birds that they used to be powerful and hugely respected, and that the new city would return the bird community to its rightful place in the hierarchy of species and deities. The first task, Peisthetaerus announces, is to build 'a wall of huge baked bricks' around their new city '[a]nd when it has been set up, Zeus should be told to hand over his power' (173). The hoopoe gives Peisthetaerus and Euelpides a root to chew on that precipitates the growth of wings.

In addition to planning a new city significantly different from the Athens dominated by grievances and lawsuits, the birds rewrite some of the moral bases for human relations. No longer will it be a transgression for a son to hit his father; like the fighting cock who spiritedly challenges his father it will be seen, says the chorus leader, as 'the most natural thing in the world' (179). Runaways, slaves, ex-convicts, and rebels will all be welcome in the new city. They name the city *Nephelokokkygia*, which David Barrett translates as 'Much Cuckoo in the Clouds', others as 'cloud-cuckoo-land'.[68] Peisthetaerus sends Euelpides to help build the city wall (and, rather oddly, that is the last we see of the latter), while Peisthetaerus organizes a naming ceremony. His attempt to make a sacrifice of a goat is comically interrupted by a series of intruders: first a poet; second an oracle man; third a surveyor; fourth an inspector; and fifth a statue seller. After successfully rebuffing them all, a messenger arrives to announce that the wall is complete and that it is 600 feet high and wide enough at the top for two chariots, but a second messenger follows soon after to announce that one of the gods, who we later find out is Iris, has slipped through the guarded gates. After Iris's capture, Peisthetaerus sends her packing but not before claiming ultimate sovereignty, taunting Iris with a threat of sexual violence, and threatening Zeus with a 'squadron of fire-bearing eagles [to] burn down his palace' (196).

Peisthetaerus' endeavour to establish the peaceful city is once more interrupted as a new set of visitors arrive: first a rebellious youth who is attracted by the utopia's radical stance on father/son relations; second a poet, Cinesias who is after a set of wings as he thinks flying will inspire his poetry; third an informer for the courts, who is also after a set of wings to facilitate his spying more efficiently; and fourth Prometheus who arrives in disguise and secretly apprizes Peisthetaerus of the knowledge that the gods are floundering and are planning to request a peace treaty. Immediately after Prometheus' departure, an entourage of Poseidon, Heracles, and the god of the Triballians

---

[68] The earliest known usages of the phrase 'cloud-cuckoo-land' come from the following translations of *The Birds*: H. R. Cary, *The Birds of Aristophanes* (London: Taylor and Hessey, 1824) and B. H. Kennedy, *The Birds of Aristophanes* (London: Macmillan and Co., 1874).

arrives, and negotiations begin. Through wit and cunning, Peisthetaerus successfully secures Zeus' sceptre for the bird city, and, less easily, the character, Sovereignty, as his wife. The play ends in celebratory fashion with the new city *Nephelokokkygia* fully established, and Peisthetaerus victorious; feasting and revelry at the wedding of Peisthetaerus and Sovereignty close the play.

The dramatization of this utopian scheme – through the generic conventions of Old Comedy – makes it difficult to assess the interplay of genuine utopian thought, satirical debunkery, and serious political comment. Wayne Ambler remarks that *The Birds* is 'a wild and crazy comedy, [...] a fantasy whose events are as impossible as those of *A Midsummer Night's Dream*'.[69] Nicholas D. Smith writes, 'most of the utopian elements in Aristophanes's comedies are presented with obvious irony', but at the same time admits that there is 'the reflection of genuine utopianism in these themes'.[70] Dora C. Pozzi emphasizes the 'free[dom] from the bounds of logic' that the mythical allusions in the play – such as the myth of Tereus and Procne – inspire.[71] Fantastical comedy destabilizes an ardent utopian vision, but is at the same time capable of registering utopian otherworldliness; the movement beyond familiar scripts makes visible alternative ways of imagining society.

Devin Stauffer ponders whether Aristophanes supports Peisthetaerus in his act of utopian schematizing and concludes that '[t]here does not seem to be a simple, unambiguous answer to this question'.[72] Early in the play, Peisthetaerus is familiar to a modern reader in his role as part of an absurdist double act:

> **Peisthetaerus** Blast the bird, I nearly died of fright when he came out.
> **Euelpides** My jackdaw was so scared he flew away.
> **Peisthetaerus** You mean *you* were so scared you let go of him: coward!
> **Euelpides** And *you* were so scared you fell down in a heap, *and* let go of your crow.
> **Peisthetaerus** I never let go of her, what are you talking about?
> **Euelpides** Where is she now?
> **Peisthetaerus** [*pompously*] She flew away of her own volition.
>
> 158

---

[69] Wayne Ambler, 'Tyranny in Aristophanes's *Birds*', *The Review of Politics* 74 (2012): 185–206, 186.
[70] Nicholas D. Smith, 'Political Activity and Ideal Economics: Two Related Utopian Themes in Aristophanic Comedy', *Utopian Studies* 3 (1992): 84–94, 84.
[71] Dora C. Pozzi, 'The Pastoral Ideal in *The Birds* of Aristophanes', *The Classical Journal* 81.2 (1986): 119–29.
[72] Devin Stauffer, 'Leo Strauss's UnSocratic Aristophanes?', in *The Political Theory of Aristophanes: Explorations in Poetic Wisdom*, 342.

The Marx brothers, Laurel and Hardy, and *Waiting for Godot*'s Vladimir and Estragon are modern versions of this pair of knockabout comedians: ordinary blokes, down on their luck, looking for comfort, some peace, and a life more affirming than the cold, confusing real world within which they are trapped. Thus, in the context of the early sections of the play, where spectators are invited to laugh at the childish banter between Peisthetaerus and Euelpides, Peisthetaerus emerges as an improbable hero. Unlike the instigators of utopian schemes in classical utopias (such as the Philosopher Kings in Plato's *The Republic* or King Utopos in More's *Utopia*), who are elites, leaders, or nobles, in *The Birds*, it is a pair of unremarkable Athenian citizens, and rather silly ones at that, to whom this privilege is granted.

The challenge of reading the utopian politics of *The Birds* extends to accounting for the new utopian society itself. Gregory W. Dobrov describes the bird community as an 'enigmatic utopian city',[73] while Carroll Moulton refers to Peisthetaerus' 'ambiguous "utopia"',[74] a phrase that forms the subtitle of Ursula Le Guin's critical utopia, *The Dispossessed: An Ambiguous Utopia*.[75] In addition to being an unlikely founder of utopia, Peisthetaerus conflates the roles of founder/utopian citizen and visitor to utopia, roles that are usually disaggregated in prose utopias.[76] The separation of roles in prose utopias helps to provide interpretative stability: for example, Raphael Hythloday in More's book is the visitor to utopia, his outsider status strengthening his credibility as a trusted appraiser of the utopian scheme. What *The Birds* gains is what is often lacking in the prose tradition: registration of human agency. This itself, however, is troubling: on the one hand the ability of Peisthetaerus to refuse the social role prescribed for him and to make society anew unleashes a dynamic utopian energy that creatively rethinks the parameters of both the human subject and the social world. However, as many scholars have pointed out, the enjoyment Peisthetaerus appears to experience from a sustained exercise of power is in tension with the harmonious, peaceful new city he seeks to establish. Yet, David Konstan notes, 'the birds preserve, even in their walled city, a kind of natural solidarity among themselves that needs no law to

---

[73] Gregory W. Dobrov, 'Introduction', in *The City as Comedy: Society and Representation in Athenian Drama*, ed. Gregory W. Dobrov (Chapel Hill, NC: University of North Carolina Press, 1997), xii.

[74] Carroll Moulton, *Aristophanic Poetry* (Göttingen: Vandenhoeck und Ruprecht, 1981), 101.

[75] Ursula Le Guin, *The Dispossessed: An Ambiguous Utopia* (New York: Harper and Row, 1974).

[76] Examples of prose utopias with a separate guest and utopian founder/citizen include Thomas More's *Utopia* (1516), Edward Bellamy's *Looking Backward* (1887), William Morris' *News from Nowhere* (1890), H. G. Wells' *A Modern Utopia* (1905), and Marge Piercy's *Woman on the Edge of Time* (1976).

enforce it. Cloudcuckooland sends packing those emissaries from the real city who come bearing anything that smacks of political structure or contention'.[77] Despite Peisthetaerus' will to power, he has no desire for a litigious culture, property, wealth, or slaves, and is inspired by the primitive nobility of the bird community. Konstan responds to these apparent paradoxes in the play by identifying four different types of utopia: the anomian (absolute lawlessness), antinomian (reversal of laws/norms), the eunomian (just laws/norms), and the magalonomian (excessive/without laws or boundaries, promoting ambition and desire), and argues that *The Birds* expresses them all.

Following Konstan, and in contrast to readings proffered by critics such as F. E. Romer, who contends that the new utopian city is 'reminiscent of Athens and no less dependent on law and the political power of vested interests than Athens',[78] I would suggest that the new utopia is demonstrably different from the Athens Peisthetaerus flees, and in many ways anticipates the prose tradition that follows. Like More's *Utopia* (which originally existed as a peninsular but was deliberately cut off by the utopians from the mainland to create an island) *Nephelokokkygia* is marked out and separated from the surrounding space by a 600-foot wall constructed by the new utopians themselves. Also like More's society, which has a 'permanently garrisoned' tower,[79] the wall in Cloudcuckooland is vigilantly guarded by jackdaws. The paradox of a material locale and a nebulous space, again a feature common to prose utopias, is also a striking attribute of Aristophanes' play. The physical density of the bricks constructing an indisputable and protected boundary materially spatializes the good place, but this is simultaneously a 'noble city in the skies' (197) and as such is ungrounded and free-floating. Thus, one of the recurring features of utopia – the placeless place, or the good society, which is at the same time, nowhere – is explicitly imagined in *The Birds*. It might be a comical and fantastical depiction, but no less so than in More where the geographical coordinates of Utopia remain unknown because someone 'started coughing rather loudly' when the visitor to Utopia, Raphael, revealed them,[80] or in Edward Bellamy's *Looking Backward* (1888) where Julian West – through mesmerism – falls into a trance and wakes up in utopia over 100 years later, or indeed in Joanna Russ's *The Female Man* (1975), where the utopian planet of Whileaway is guarded by talking gnats.[81]

---

[77] David Konstan, 'The Greek Polis and Its Negations: Versions of Utopia in Aristophanes' Birds', in *The City as Comedy*, 10.
[78] F. E. Romer, 'Good Intentions and the ὁδὸς ἡ ἐς κόρακας', in *The City as Comedy*, 52.
[79] Thomas More, *Utopia* (London: Penguin, 2003), 49.
[80] More, *Utopia*, 12.
[81] Edward Bellamy, *Looking Backward 2000-1887* (Oxford: Oxford University Press, 2007); Joanna Russ, *The Female Man* (New York: Bantam Books, 1975).

Classic utopian fiction has tended to interpellate its reader as a critical friend. Often the visitor to utopia mediates the new utopian world and expresses a questioning but open demeanour with which the reader is encouraged to identity. Frequently there are sceptics or dissenters either in the surrounding narrative (this is the case in Book 1 of *Utopia*) or in the utopian society itself (for example in William Morris' *News from Nowhere*, where Clara's grandfather, a 'grumbler', yearns for the pre-utopian days of 'unlimited competition'[82]). These characters serve to produce a dialogic text where the reader becomes immersed in contemplation of the competing attractions of the utopia versus the hostilities of the non-utopian world. However, in Old Comedy, the utopia is dramatized quite differently. The complex hierarchies of discourse produced by literary narrative framing are replaced in Old Comedy by a less rhetorically mediated production. In performance, the *parabasis*, delivered by the chorus of *The Birds* directly to spectators offers a different kind of mediation:

> Listen, you men down there in the half-light! Shadowy, impalpable, dreamlike phantoms: feeble, wingless, ephemeral creatures of clay, dragging out your painful lives till you wither like the leaves and crumble again to dust! Pay attention to us, the immortals.
>
> 177

Contrary to the subtler manipulations of utopian fiction, here spectators are peremptorily directed to pay attention and firmly positioned as subjugated citizens living thwarted lives. Thus, in place of the process of gradual familiarization with the strange utopian world and the estrangement of the familiar non-utopian world, *The Birds* uses alternative methods for promoting the attractions of the utopia. As Niall W. Slater notes, 'in performance it must have been ravishing – and that is the point. It means to entice the viewers just as lovers use gifts of birds to persuade their reluctant beloveds'.[83] This excessive, sensual vision – a full chorus dressed in extravagant and colourful bird costumes speaking of a wondrous new community – serves to compel and seduce spectators, who are addressed directly in a live encounter.

Yet, this charged encounter is potentially mitigated by the production of a particular mode of attention encouraged by conventions of the comic genre that appear to permit spectatorial indulgence of outrageous flights of fancy, obscenities, political subversion, and blasphemy. As I have established, the prose tradition of utopias emerges from a genre mix of travel writing, political

---

[82] William Morris, *News from Nowhere* (London: Penguin, 1993), 173; 174.
[83] Niall W. Slater, 'Performing the City in *Birds*', *The City as Comedy*, 91.

treatise, journal, and epistolary writing, which tend towards a realist mode in form and an earnestness of register. For example, More works hard to produce plausibility through the framing of his utopian narrative inside letter correspondence among several non-fictional personalities, and through spending half of his text – Book 1 – carefully outlining the dysfunctions of his contemporary society. In contrast, the aesthetics of Old Comedy, as we have seen, are both anti-realist in form and witty in register. The spectating positions promoted by Old Comic conventions – whilst expectant of the unruly – are simultaneously radically unstable. This radical instability extends to the critical scholarship on the play. Dobrov notes that '[f]rom its origins in Hellenistic scholarship, the controversy over the meaning of *Birds* developed by the end of the nineteenth century to the point where a bibliography could classify work on the play under six categories, each representing a distinct band in the interpretative spectrum'.[84]

The disruptive character of Old Comedy makes it difficult to perceive a consistent utopian politics in *The Birds*. However, while direct address and early, abrupt, and unmediated appearances of the utopian society differentiate Old Comedy from classic prose utopias, they resonate at the same time with some of the formal features of the critical utopia. As outlined in Chapter 1, Tom Moylan coined this term to describe a new form of predominantly feminist utopian fiction emerging in the 1970s. Rejecting static, blueprint utopianism, the critical utopia (as exemplified in the work of authors such as Ursula Le Guin, Marge Piercy, Sally Miller Gearhart, Samuel R. Delaney, and Joanna Russ) preserves the utopian impulse, the desire to move beyond existing social and political delimitations, without producing perfected, static worlds vulnerable to the charge of totalitarianism.[85] Critical utopias move away from a realist aesthetic and employ more experimental, deconstructive forms. For example, a dynamic shifting temporality in Piercy's *Woman on the Edge of Time* (1976) disrupts linear realism. In Russ's *The Female Man* (1975), gone is the lengthy introductory narrative preparing the reader for encountering utopia common to classic utopias; instead, the utopian character, Janet, speaks in the first person on the first page of the novel. There is also no longer an attempt to represent utopia as flawless. Non-utopian moments, actions, practices, and emotions occur within the utopian space, these permitted as the inevitable effects of human social interaction. Furthermore, the comic mode, particularly in *The Female Man* but also in *Woman on the Edge of Time*, is a critical component of the aesthetic.

---

[84] Gregory W. Dobrov, 'Language, Fiction, and Utopia', in *The City as Comedy*, 96.
[85] See Karl Popper, 'Utopia and Violence', *World Affairs* 149.1 (Summer 1986): 3–9.

However, the critical utopia is historically specific: it is a genre emerging from late 1960s left countercultures and second-wave feminism, and an aesthetic that discovers a means of salvaging utopian fiction after the nightmares of early- and mid-twentieth-century history. The formulation of the critical utopia directly reflects twentieth-century historical concerns, but the concept – particularly its theorization of form – nevertheless speaks to some of the elements of this ancient play. The permeability of the utopian boundary, the accommodation of flaws within the utopian space, and the inclusion of wit and irony are features that the play and critical utopias have in common. By noticing that some of the characteristics deemed to emerge newly in critical utopian fiction of the 1970s were in fact visibly present in the utopian plays of ancient Greece encourages us to rethink some of the critical framework of utopian literary studies that privileges prose fiction as the model utopia at the expense of other utopian forms. Registering *The Birds* as a utopia allows us to appreciate how the play sustains a utopian desire for a better way of being in the world at the same time as destabilizing an earnest attempt at utopian blueprinting.

Aristophanes' *The Assemblywomen*

Aristophanes' other utopia, *The Assemblywomen* (*Ecclesiazusae*), was likely to have been performed between 393–391 BCE. From the surviving plays, it was his penultimate (the last was *Wealth* [388 BCE]) and was written twenty or so years after *The Birds*. The Peloponnesian War had ended in 405 BCE, which left Athens completely defeated and shorn of its empire. After a period of tyrannous rule by Spartan-sympathizing oligarchs, a civil war ensued as the regime was challenged by an army of exiled citizens under the leadership of Thrasybulus, who, after some months returned to Athens and successfully reinstated the democratic constitution. Although Athens experienced a degree of economic recovery after this, it also disastrously resumed hostilities with Sparta. David Barrett notes: '[t]he state of war dragged on, [which resulted in] a drain on money and manpower: the future was obscure, the economy shaky, counsels divided, and the glory of Athens (it seemed) a thing of the past'.[86] *The Assemblywomen* cannot be dated precisely, and thus it is difficult to know with accuracy the exact historical context for the play's production, but it is known that there were real concerns about poverty, justice, the operations of power, and the political future of the city.

---

[86] David Barrett, Introductory Note to *The Assemblywomen*, in Aristophanes, *The Birds and Other Plays* (London: Penguin, 2003), 217.

The play begins with the heroine, Praxagora, gathering a bundle of items from her house – '*her husband's cloak and shoes, a walking-stick, a false beard and a bundle of ceremonial headwreaths*' – and walking out onto the street in the early hours of the morning while it is still dark.[87] In an address to her lamp Praxagora reveals she has initiated a plot. The chorus leader and other women arrive, also with beards and clothing taken from their husbands and we learn that one has 'grown an absolute forest under [her] armpits' and another discarded her razor, 'so as to get hairy all over and not look like a woman at all' (224). Fairly soon, we discover Praxagora's plan, which is for women to enter the Assembly in disguise as men and speak to a motion proposing that the Assembly passes control of Athens to the women since they are so adept at managing their homes. Praxagora's argument is that women are predictable and therefore dependable. Furthermore, women's maternal dispositions means that 'they will naturally be concerned for the safety of our soldiers' and 'ensure them an adequate supply of food' (230). The final part of Praxagora's argument highlight's women's 'resourceful' natures 'when it comes to ways of raising money', and because women know 'all the tricks already' they are much less likely to be duped' (230). Praxagora has become skilled in speechmaking through overhearing speakers and studying their technique when she lived 'up on the Pnyx' (230).

While the women head towards the Assembly the scene turns to their husbands left behind. Praxagora's husband, Blepyrus, appears in the street '*dressed in Praxagora's yellow undergown and a pair of pretty Persian slippers*' (233). The ribaldry is amplified by Blepyrus' confession of his constipated state; he asks the audience: '[h]ey, anyone out there with any experience of bottoms? [...] Oh, Goddess of Childbirth, can you look on unmoved as I crouch here, bulging, but bunged up? It's just like a scene in some low comedy' (235). This scatological and meta-theatrical humour is expressive of the popular grotesque, the popularity of which is performatively reproduced through the breaking of the fourth wall, and the interpellation of spectators as knowing indulgers of such vulgarisms. Spectators are permitted to take pleasure in the toilet humour through their simultaneous positioning as shrewd participants in meta-theatrical jokes. This scene also serves to reinforce the women's case: while Praxagora reveals an adroit command of rhetoric and speechmaking, an impressive ability to plot a takeover, and clever appropriation of male clothing to achieve her aims, her husband appears comically desperate to relieve his bowels and emasculated in his wife's nightie and slippers.

---

[87] Aristophanes, *The Assemblywomen*, in *The Birds and Other Plays*, trans. David Barrett and Alan H. Sommerstein (London: Penguin, 2003), 222. All further references are to this edition and appear in the main body of the text.

We then hear from Chremes, a man returning from the Assembly, that Praxagora – 'a good-looking young man with a pale face' (236) – made a speech that referred to women's intelligence, good financial management, discretion, as well as the likelihood of there being 'no informing, no prosecuting, no conspiring to overthrow the democracy' (237) with women in charge. Praxagora's motion was passed: '[t]he general feeling was, that as this was the only method that hadn't yet been tried, they might as well try it' (237). After some crude joking about sexual demands, Blepyrus and Chremes seem to take it in their stride, and Praxagora sets out her plan for a society without theft, envy, poverty, and rivalry but wonders, '[w]hat worries me is whether the audience here will be ready to try out new methods instead of muddling along for ever with the old ones that we know only too well' (241). In *The Birds* the only preparation spectators receive for their encounter with the utopian scheme is the emphasis on Athens as a tiresome, litigators' city. In *The Assemblywomen*, Praxagora's motion was submitted in response to a call 'for proposals on how to save Athens', thus the seemingly intractable problems to which the utopian scheme purports to respond are explicitly placed in the foreground; furthermore, as we have seen, Praxagora articulates the advantages of women's rule on several occasions, and she now engages directly with spectators as critically thinking sceptics (235). All this takes place before the utopian city has been established.

Praxagora's scheme is radically utopian, not just because it overturns patriarchal rule, but also because it institutes a proto-communist economy: 'everyone is to have an equal share in everything and live on that [...]. There will be one common stock of necessities for everybody, and these will be shared equally. [...] I shall declare all land, all money, and all private possessions to be common property' (242). The women's role will be to manage the common stock and the affairs of the state efficiently and fairly. As part of the process of defamiliarizing the fetish of private property – common to many a utopia to come – Praxagora claims: '[n]o one will be motivated by need: everybody will have everything – leaves, cutlets, cakes, warm cloaks, wine, head-wreaths, chickpeas. So what advantage will there be in hanging on to one's wealth?' (242) Thus, in addition to establishing collective ownership of property, this new society is also overlain with an appeal to the sensual appetites, resonant of the golden age: good food, warmth and comfort, decorative adornment, and wine.

Sexual activity too – along with its democratization – is selected as an important sphere of human interaction in need of rethinking in the new utopia. Anyone who wants to have sex with someone young and attractive will need to sleep with 'the plain unattractive' (243) one first. Perhaps more far-reaching are the accompanying implications of this rethinking of sexual relations (a kind of proto free love movement) – the replacement of the private, patriarchal family with the collective fathering of children, who 'will regard all older men as fathers' (249). Although not permitted in More's *Utopia*, this libertarian approach to sex and reproduction is repeated positively in several canonical nineteenth- and twentieth-century utopias.[88] Even in More's text, divorce is permitted and there is the (rather peculiar) stipulation that men and women show themselves naked to each other before marriage, recognition it seems that at least some conservative rules determining sexual behaviour should be abolished in the interests of happier sexual relations. Marriage is significantly absent from Plato's *The Republic*, and as in *The Assemblywomen*, women and children are held in common. I will return to comparisons with *The Republic* later.

Defamiliarizing ideological norms upholding private property regimes (a process commonly reproduced in utopian literature through the ages) takes the familiar form of Socratic dialogue in the play:

> **Blepyrus** [...] supposing somebody has too much to drink at dinner, and starts knocking people about. How's he going to pay compensation? Eh? That's got you!
> **Praxagora** It'll be stopped out of his food allowance. He'll think twice before committing assault again, once his stomach has had to suffer.
> **Blepyrus** And there won't be any thieves?
> **Praxagora** How can anyone steal what he owns already? [...] If this fellow wants to take your cloak, give it to him. Why fight about it, when you can go to the common store and get a better one?
>
> 245

The viewpoint of the sceptical spectator is aligned with Blepyrus, who in turn facilitates Praxagora's fully rational explication of the workings of the utopian city. Anticipating the utopian tradition to come, a dynamic debate of utopian value is established through this dialogue between proponent and sceptic, while the spectators are encouraged to open themselves up to speculative thinking.

Scene two opens with Chremes organizing his possessions to contribute to the common stock. A character named Citizen arrives, and in an aside reveals his plans not to volunteer his possessions at least until he knows 'what

---

[88] In Morris' *News from Nowhere* (1888), although monogamy is usual, there is no marriage contract, and utopians are free to engage in romantic and sexual encounters with others if they please. In several critical utopias (e.g. Piercy's *Woman on the Edge of Time* and Le Guin's *The Dispossessed*) monogamous marriage is replaced by a freer approach to love, sex, and parenting.

it's all about first' (248). In an exchange with Chremes he voices the most common argument against utopia: '[g]rabbing, not giving, is what comes natural to us' (248). After failing with this line of critique, he changes tack by alluding to the frequent U-turns of the Assembly in the past, to which Chremes responds: '[y]es, but that was different. That was when *we* were in charge. Now the women are running things' (248). The two men meet again at the *agora* where Chremes is depositing his goods; on learning of the feast planned for all citizens ('the couches are piled high with cushions and rugs, the drinks are ready for pouring, the perfumers are standing by; the stoves are aglow, waiting to grill your fish; the meat is on the spit, the cakes in the oven' [251]), Citizen appears to devise a plan to keep his property 'without losing [his] share of all this public feasting' (252). Significantly, nothing comes of this, and we see nothing more of Citizen in the rest of the play.

Scene three reverts to a ribald demonstration of the new laws on sexual interaction – in this example as hilarious slapstick. The scene revolves around a young man being fought over by a young woman and an old 'hag', who is later joined by a second and then third 'hag'. Citing the new laws, the 'hags' insist on their rights to sex with him before he is allowed to sleep with the young woman. With plenty of crudities and physical humour, the scene ends with the following stage direction: '[*t*]*he two women haul him into second hag's house and the door is slammed shut*' (261). Although Praxagora champions a series of plausible arguments for the utopian arrangements, this vignette – whilst bawdily comical – seems to suggest that the scheme is not flawless.

However, scene four – the conclusion to the play – ends with happy, harmonious revelry. The setting is '[*a*] *lively street scene, somewhere in Athens. The public banquet is nearly over and many citizens [...] have already come away from it, in festive mood; they carry torches and seek female company, which is easily found. There is music and dancing. The chorus mingle with the throng*' (261). This is extended beyond the play: through a further breaking of the fourth wall, the chorus leader makes a direct appeal to spectators: 'anyone in the audience who's enjoyed the play [...] can come along too, you're welcome to everything' (261). The final lines make further references to culinary delights and feasting, and an appeal to winning first prize. Significantly at the close of the play, the utopian city is still in full swing, rather than undermined by Citizen or any other sceptic, and instead of the sexual harassment of some young man, sexual encounters appear to be amorous and consensual.[89]

---

[89] There was a private production of *Peace* directed by Michèle Heydorff in 1995 as part of the festival, 'Wine and Utopia', which took place in the Minervois in the South of France. The production offered 'a depiction of a pastoral, village utopia', and before every performance audience members partook in a lavish feast of country food and copious

Yet, despite *The Assemblywomen*'s adoption of recognizable utopian characteristics, several scholars argue that the play is not utopian, or even that it is *anti*-utopian.[90] Sargent claims that Praxagora's 'legislation failed not because it was bad but because the human race was not capable of the required altruism. This is a standard reason given for rejecting utopias'.[91] This aligns with Sargent's claim that Aristophanes was the first anti-utopian, but it is not clear how this interpretation is arrived at: the play closes in full celebratory mode after the inauguration of the new utopian state. For scholars, such as Edith Hall, the play is 'an absurdist flight of comic fantasy', and Chremes' arrangement of his goods to donate to the new utopian state resembles citizens preparing to take part in the opening procession of the Panathenaea (an important festival marking the New Year). Hall considers the analogical new era in the play to be that of 'female power and communism, characterized by the joint ownership of possessions which now ludicrously march in festival procession'.[92] A common starting point for scholars, who do not consider the play to be engaging sincerely with utopian ideas is the assumption that women's rule and common ownership of goods is *de facto* ludicrous and unimaginable in this context outside of satire. Froma I. Zeitlin rules out the possibility of female agency in these dramas as ever functioning as an end in itself; she considers more complex and extended female characterization as serving as 'antimodels' or 'hidden models' for masculinity.[93] Peter Nichols describes the new utopian state as 'at once comical and chilling' and later states: 'Aristophanes elucidates the madness and tyranny attendant upon abolition of the private life and the affront to human nature associated with the abolition of private property.'[94] This is a pronounced example of the political partiality of scholarly responses to Aristophanic comedy, a partiality that is, of course, present in every act of interpretation.

---

amounts of wine. Malika Bastin-Hammou describes it as 'a fantasy version of rustic authenticity, the indulgence of agrarian pleasure', and the manifestation of 'a dream of gathering different people together [...] around a collective feast'. ['Aristophanes' *Peace* on the Twentieth-Century French Stage: From Political Statement to Artistic Failure', in *Aristophanes in Performance 421BC–AD2007: Peace, Birds and Frogs*, ed. Edith Hall and Amanda Wrigley (London: MHRA and Maney Publishing, 2007), 253.]

[90] See also Kenneth S. Rothwell *Politics and Persuasion in Aristophanes' Ecclesiazusae* (Leiden and New York: E. J. Brill, 1990) for a reading of the play as deeply ironic.
[91] Sargent, *Utopianism*, 18.
[92] Edith Hall, 'Comedy and Athenian Festival Culture', in *The Cambridge Companion to Greek Comedy*, 309.
[93] Froma I. Zeitlin, 'Playing the Other: Theater, Theatricality, and the Feminine in Greek Drama', in *Nothing to do with Dionysos?*, 69.
[94] Peter Nichols, 'The Comedy of the Just City: Aristophanes' *Assemblywomen* and Plato's *Republic*', 259–74, 260; 271.

The claim that Praxagora's utopian scheme fails depends crucially on drawing particular conclusions about the significance of the presence of the dissident citizen. Dissident detractors have been recurring presences in utopian fictional worlds from antiquity to the present. They generate a dialogic dynamic for utopian ideas, ideas inherently difficult to imagine. They provide a proxy for the sceptical reader/spectator, who is more inclined to be receptive to the utopian encounter if doubt forms part of the economy of the play's ideas. In drama, there is no mediating third-person narration qualifying the sceptical voice, so there is more potential for the sceptical voice to be destabilizing. Yet, there are other ways of interpreting a play's ideological viewpoints, and in the case of *The Assemblywomen*, Citizen's refusal to donate his property to common ownership is pitted against another citizen (importantly unrelated to Praxagora), Chremes, who happily participates in the communist scheme, simultaneously making reference to many other citizens content to do the same. As I have said, importantly the utopian scheme remains intact at the end of the play, and therefore any reading that claims the scheme fails, is moving significantly outside of the play's parameters.

Yet, although I am making a case for the play to be considered as offering a genuine consideration of utopian thinking, there is no doubt that *The Assemblywomen* simultaneously contains satire, anti-utopian viewpoints, and absurdist elements. While the dissident citizen's voice is satisfactorily counteracted, the implication is that he is left plotting against the scheme, or at least left to find a way of benefiting from the utopia without donating his property to the common store. John Zumbrunnen writes: '[p]erhaps Aristophanes means his skepticism as a convenient foil soon overtaken by the power of Praxagora's fantastic vision. Or perhaps the Dissident reflects the ironic undercurrent of the play'.[95] Moreover, it is hard to make a case for the sex scene (where a young man is fought over by three 'hags') to be other than at best crudely entertaining, and at worse, a perverse illustration (and therefore a non-endorsement of) the new utopian sex laws. While the final scene offers another utopian counteraction, this time of happy, consensual flirtation, the earlier sex scene, which is comparatively lengthy, continues to resonate, largely due to sexist and ageist assumptions that are as persistent in modernity as they are in antiquity.

To read the play straightforwardly as *either* satirical *or* as sincerely utopian is to suppress parts of the play's systems of meaning-making. As Roselli entreats, '[s]urely it is important to note both support for and opposition to

---

[95] John Zumbrunnen, 'Fantasy, Irony, and Economic Justice in Aristophanes' *Assemblywomen* and *Wealth*', *The American Political Science Review* 100.3 (August 2006): 319–33, 326.

economic reforms built into these plays'.⁹⁶ Equally the play seems to accommodate both perverse and affirmative representations of the new utopian forms of sexual interaction. Yet, crucially, I would suggest, what makes the play more utopian than anti-utopian is the eloquence and charisma of the heroine, Praxagora, whose energy, skill, and intelligence are sustained throughout the play. Erin K. Moodie points to the number of occasions where there is a close encounter between Praxagora and her women conspirators and the audience, particular through direct address: '[t]hat his female characters enjoy a nearly uncontested rapport with the audience also suggests that Aristophanes is not parodying the ideas presented in the *Assemblywomen*'.⁹⁷ Robert C. Elliott is right in his conclusion that 'Aristophanes takes his women and their ideal state seriously'.⁹⁸ As is the case with *The Birds*, approaching *The Assemblywomen* as a comical utopia that is in part satirical – satirical of both the non-utopian context of its production *and* of some of its utopian aspects – allows us to appreciate more fully the play's variety of dramaturgical and aesthetic strategies, some seemingly in contradiction with others.

Conclusion

During the fifth and fourth centuries BCE the Old Comedy of Athenian drama put utopian ideas and desires on stage for the first time. Alongside these comic plays, tragic drama utilized familiar stories and myths to construct inherently un-utopian theatre. Other narrative forms such as Homer's and Hesiod's poetry contained a few vignettes of utopian images, and although Plato's *The Republic* is undoubtedly utopian speculation, it is a philosophical dialogue, not a fictional representation of utopia. Hence, the emergence of fully realized (rather than mere glimpses of) utopias in comic form is paradoxical: Old Comedy – because of its formal plasticity and anarchic disregard for thematic and ideological discipline – is the very form that makes possible the imagination of utterly alternative worlds. As Wayne Ambler states, 'the very atmosphere of ridiculousness may [...] serve Aristophanes' higher purposes, for amid such madcap goings-on, everything becomes permissible'.⁹⁹

---

[96] David Kawalko Roselli, 'Social Class', in *The Cambridge Companion to Greek Comedy* (Cambridge: Cambridge University Press, 2014), 253.

[97] Erin K. Moodie, 'Aristophanes, The *Assemblywomen* and the Audience: The Politics of Rapport', *The Classical Journal* 107.3 (2012): 257–81, 273–4.

[98] Robert C. Elliott, *The Shape of Utopia: Studies in a Literary Genre* (Chicago and London: University of Chicago Press, 1970), 21.

[99] Wayne Ambler, 'On the Anabasis of Trygaeus: An Introduction to Aristophanes' *Peace*', in *The Political Theory of Aristophanes: Explorations in Poetic Wisdom*, 154.

The great contribution of Old Comic utopian dramas to the utopian genre is the genre's use of satirical comedy in enabling alternative depictions. Utopian satire re-emerges in More's *Utopia* both in Book 1's satirical attack on early modern European society, and in the text's comedic framing of the utopia (although More's satirical treatment of the utopia is gentle and held in check by extensive use of genres more expressive of sincerity and didacticism – letters, travel writing, and political treatise). In Old Comedy, the satirical form actively destabilizes the utopian meanings of the plays. Through the unreliability of register – with its movement from sincerity to irony, ardour to satire – Old Comedy understates what in more realist forms would approach an earnest and sober articulation of a utopian society. Nevertheless, utopian desire sustains these satirical utopian works; as Elliott observes, 'there is inevitable doubleness of effect – longing as well as laughter'.[100]

---

[100] Elliott, *The Shape of Utopia*, 5.

3

Temporary utopias of female community

Introduction

This chapter focuses on Margaret Cavendish's utopian plays *The Female Academy* (1662), *The Convent of Pleasure* (1668), and *Bell in Campo* (1662). These works are striking for several reasons but two particularly stand out: first, they form a rare trilogy of utopian *plays* during a period in which scores of utopias in literary prose were in circulation; second, they appear to be amongst the first utopian fictional works by a female author.[1] Like Aristophanes discussed in Chapter 2, Cavendish's class allegiances and their permeation of her utopian texts complicates a straightforward utopian reading (or at least a proto-socialist reading) of her work. Cavendish's ideological commitment to royalism and her aristocratic interests are repeatedly cited in scholarship on her work. Yet her audacious, separatist utopias of women are unquestionably radical for their rewriting of gendered identity and practice, particularly when considered in the context of early modern utopian thinking and aesthetics more broadly.

The early modern period was the historical moment within which utopia became rooted in the cultural imagination and began to develop, multiply, and indeed flourish. The publication of More's *Utopia* (1516) was swiftly followed by many other creative literary experiments in refashioning the world, including the following prose utopias (and these are a tiny fraction of published utopias during this period): Tomasso Campanella, *City of the Sun* (1602), Robert Burton, *The Anatomy of Melancholy* (1621), Francis Bacon, *New Atlantis* (1627), Francis Godwin, *The Man in the Moone; or, A Discourse of A Voyage Thither* (1638), Gabriel Platte, *A Description of the Famous Kingdome of Macaria* (1641), Samuel Gott, *Nova Solyma* (1648), and Henry Neville, *The Isles of Pines* (1668). Many of these utopias – including More's – were inspired by 'new world' discoveries of early colonial expansionism. Exotic far-off islands with temperate climates, beautiful environments, and

---

[1] Christine de Pizan wrote *The Book of the City of the Ladies* in 1405. It describes an allegorical city, which houses an array of famous historical women, and makes the case for the importance of valuing women.

non-European peoples offered imaginative possibilities for envisioning new forms of social relations and political community. Indeed, the much smaller number of dramatic examples of work interested in utopian themes (or science fiction in the case of the last in this list) – such as William Shakespeare's *The Tempest* (1611), William Davenant and John Dryden's adaptation of it in *The Tempest, Or The Enchanted Island* (1670) and Aphra Behn's *The Emperor of the Moon* (1687) – similarly drew on the colonial imagination to think about alternative ways of organizing social life.[2] This intersection of utopian world-making and early European colonial enterprise prompts Nicole Pohl to observe that 'Utopia is inseparable from the imaginary voyage'.[3]

Yet, this was not the case with the utopian plays of Cavendish. *The Female Academy*, *The Convent of Pleasure*, and *Bell in Campo* do not take inspiration from colonial narrative or the island utopia, but instead seek to rethink gender relations in temporary, liminal, and – in the case of *The Female Academy* and *The Convent of Pleasure* – heterotopic spaces. The utopias are temporary as the utopian boundaries within each play are ultimately breached which is followed by some form of reintegration into the non-utopian world at the dramas' close, albeit on different social terms. Unlike the material permanency of Aristophanes' bird paradise or More's island utopia, the utopian spaces in *The Female Academy* and *The Convent of Pleasure* are liminal, in-between spaces, which seem to exist in a state of ambiguous, fluid contingency. These spaces are at the same time heterotopic in the Foucauldian sense; unlike the unreal spaces of utopia, heterotopias are real. They form 'counter-sites, a kind of effectively enacted utopia in which the real sites, all the other real sites that can be found within the culture, are simultaneously represented, contested, and inverted'.[4] Theatre scholar, Joanne Tompkins, has examined the physical spaces of certain performances as heterotopias due to their 'capacity to influence an audience's understanding of the relationship between the theatre and the world outside its walls', this making them potentially potent sites of both contestation and the figuration of alternatives.[5] The convent and the academy are both heterotopic and utopian: they are actual physical spaces, subversive of the dominant culture beyond their walls, but they are simultaneously utopias – they produce new utopian communities with alternative practices and social relations.

[2] See David Cressy, 'Early Modern Space Travel and the English Man in the Moon', *American Historical Review* 111.4 (October 2006): 961–82.
[3] Nicole Pohl, 'Utopianism after More: The Renaissance and Enlightenment', in *The Cambridge Companion to Utopian Literature*, ed. Gregory Claeys (Cambridge: Cambridge University Press, 2010), 53.
[4] Michel Foucault, 'Of Other Spaces', *Diacritics* 16 (Spring 1986): 22–7, 24.
[5] Joanne Tompkins, *Theatre's Heterotopias: Performance and the Cultural Politics of Space* (Basingstoke: Palgrave, 2014), 27.

In *Bell in Campo* the utopia does not materialize in spatial form; the utopia in this play is located in the practices and processes of women's self-organization – leaving the domestic sphere, building an Amazonian army, training themselves to become disciplined warriors, and fighting successfully on the battlefield. While reflecting some key interests of male utopian art of the period, Cavendish's plays are at the same time markedly dissimilar both in form and theme, and it is this difference the chapter will go on to discuss. But first a brief overview of early modern utopian literature will provide a context for appreciating Cavendish's particular intervention.

Utopian literary contexts

Reverberations of More's *Utopia* were felt in the publication of an abundance of utopian texts across Europe during the succeeding century and beyond, as well as in the inclusion of the world 'utopia' in an English dictionary in 1611.[6] Both the variety of utopian content (golden age visions, millenarian thinking, political state-building, the earthly paradise, ideal monarchy, radical democracy) and the range of literary forms (drama, prose, poetry, sermons, letters, pamphlets) were vast and prevalent. Pohl groups the diverse array of utopian depictions in the early modern period into two categories: the 'archistic' and the 'anarchistic'. The former involved bold new societies tightly regulated and controlled by statutory or governmental laws, systems, and processes in the delivery of the common good; the latter promoted self-governance with a view to maximizing freedom and autonomy.[7] The archistic can be mapped on to the 'city utopia' and the anarchistic onto the 'body utopia' (see Chapter 1). During the early modern period, there was, as Krishan Kumar states, an assertion of the 'primacy of the city against the anarchic countryside': city utopias 'pitted reason against the formless chaos of nature'.[8] Campanella's *City and the Sun* and Bacon's *New Atlantis* (in addition to More's *Utopia*) offer two of the most well-known examples of the archistic utopia, which presented an ideal city imagined through the application of rational philosophy and modelled on Hellenic ideals.

The anarchistic utopia combined an interest in self-governance, freedom, and autonomy with Arcadian abundance and the carnivalesque revelry of the Land of Cockaygne, the latter drawing inspiration from the idea of the Golden Age in Hesiod, which also runs through Old Comedy (as discussed in Chapter 2). Spanish novelists Antonio de Guervara and Miguel de Cervantes drew on this anarchistic utopian form to document the utopian desires of

[6] Pohl, 'Utopianism after More', 57.
[7] Ibid., 52.
[8] Krishan Kumar, *Utopianism* (Milton Keynes: Open University Press, 1991), 15.

rural migrants in conflict with farmers in *Libro Llamado Menospecio de Corte y Alabança de Aldea* (1591) and *Don Quixote de La Mancha* (1605) respectively.⁹ An exemplar of the anarchistic utopian interest in the liberated self is François Rabelais' *Abbey of Thélème* (1534), where, the Abbey welcomes both men and women into its libertarian space, within which its inhabitants are free to pursue their own desires and interests.

However, this kind of binaristic categorization inevitably suppresses the internal differences within utopian texts – and More's *Utopia* is a case in point. While clearly an example of alternative state-building informed by rational engagement with political philosophy, *Utopia* is simultaneously a creative, imaginative work, which is, as Lee Cullen Khanna describes, 'the mirror opposite of More's historical location'.¹⁰ In this way, More's vision is outside of historical temporality, which in turn, marks it as feminine: 'one could argue that the genre itself is feminized by its secondary and relational status in conjunction with the implicitly inscribed masculine "reality" or history'.¹¹ Furthermore, its playful, slippery use of language as discussed in Chapter 1 – its deconstructive moments of undoing – along with its deployment of jokes (utopian toilets are made of gold, remember) act as a feminine teasing of the more serious, masculine pursuit of state-building. The political implications of this form of gendering – the way, as Khanna, observes, that 'such a division mimics a gender ideology that casts the feminine as pleasurable distraction from masculine work and duty' – will become relevant once more when we move on to consider Cavendish.¹²

Meanwhile, alongside the plentiful examples of utopias inspired by colonial conquest there was also a proliferation of proto-communist utopian representations of economic equality emitting from the civil war discourse of the radical religious sects during the 1640s and 1650s, such as the Levellers, Diggers, Ranters, Anabaptists, and Fifth Monarchists. Prominent examples include Gerrard Winstanley's *The Law of Freedom* (1652) and Fifth Monarchist, Mary Cary's, *A New and More exact Mappe of New Jerusalems Glory when Jesus Christ and his Saint with him shall reign on earth a Thousand years, and possess all Kingdoms* (1651).¹³ Winstanley's revolutionary vision of political

---

[9] Pohl, 'Utopianism after More', 56.
[10] Lee Cullen Khanna, 'Utopian Exchanges: Negotiating Difference in Utopia', in *Gender and Utopia in the Eighteenth Century: Essays in English and French Utopian Writing*, ed. Brenda Tooley and Nicole Pohl (London: Routledge, 2007), 18.
[11] Ibid.
[12] Ibid.
[13] 'The Diggers' was the name later applied to a group who called themselves the 'True Levellers', 'true' reflecting their more radical stance on economic justice compared to the more moderate Levellers. The Diggers emerged during the turmoil of the English Civil War and were agrarian communists and pacifists. The Fifth Monarchists (or The Fifth Monarchy Men as they called themselves) believed that the second coming of Christ was

economy extended simultaneously to a total rethinking of the human subject and social relations. Cary's intervention – less communistic and more, as Robert Appelbaum describes it, a vision of 'radical amelioration, projected onto an ideal canvas of millenarian destiny' – is at the same time significant for its feminist impulses, particularly evident in her bold defence of women preachers and prophets.[14]

Other notable utopian contributions by women (published shortly after Cavendish's utopian plays) include Aphra Behn's 1684 poem 'The Golden Age' and Mary Astell's *A Serious Proposal to the Ladies* (1684). Behn's poem – a translation and adaptation of the opening chorus of the Italian writer Torquato Tasso's pastoral play *Aminta* (1573) – quite significantly expands on the original. As well as depicting nature as verdant and animated, Behn imagines the golden age as a liberating time for women: as, according to Heidi Laudien, 'a time without a gendered social structure, where both young maids and swains are encouraged to seize the day and to live for the moment'.[15] In *A Serious Proposal to the Ladies* (1695), Astell invents a 'female monastery' where, as Alessa Johns observes, women achieve 'subjectivity and independence in the context of an ideal society in which they do not assert identity but model themselves after each other, imitating the copies of heavenly originals they experience around them'.[16] Astell's community of women appears to have directly influenced Sarah Scott's 1762 utopian novel, *Millenium Hall*.[17]

Dramatic examples of utopia are very few in number. As mentioned, there are Rabelais' *Abbey of Thélème* and Tasso's *Aminta*, and, there is Shakespeare's *The Tempest*. The latter is not a utopia *per se*; it is a debate of utopian ideas (at least it is so in part). Its story of travel, shipwreck, an exotic island, islanders imagined as other, and different languages and cultures are clearly inspired by contemporary travel narratives and the utopian possibility of what the colonial imagination projects as fertile opportunity. Gonzalo's famous 'commonwealth' speech evokes the 1609 Bermuda pamphlets and paraphrases

---

imminent and that this would bring with it the establishment of the fifth monarchy (the four previous being the Babylonian, Persian, Macedonian, and Roman). See Christopher Hill, *The World Turned Upside Down: Radical Ideas During the English Revolution* (London: Penguin, 1991); Diane Purkiss, *The English Civil War: A People's History* (London: Perennial, 2007).

[14] Robert Appelbaum, *Literature and Utopian Politics in Seventeenth-Century England* (Cambridge: Cambridge University Press, 2002), 152.
[15] Heidi Laudien, 'Aphra Behn: Pastoral Poet', *Women's Writing* 12.1 (2005): 43–58, 49.
[16] Alessa Johns, 'Mary Astell's "Excited Needles": Theorizing Feminist Utopia in Seventeenth-Century England', *Utopian Studies* 7.1 (1996): 60–74, 60.
[17] Ruth Perry describes *Millenium Hall* as 'an imaginative fulfilment of Mary Astell's first book' (Ruth Perry, 'Mary Astell's Response to the Enlightenment', in *Women and the Enlightenment*, ed. Margaret Hunt, Margaret Jacob, Phyllis Mack, and Ruth Perry [New York: Haworth Press, 1984], 112).

Montaigne's views on natural justice in his essay 'On Cannibals', which documented his observations of Brazilian natives whom he considered to be living peaceful, utopian lives. Gonzalo's utopian speech – with its proto-Rousseauian vision of the benevolent capacity of human nature combined with evocations of a munificent natural world resonant of the golden age – competes against other projections of the good life. Prospero's reign on the island contains suggestions of a skewed form of More's utopia – with its colonial beginnings, emphasis on education, and the deployment of slavery as punishment for transgression. While the play closes with Prospero restored as Duke of Milan, Caliban repentant, Ariel freed, and Naples and Milan united through the marriage of Miranda and Ferdinand, both Prospero's and Gonzalo's utopian projections are found wanting.

Margaret Cavendish: biographical contexts

It is difficult to appreciate Cavendish's artistic output without taking some account of what we know of her life. Her aristocratic roots and royalist allegiances significantly structure the direction of her life and work. Born Margaret Lucas in 1623, she lived with her mother Elizabeth Lucas (her father died when she was an infant) at St John's Abbey in Colchester, Essex, until moving to Oxford in 1642 to become one of Queen Henrietta Maria's Ladies-in-waiting. She then followed the Queen into exile in Paris in 1644. In 1645, she married William Cavendish, first Marquis, then Duke, of Newcastle, a marriage by all accounts that seemed to be fulfilling and happy. William had two surviving children from his first marriage and although he and Margaret tried for a child, Margaret never became a mother. They lived in both Rotterdam and Antwerp before returning to England after the Restoration and set about restoring the Cavendish estates.

As was commonly the case for women of her rank, Cavendish did not benefit from a formal education, but she did have access to libraries and rudimentary schooling from a private tutor. She seemed to be self-taught on a wide range of topics usually only accessible to male thinkers and writers. She also associated with contemporary writers and philosophers (such as Hobbes and Descartes) who were part of her, William's, and her brother-in-law's social circle. That Cavendish published her creative works at all was audacious enough (she was one of the first women to publish literary writing in her own name) but to publish across multiple forms and genres and on a variety of subject matter was a provocation too far for many. She published poems, plays, prose fiction, philosophy, scientific compendiums, orations, letters, aesthetic theory, and science fiction. Cavendish's highly original, genre-blurring, philosophical-scientific-fantastical utopian prose fiction *The Blazing World* (1666) is described by Christopher Marlow as 'a generous and generative exemplar both for women's literary achievement and the literary mode that would come to be known as science fiction'.[18] Cavendish's bold intervention into a masculine sphere combined with an unconventional self-display: she was known to experiment with unusual, sometimes masculine clothing, and expressed other eccentricities such as bashfulness at the same time as being considered extravagant and ostentatious. This potent mix of a performance of public intellectualism and gender transgression is a useful context for understanding Samuel Pepys' much-cited dismissal of Cavendish as 'a mad, conceited and ridiculous woman'.[19]

This hostility towards Cavendish has endured across the centuries. Frank E. Manuel and Fritzie P. Manuel include an extraordinary appraisal of *Blazing World* in their lengthy study of utopian thought in the western world. They claim that this monumental, generically experimental, and politically penetrating text 'has much in common with the delusions of Dr. Schreber analyzed by Sigmund Freud in a famous paper. Uncounted utopian worlds of this stripe, many of them highly systematized, are being conjured up every day, in and out of hospitals, though few of them are ever set in print'.[20] They consider the work to be incoherent and disruptive: a 'personal daydream with its idiosyncratic fixations' which must 'be excluded'.[21] For a utopia to be counted it must have 'some measure of generality, if not universality, or it becomes merely schizophrenia'.[22] The idea of *The Blazing World* as a delusional fantasy reverberates in John Carey's rude titling of his chapter on the text, 'The Empress's New Clothes'. He describes *The Blazing World* as 'tedious and rambling', a text that 'endorses tyranny, aristocratic privilege, opulence, and self-aggrandizement'.[23] Another infamous dismissal of Cavendish came from Virginia Woolf: '[w]hat a vision of loneliness and riot the thought of Margaret Cavendish brings to mind! as if some giant cucumber had spread itself over all the roses and carnations in the garden and choked them to death'.[24] Particularly bruising coming from an icon of feminism, the comments repeat

---

[18] Christopher Marlow, '"Worse in Singularity"?: Kant, Derrida, and Aesthetics in Margaret Cavendish's *The Blazing World*', *Restoration* 41.1 (Spring 2017): 59–80, 73.
[19] Samuel Pepys, *The Diary of Samuel Pepys*, ed. Robert Latham and William Matthews, 11 vols (London: G. Bell and Sons, 1976), 9: 123.
[20] Frank E. Manuel and Fritzie P. Manuel, *Utopian Thought in The Western World* (Oxford: Blackwell, 1979), 7.
[21] Ibid.
[22] Ibid.
[23] John Carey, ed. *The Faber Book of Utopias* (London: Faber, 1999), 78.
[24] Virginia Woolf, *A Room of One's Own* (New York: Harvest Books, 1989), 64.

some of the earlier anxieties about Cavendish – that her agency was somehow grossly inappropriate, damaging even. Hero Chalmers refers to critics' frequent linking of Cavendish's 'unprecedently self-assertive stance as a woman writer to supposed psychological eccentricity'.[25]

Despite the prejudices she endured in her own time, an opportunity was simultaneously afforded for Cavendish to experiment with literary form, genre, and subject matter. Emma Rees refers to the ways in which her 'anomalous role as a writing woman' endowed her with a 'license to propagate at times uncompromisingly contentious ideas which a *man* – in the context of the age, the only proper pretender to the title of "writer" – would not have dared to have published'.[26] Unburdened by the limitations of the appellation 'writer', Cavendish exploited the 'freedom' of this exclusion in her creative navigation of multiple genres and her probing of normative gender and sexuality politics. Similarly, while Cavendish failed to fulfil her wifely responsibilities of bearing a child, this, for Rachel Warburton, meant that 'Cavendish's non-reproductive marriage to an older man who already had heirs for his estate places her outside of heteronormativity'; instead 'her focus [was] on her un(re)productive writing pursued for her own fame and benefit'.[27] Thus the attenuation of her experience of wifeliness – while painfully curtailing her feminine identity – simultaneously opened space for her to develop her writing.

Carey's denunciation of Cavendish's utopianism for its aristocratic investments is similar to the scholarly alignment of Aristophanes' class identity and the politics of his work, as discussed in Chapter 2. Often in the case of intellectual engagements with Aristophanes, the critical assumption has been that his class interests inevitably placed restrictions on the radical political potential of his work. Several scholars consider Cavendish's exile *as a royalist* peculiarly resonant in her writing. Erika Mae Olbricht speaks of 'a representation of rigid class difference, a disavowal of social mobility, and the fantasy of class permanence insured by both of these'.[28] Karen L. Raber claims that '[t]o the exile, especially the aristocratic exile, there was no comfort from or liberation in dissolving the structures on which power, place, and privilege

---

[25] Hero Chalmers, 'Dismantling the Myth of "Mad Madge": The Cultural Context of Margaret Cavendish's Authorial Self-Presentation', *Women's Writing* 4.3 (1997): 323–40, 323.

[26] Emma L. Rees, *Margaret Cavendish: Gender, Genre, Exile* (Manchester: Manchester University Press, 2003), 3.

[27] Rachel Warburton, '"[A] Woman hath no … Reason to desire Children for her Own Sake": Margaret Cavendish Reads Lee Edelman', *Lit: Literature Interpretation Theory* 27.3 (2016): 234–51, 239–40.

[28] Erika Mae Olbricht, 'Using Sex: Margaret Cavendish's "The Lady Contemplation" and the Authorial Fantasy of Class Permanence', *Pacific Coast Philology* 38 (2003): 77–98, 78.

depended'.[29] Perhaps this is so, and yet I would argue that Cavendish's exclusion from political life prompted a more complicated relationship with discourses of authority, and her interest in female social and political value troubles a simple narrative of aristocratic self-interest.[30] For Chalmers, '[t]he authority and self-sufficiency of the women' in Cavendish's female-only spaces in her utopian plays 'may be linked to the Interregnum royalist need to promulgate the notion that the feminised space of retreat is in some sense the centre of power'.[31] Chalmers further suggests that '[t]he existence of a stateless King in exile lends credibility to such an idea, with the nexus of power residing beyond its state apparatus'.[32] While Chalmers' association of a safe feminine retreat with an exiled royal authority is insightful, it nevertheless performs a displacement of the specific challenges offered by the plays' audacious gender performances. Emma Rees alludes to the radical alterity of Cavendish's marginality in terms of being triply exiled – as a woman writer, as a royalist, and as a royalist engaged in theatrical work. Due to this triple exile, Cavendish's voice, Rees argues 'was subversive almost as soon as it was articulated'.[33]

Happily, Cavendish has attracted very favourable attention in the late twentieth and twenty-first centuries. The International Margaret Cavendish Society, established in 1997, marks a point of arrival of a resurgence of interest in her, and has disseminated research on her work through annual conferences. Scholarly engagement with Cavendish's work has flourished and there now exists a rich and vibrant, multifaceted body of critical work on her life and writings. There are plans in process to publish *The Complete Works of Margaret Cavendish*,[34] and her writing has provided inspiration to contemporary novelists: the title of Siri Hustvedt's *The Blazing World* (2014) comes from Cavendish's utopia of the same name, and Cavendish is the subject of Danielle Dutton's 2016 novel *Margaret the First*. The causes of such a hostile reception in her own time until relatively recently – an upturning of

[29] Karen L. Raber, 'Warrior Women in the Plays of Cavendish and Killigrew', *Studies in English Literature, 1500–1900* 40.3 (2000): 413–33, 430.
[30] I am grateful to Elaine Hobby for pointing out to me that Cavendish's own background was upper gentry, not aristocracy. She married up, and yet, interestingly, emphasized her ancient gentry lineage in her autobiography, suggesting that this was the height of honour. This mixed identity may have affected her overt (and unconscious) positioning. See Margaret Cavendish, 'A True Relation of my Birth, Breeding, and Life', in *Natures Pictures Drawn by Fancies Pencil to the Life. Written by the thrice Noble, Illustrious, and Excellent Princess, the Lady Marchioness of Newcastle* (London, 1656), 368–91.
[31] Hero Chalmers, 'The Politics of Feminine Retreat in Margaret Cavendish's *The Female Academy* and *The Convent Of Pleasure*', *Women's Writing* 6.1 (1999): 81–94, 89.
[32] Ibid.
[33] Rees, *Margaret Cavendish*, 7.
[34] See the project's webpage: http://digitalcavendish.org/complete-works/

gendered expectations, wide-ranging subject matter across several intellectual fields, a confident pursuit of unconventional literary practice, and a radical experimentation with genre – are all now the very grounds for her celebration. In fact, the inextricable intersection of these characteristics is often of primary interest to Cavendish scholars, perhaps best exemplified by the title of Rees' monograph, *Margaret Cavendish: Gender, Genre, Exile* (2003). Warburton refers to Cavendish's 'generic hybridity' as 'verging on promiscuity' but sees this as 'precisely what makes her [...] compelling, as it marks a peculiar, perhaps even queer, refusal of form'.[35]

Cavendish and literary experimentation

Cavendish – like George Bernard Shaw, the subject of Chapter 4 – composed extensive peritextual material to accompany her plays, poems, and prose. In her address to readers which formed part of the front matter to *Playes* (1662), she wrote (and it is worth quoting this excerpt in full):

> Although I expect my Playes will be found fault with, by reason I have not drawn the several persons presented in a Circular line, or to a Triangular point, making all the Actors to meet at the latter end of the Stage in a flock together; likewise, that I have not made my Comedies of one dayes actions or passages; yet I have adventured to publish them to the World: But to plead in my Playes behalf, first, I do not perceive any reason why that the several persons presented should be all of an acquaintance, or that there is a necessity to have them of one Fraternity, or to have a relation to each other, or linck'd in alliance as one Family, when as Playes are to present the general Follies, Vanities, Vices, Humours, Dispositions, Passions, Affections, Fashions, Customs, Manners, and practices of the whole World of Mankind, as in several persons; also particular Follies, Vanities, Vices, Humours, Passions, Affections, Fashions, Customs, Fortunes, and the like, in particular persons; [...] For since the world is wide and populated, and their various actions dispersed, and spread about by each particular, and Playes are to present them severally, I perceive no reason they should force them together in the last Act [...].[36]

---

[35] Warburton, '"[A] Woman hath no ... Reason to desire Children for her Own Sake"', 235.
[36] Cavendish, 'To the Readers', Front Matter to *Playes*, 1662, in *The Convent of Pleasure and Other Plays*, ed. Anne Shaver (Baltimore and London: The Johns Hopkins University Press, 1999), 255–6.

From Cavendish's address to the reader, we can see she is clearly well-versed in the Aristotelian rules of drama but has good reason to depart from them. Joyce Devlin Mosher observes that Cavendish's 'short scenes demand a rapid pace and effect a dislocation of the three unities – place, time, and action – of neoclassical drama'.[37] We should note that the unities were understood to refer to time, place, and persons in the early modern period, although Mosher's point still stands.[38] Crucially, this disruption of generic convention is at once a political disruption; as Mosher further observes, Cavendish 'transgresses the rules of dramatic composition so her characters may transgress the boundaries of gender'.[39] Cavendish is also alert to the critical reception that such literary rule breaking is likely to incite.

As part of disrupting the classical rules of drama, Cavendish's plays include, as Katherine R. Kellett writes, 'a spectacular (and usually subversive) hybridity of theatrical conventions, including pastoral romance, cross-dressing, and masque, stubbornly resisting classification'.[40] An additional consideration is the status of her drama: none of Cavendish's plays were staged during her lifetime. In an epistle preceding *Plays, Never Before Printed*, 1668, Cavendish declared, 'I regard not so much the present as future Ages, for which I intend all my Books'.[41] She claimed to be worried that those who had watched her plays in the theatre would be bored of reading them in print. The 1662 plays, at least, were almost certainly composed during the 1650s when Cavendish was in continental Europe and the London public theatres were closed. There was therefore good reason for her to write for reading rather than for publication. Yet there is not a scholarly consensus on whether the plays were intended as closet dramas – plays created by the playwright to be read aloud in private social circles rather than staged publicly in a theatre.

A full stage play with all the implications of that public, multisensuous event seems more impressive, more ambitious than the comparatively constrained form of closet drama. However, as Kamille Stone Stanton notes, the idea of closet drama as 'a private and limited genre' took on a different

---

[37] Joyce Devlin Mosher, 'Female Spectacle as Liberation in Margaret Cavendish's Plays', *Early Modern Literary Studies* 11.1 (May 2007): 1–28, 4.
[38] See Farley-Hills, 'Jonson and the Neo-classical Rules in *Sejanus* and *Volpone*', *Review of English Studies* 46 (1995): 53–73.
[39] Mosher, 'Female Spectacle as Liberation in Margaret Cavendish's Plays', 4.
[40] Katherine R. Kellett, 'Performance, Performativity, and Identity in Margaret Cavendish's *The Convent of Pleasure Studies*', *SEL Studies in English Literature 1500–1900* 48.2 (Spring 2008): 419–42, 420.
[41] Cavendish, 'Author's Epistle Preceding *Plays, Never Before Printed*, 1668', *The Convent of Pleasure and Other plays*, ed. Anne Shaver (Baltimore, MD: The Johns Hopkins University Press, 1999), 273.

understanding after theatres closed in 1642.[42] The closure of the theatres and banning of public performance for a period of nearly twenty years meant that dramas had to take 'the form of a page-play, and because the prohibition did not in any way extend to printed plays, their use as a vehicle for political, commentary, discussion, and debate became more explicit'.[43] Stanton argues that regardless of when Cavendish's plays were written (and we do not know the exact dates), it is possible that she consciously elected to write in the genre of closet drama; if so, Stanton reads such a decision as encouraging 'a political reading' due to the connection of closet drama with clandestine politics during the period of the interregnum.[44] Furthermore, in writing plays, Cavendish was, as Elaine Hobby observes, 'freed from the need to commit herself to an authorial stance', and writing page plays that were not performed in public allowed her to experiment 'more freely than in any other works with outrageous and remarkable female characters'.[45]

Whatever Cavendish's intentions, there have been successful efforts to perform Cavendish's plays in recent times. Gweno Williams has talked in detail about her staging of *The Convent of Pleasure* and how easily the play lends itself to performance. Hobby makes the point that the later plays published in *Plays, Never before Printed, 1668* – which includes *The Convent of Pleasure* – demonstrate a greater awareness of theatrical performance than in the plays published in her 1662 collection *Playes*.[46] One of the earliest of the three plays discussed here, *The Female Academy* – with its lengthy discourses – is indeed the more readerly and least theatrical of the three. While it is difficult to garner the intentions of Cavendish regarding the status of her dramatic works, their ambiguous forms go hand in hand with her more general departure from dramatic rules and conventions.

A further generic anomaly is Cavendish's tendency to amalgamate quite different aesthetic modes. Sarah Hutton notes the presence of a 'Lucianic blend of seriousness and comedy' in both Cyrano de Bergerac's *Histoire comique* and More's *Utopia*, and 'it is Lucian's special brand of intellectual satire-cum-science-fiction that matches *Blazing World* most exactly'.[47] We

---

[42] Kamille Stone Stanton, '"An Amazonian Heroickess": The Military Leadership of Queen Henrietta Maria in Margaret Cavendish's *Bell in Campo* (1662)', *Early Theatre* 10.2 (2007): 71–86, 76.
[43] Ibid.
[44] Ibid.
[45] Elaine Hobby, *Virtue of Necessity: English Women's Writing 1649–88* (London: Virago, 1988), 105.
[46] Hobby, *Virtue of Necessity*, 106.
[47] Sarah Hutton, 'Science and Satire: The Lucianic Voice of Margaret Cavendish's *Description of a New World Called the Blazing World*', in *Authorial Conquests: Essays on Genre in the Writings of Margaret Cavendish*, ed. Line Cottegnies and Nancy Weitz (London: Associated University Presses, 2003), 171.

thus encounter a further connection with Aristophanes as Lucian (writer and philosopher born in 120 CE in Samosata, then a province of the Roman Empire) was (unusually for the time) a great admirer of Aristophanic Old Comedy, which found its way into his work. Ralph M. Rosen writes, 'it is difficult for us to find readers in this period who showed an interest in understanding Old Comedy on its own terms, i.e., as a genre of satire in continual tension with a need to generate laughter and a pretense of seriousness and moral efficacy'.[48] Rosen considers Lucian's writing to evidence a comprehension of Old Comedy 'deeper and shrewder than the critics of his time seemed capable of, and an ability to exploit for his own literary purposes the various strategies that made Old Comedy so complex and dynamic'.[49] Hence, Cavendish's Lucianic merging of different modes – such as the serious and the comic, the earnest and the ironic – simultaneously contains reverberations of Aristophanic comedy, an idea I will return to when discussing Cavendish's plays.

Gendering utopia

That utopia has the potential to envision a radical rethinking of the human subject, a total reimagination of social relations, and a fundamental remodelling of human society, makes it a form peculiarly enabling of the feminist imagination. Historian Sheila Rowbotham cites '[b]reaks, adventures, [and] glimpses' as having been taken up by feminists 'who know that the problem of moving from existing needs to transforming the scope and capacity to desire is especially knotty for women because there is social inequality and biological difference to fortify the refrain – "You can't change human nature"'.[50] Feminism itself is in some part utopian; as Anne K. Mellor writes, '[f]eminist theory is grounded on the assumption of gender equality, a social equality between the sexes which has never existed in the historical past'.[51] Yet, the utopian literary canon has tended to reproduce sexist perspectives on women's place in utopia. In More's *Utopia* women gain more rights and an appearance of equality in certain aspects (for example, men and women wear the same clothes and both work outside the house); however,

---

[48] Ralph M. Rosen, 'Lucian's Aristophanes: On Understanding Old Comedy in the Roman Imperial Period', in *Athenian Comedy in the Roman Empire*, ed. C. W. Marshall and Tom Hawkins (London: Bloomsbury, 2016), 142.
[49] Rosen, 'Lucian's Aristophanes', 144.
[50] Sheila Rowbotham, 'Hopes, Dreams and Dirty Nappies', *Marxism Today* (December 1984): 8–12, 10.
[51] Anne K. Mellor, 'On Feminist Utopias', *Women's Studies* 9 (1982): 241–62, 243.

women crucially remain within a patriarchal structure: '[w]ives are subordinate to their husbands, children to their parents, and younger people generally to their elders'.[52] While Plato and Campanella abolish the family and provide greater equality for women, many utopias – and Bacon's *New Atlantis* and More's *Utopia* are prime examples of this – maintain the family unit and separate gendered spheres with women subservient within these structures. Utopian scholar Lyman Tower Sargent claims that '[m]ost utopianists since 1850 argue for a clearly inferior role for women' and we see this repeated in the late nineteenth-century to early twentieth-century cluster of utopian novels.[53] Edward Bellamy's *Looking Backward* (1888), William Morris' *News from Nowhere* (1890), and H. G. Wells' *A Modern Utopia* (1905) all propose their alternative visions of human society from the perspective of a benevolent masculinity which bequeaths the sidelines as the location for their female utopians, who are reproduced primarily as love interests or in other supporting roles.

A repeated narrative pattern in the classical utopia follows a male visitor from the reader's present to the utopian society, where he enters into dialogue with a male utopian citizen. This dialogue offers a dialectical exchange of strange and unfamiliar sights, and stories and explanations of the alternative world, which incrementally undermines the foundations of the non-utopian society from which the visitor has travelled. Frances Bartkowski makes the point that '[b]eginning with Thomas More's *Utopia* the question of women in utopia is always asked and usually summarily answered. Their "condition" is usually seen as improved relative to the narrator's present, though women themselves tend not to participate in shaping this future in any dramatic way'.[54] Indeed, female utopians tend to be decorative supplements to, or support for, the focus on masculine enlightenment and state-building.

While these utopias have prioritized political structures, social regulation, and legal systems, Kate Lilley suggests that 'utopian writing by women has tended to focus strategically on the possibilities and problems of gendered social life and the weight of custom'.[55] This has meant a preoccupation in feminist utopias with 'micropolitical questions of sexuality, maternity,

---

[52] Thomas More, *Utopia*, trans. Paul Turner (London: Penguin, 2003), 60.
[53] Lyman Tower Sargent, 'Women in Utopia', *Comparative Literature Studies* 10.4 (1973): 302–16, 304–5.
[54] Frances Bartkowski, *Feminist Utopias* (Lincoln, NE and London: University of Nebraska Press, 1989), 9.
[55] Kate Lilley, 'Blazing Worlds: Seventeenth-Century Women's Utopian Writing', in *Women, Texts and Histories 1575–1760*, ed. Clare Brant and Diane Purkiss (London and New York: Routledge, 1992), 118.

education, domesticity and self-government – while declining the burden of representing a fully articulated model of a new political order'.[56] An expression of female desire – at times as the undoing of epistemic norms or speculating with images and narratives of fantasy – has been a way of prising open and interrupting patriarchal history. As part of this, female visitors and utopians in feminist utopias have often disrupted the construction of the singular and unified subjectivity common in male-authored utopias; Joanna Russ's *The Female Man* (1975) is a good example of this as its four protagonists, Joanna, Janet, Jael, and Jeanine merge the visitor/utopian roles and are at once individuated people and a collective expression of one subject. Significantly, such experiments with 79 multiple female selves are present in Cavendish's work; Khanna highlights this tendency in *Blazing World*: '[b]y constructing varied subject positions for women, her fiction releases the utopian genre from conventional binary oppositions in the depiction of the desire for the good life'.[57]

A further contribution to the utopian genre has involved complicating the dualistic archistic and anarchistic traditions of utopian narrative. Khanna sees Cavendish's work as anticipating later feminist utopias in its tendency 'to close the gap between the vision of utopia as natural paradise in arcadian settings and that of cultural construct, set in the city'.[58] Melding these two types of utopian construction reduces the gap 'between representations of "the good life" as the gratification of sensual pleasures, and representations that focus on the predominance of reason in ordering moral life and the good state'.[59] This reframing of the conventionally separate processes of cognition and emotion anticipates the affective turn experienced in the twenty-first century. Yaakov A. Mascetti refers to Cavendish's 'opposition of imagination and wit to the crude and disenchanted reality produced by male thinkers of her time'.[60] Thinking-feelings – an inseparable coalescence of intellect and sensibility – might be considered to underpin the terms of communication of Cavendish's utopian dramas.

Connected to this reformulation of utopian social structures and relations is a deviation from the utopian dialogic experience and its concomitant investment in processes of both individual and collective enlightenment.

[56] Ibid.
[57] Khanna, 'The Subject of Utopia', 15.
[58] Ibid.
[59] Ibid.
[60] Yaakov A. Mascetti, 'A "World of Nothing, but Pure Wit": Margaret Cavendish and the Gendering of the Imaginary', *Journal of Literature and the History of Ideas* 6.1 (January 2008): 1–31, 2.

Zelia Gregoriou states that '[n]ot all utopian travels recapitulate the Platonic myth of the cave and the turn towards the light, i.e. toward a newly found and "end-state" truth' where there is a 'solipsistic journey toward the deep, inner self', which is the 'site of transformation'.[61] Transformative in other (feminist) utopias is the 'adventure on the surface of cultural performances through which travellers encounter, interact and cooperate with others toward new learnings'.[62] Platonic enlightenment – enabled by the colonial picaresque adventure to a utopian island – is replaced instead in Cavendish's utopias by a reworking of gender and genre to produce a more diffuse, heterotopian space within which temporary utopian communities of women experiment with new ways of living. In similar terms Lilley suggests that the 'privileging of sexual, social and educational over legal and/or political reform in [women's] utopian writing [...] is not a mark of generic failure or incapacity, but of specifically gendered insight into the diffuse, informal, ideological mechanisms by which women are controlled'.[63]

As was the case with Aristophanes' utopian plays, Cavendish's dramatic utopias are much more proximate to the non-utopian world of the reader/spectator than the distant, estranged worlds of early modern utopian prose. What is peculiarly distinctive to Cavendish's utopian dramas, however, is the temporariness of the utopia; none of the utopias in her plays is permanent, or even long lasting: they all close with the women reintegrating into the non-utopian (albeit altered to various degrees) world. Rowbotham states: '[u]topia is not necessarily frozen in the future. It is not necessarily the polar opposite to strategy. It intertwines with the assessment of the odds. [...] It reveals a terrain in which we can manoeuvre to advantage'.[64] There is scholarly debate over how to read the inevitably disheartening endings of Cavendish's plays, which I discuss in the next sections, but Rowbotham's insight is a useful reminder of the importance of considering utopia's relationship with the here and now. In this sense, it is striking that Cavendish's utopian plays contradict Appelbaum's characterization of the seventeenth-century literary utopia as changing from 'a tool of contestatory discourse to a device of compensatory diversion'.[65] He argues that 'the utopian imagination was becoming autonomous [...] as the recognition and articulation of a realm of feeling which existed *apart* from political action, or *against* political action'.[66]

---

[61] Zelia Gregoriou, 'Pedagogy and Passages: The Performativity of Margaret Cavendish's Utopian Fiction', *Journal of Philosophy of Education* 47.3 (2013): 457–75, 472.
[62] Ibid.
[63] Lilley, 'Blazing Worlds', 128.
[64] Rowbotham, 'Hopes, Dreams and Dirty Nappies', 9.
[65] Appelbaum, *Literature and Utopian Politics in Seventeenth-Century England*, 198.
[66] Ibid.

In contrast, Cavendish's utopias are intertwined with the social-political world within which they were produced.

Appelbaum discusses only Cavendish's *Blazing World* in his study of seventeenth-century literature and utopian politics, paying no attention to her utopian plays. In her chapter on Renaissance and enlightenment utopias in *The Cambridge Companion to Utopian Literature*, Pohl makes two brief references to *Blazing World* and does not mention Cavendish's utopian drama. Sargent's excellent online resource 'Utopian Literature in English: An Annotated Bibliography From 1516 to the Present' includes *Blazing World* but only one of the three utopian plays (*The Convent of Pleasure*). As we have seen, Carey's *The Faber Book of Utopias* includes a dismissive short section on *Blazing World*, but there is no reference to her utopian drama. Indeed, there is a repeated pattern of overlooking Cavendish's contribution to utopian aesthetics from within the field of Utopian Studies – particularly her dramatic utopias. As would be expected, there is more attention to these works from within early modern and Cavendish studies, but still, there are few publications examining *The Female Academy*, *The Convent of Pleasure*, and *Bell in Campo* as *utopian* works.

I am interested in the plays' sensitivity to the challenges of materializing utopian worlds. Like utopias from Old Comedy, Cavendish's plays are not straightforward animations of utopian communities. The all-female space of sensual delights in *The Convent of Pleasure* is ambivalently present. It is absent in the first two acts, where it exists only in reports. In its later scenes, it emerges as an amorphous space, first a pastoral scene of maypole festivities, then a seascape. *The Female Academy*'s interest in discourse, understanding, learning, speech, and audience is engendered from what Jane L. Donawerth and Carol A. Kolmerten describe as 'the nascent feminism of the movement to acquire education for women in seventeenth-century Europe'.[67] *Bell in Campo* turns from education to bodily empowerment, discipline, and camaraderie with a dramatization of female warriors that preempt the Amazonian women in much later utopias such as Monique Wittig's *Les Guérillères* (1969) and Sarah Hall's *The Carhullan Army* (2007). All three of Cavendish's plays constitute striking historical precursors to modern and contemporary utopian interests in subjectivity, contingency, and affective ways in which attachments dislodge and reconfigure in new, feminist arrangements.

---

[67] Jane L. Donawerth and Carol A. Kolmerten, 'Introduction', in *Utopian and Science Fiction by Women: Worlds of Difference*, ed. Jane L. Donawerth and Carol A. Kolmerten (Liverpool: Liverpool University Press, 1994), 4.

The Female Academy

The female academy is a school for young upper-class women to become educated and learn the art of public speaking and debate within an exclusively female space. 'Lady speakers' take it in turns to offer meditations on particular questions, such as 'whether women are capable to have as much wit or wisdom as men'.[68] Other themes include discoursing, women's behaviour, truth, friendship, theatre, vanity, vice and wickedness, boldness and bashfulness, virtuous courtships, and the wooing of suitors. Alternating with these scenes are phallic interruptions where gentlemen at first listen in frustration at an open grate which allows them to hear and see the lady speakers therein. The men's anger at the voluble women, who withhold themselves from male company moves the men to establish a male academy; however, somewhat comically, the men struggle to think of topics to speak on besides their exasperation with the women and – to their intense irritation – they are completely ignored by the women. They consider forcing their way into the female academy but decide against and engage instead in sexist banter.

One brief scene includes two gentlemen engaging more constructively with the women's orations, but mostly the alternating scenes are short vignettes comprising sexist speeches from the male academy opining the many poor qualities of the female sex. Indeed, the men become increasingly vexed at the lack of attention paid to them by the women in the academy. Their next tactic is to blow trumpets at the women making so much noise that the women speakers will not be able to continue their discourses. This boorish interruption is followed by the final scene of the play, wherein a matron questions the gentlemen about their churlish behaviour. In response to the men pleading their cause (the women have cloistered themselves and the men have been shut out, and this is a dangerous precedent to set for other young ladies who should be open and accessible to male attention), the matron tells them that the women are staying at the academy only to learn to become good wives. The matron advises the men to ingratiate themselves with the ladies' parents and offers to act as mediator between the sexes with a view to facilitating romantic encounters.

The first debate the women hold – on gender and wit and wisdom – appears to reproduce familiar gendered ideas about male wisdom and female wit. Linda R. Payne observes that Cavendish 'seemed to consider the kind of ordered logic and "rules" which much of her audience expected from

---

[68] Cavendish, *The Female Academy*, ed. Sharon L. Jansen (Steilacoom, WA: Saltar's Point Press, 2017), 110. All further references are to this edition and appear in the main body of the text.

literature to be a masculine trait. [...] Women are strong on fancy, while reason is a man's domain'.[69] The Lady Speaker claims that wit 'is the daughter of Nature, the Lady Wit' (110) whose 'accouterments' and 'humor' (as in the bodily fluids) are 'various': 'sometimes she is merry and jesting, other times pleasing and delightful, sometimes melancholy, sometimes fantastical, other times spiteful and censorious, and oft times wild and wanton unless Discretion rules and leads her, who keeps her within the bounds and pales of modesty' (110-1). Lady Wit's daughters are the nine muses who live single lives but are wooed by poets, the younger of whom are 'amorous lovers' and the older 'Platonic lovers'. However, the Lady Speaker concludes the section on wit by declaring that 'there are good wits which have foolish judgments, for though Wit and Wisdom are sisters and brothers, both the children of Nature, yet for the most part the brother is a mere fool and the sister hath a great wit, but some have masculine wits and effeminate judgments, as if their beams were hermaphrodites' (112).[70] Hence, there is both a dislodging of the alignment of wisdom and masculinity as well as a complication of gender binaries.

Foregrounding a feminine emphasis on fancy, sensibility, and fantasy is at once repetition of a normative gendered fiction and simultaneously a discursive destabilization of the dominance of masculine reason, wisdom, and truth. After arguing that actually most men wrongly think themselves to be wise, the Lady Speaker states, 'women seem to all outward appearance to have a natural antipathy' to wisdom, 'abhorring his severe and strict rules, hating his medicable admonitions, his profitable counsels and advice, his wary ways, his prudent forecast, his serious actions, his temperate life and sober disposition' (115). This description of wisdom is arresting for its likeness to the priorities and values of More's *Utopia*, where the greatest pleasures of the utopians are located in life-long intellectual pursuits within an acetic lifestyle – functional, smock-style clothing, early bedtimes, and no alcohol. While *The Convent of Pleasure* elaborates on this to a much greater

---

[69] Linda R. Payne, 'Dramatic Dreamscape: Women's Dreams and Utopian Vision in the Works of Margaret Cavendish, Duchess of Newcastle', in *Curtain Calls: British and American Women and the Theater, 1660-1820*, ed. Mary Anne Schofield and Cecilia Macheski (Athens: Ohio University Press, 1991), 21.

[70] Jansen's notes in *The Female Academy* explain 'hermaphrodite' as referring both to the physical presentation of the attributes of both sexes and, potentially, to the more abstract condition of containing opposite features but do not explain the meaning of 'beam' in this context. Included in *OED* definitions, 'beam' is understood as 'the main trunk of a stag's horn which bears the branches or "antlers"', (*Oxford English Dictionary Online*, Oxford: Oxford University Press, https://www.oed.com/view/Entry/16505?rskey=ATXJTK&result=1#eid). This definition might be the context for Cavendish's figurative use of the word.

extent, we can see in *The Female Academy* that sensual pleasures, creativity, and fantasy are essential components of a utopian social space for women.

Like the 600-foot-high wall that forms the perimeter of the utopia in Aristophanes' *The Birds* – and similar to the bounded space of More's island utopia – the academy is a physically circumscribed space. However, in Cavendish's play, as I have said, there is a grate that provides an opening to the outside world, which in turn facilitates communication between the utopian and non-utopian zones. Critics have tended to interpret this as female control of the male gaze: male spectators have partial visual access to the female orators, who control the spectacle and the oration. One such critic is Susan Wiseman, who claims that the play 'presents the male gaze as controlled by and subjected to the female object of the gaze, rather than vice versa'.[71] Alyce R. Baker-Putt develops this reading further: '[w]hile the men in the play are not blinded, they still feel castrated, because they do not possess full scopophilic access to the women. [...] Because the men's scopophilia is not satisfied, their domination, including sexual domination, is not achieved'.[72] Male sexual aggression and frustration accrues in response to a potent mix of female volubility and withdrawal from the sexual economy; 'the men are very angry that the women should speak so much and they so little', says the first gentleman (115); and a little later he continues, 'they rail extremely that so many fair young ladies are so strictly enclosed as not to suffer men to visit them in the academy' (116). The men's bellicosity and sexual vexation is captured in the following exchange:

> **First Gentleman** The gentlemen will turn trumpeters, for a regiment of gentlemen have bought every one of them a trumpet to sound a march to the academy of ladies.
> **[Second] Gentleman** Faith, if the ladies would answer their trumpets with blowing of horns, they would serve them but as they ought to be served.
> **First Gentleman** Women will sooner make horns than blow horns.
>
> 146

The phallic references to cuckolding with its insinuations of female trickery work to keep in view the patriarchal aggression against which the Academy is founded.

---

[71] Susan Wiseman, 'Gender and Status in Dramatic Discourse: Margaret Cavendish, Duchess of Newcastle', in *Women, Writing, History 1640–1740*, ed. Isobel Grundy and Susan Wiseman (London: Batsford, 1992), 165.
[72] Alyce R. Baker-Putt, 'Defining the Female Self Through Female Communities: Margaret Cavendish's *The Female Academy, The Convent of Pleasure*, and *Bell in Campo*', *Shakespeare and Renaissance Association of West Virginia* 29 (2006): 37–46, 39.

However, although the grate facilitates transgression of gendered authority and sexual power, it simultaneously makes vulnerable the utopian space. It provides an opening to the outside world, which is exploited: first by the constant surveillance of what takes place within the Academy; and second through the piercing interruption of the women's dialogues by men blowing trumpets. Thus, while the grate enables the women to assert themselves beyond the small jurisdiction of the Academy (and their orations have a beneficial effect on at least two of the men outside) it simultaneously proves the utopia's undoing. It is the means by which the Academy is breached: the coordinated noisy disturbances mean that the women can no longer continue with their orations. This disruption prompts the matron to meet with the gentlemen and agree to act as mediator with a view to gender reconciliation and the re-establishment of heteronormative sexual practice.

The grate makes the utopian space potentially accessible and in doing so offers a permeability, which is very different to More's self-contained, cut-off landmass, a landmass deliberately created by the utopian settlers who severed the peninsula to establish an island. As noted in Chapter 1, representation of a utopian society through the use of drama means utilizing bodies on stage, spoken dialogue, costume, sets, and props to signify this other world. Even closet drama was read aloud and thus the text on the page was mediated through speaking voices. This performative application of the utopian text both animates and places constraints on the abstract potential of the writing, this constraint observable in the familiarity of theatrical sign systems (bodies, voices, objects). In this sense, encounters with the non-utopian world (encouraged by the grate) reflect the materiality of the aesthetic context within which these utopian plays exist. This proximity was also a key feature of Aristophanes' *The Birds*. However, the access points in Aristophanes' play were heavily guarded, would-be intruders prevented entry, and trespassers evicted, and thus the occasional breach was robustly managed.

While the access the grate provides in *The Female Academy* is ultimately the Academy's undoing, it simultaneously anticipates the more porous borders of the contemporary utopian plays discussed in Chapter 6, and many utopian novels authored by women written during the twentieth and twentieth-first centuries. The separatist female utopia of Charlotte Perkins Gilman's *Herland* (1915) for example recalls *The Female Academy* in its population of prominent societal roles with older women but also in the breach of the utopian community by three male intruders, one of whom attempts to rape a Herlander. However, whereas the implication in *The Female Academy* is that there will be a dissolution of this community after the close of the play and a concomitant reintegration of these women into the patriarchal reproductive economy, the utopia of Herland survives the breach:

one of the male visitors integrates into the community and the other two return to their non-utopian world (one with a Herlander). Similarly, in other feminist utopias, such as Joanna Russ's *The Female Man* (1975), Marge Piercy's *Woman on the Edge of Time* (1976), and Sally Miller Gearhart's *The Wanderground* (1979), the boundary separating the utopian from the non-utopian space is porous and permeable. The act of breaching the utopian perimeter brings attention to the border as an intersection of imaginative utopian hope and political critique of the prevailing system.

The Convent of Pleasure

Published six years after *The Female Academy*, *The Convent of Pleasure* similarly takes place in a discrete physical building but this time there is no grate or other opening through which intruders can breach the utopian boundary. A rich aristocratic heiress, Lady Happy, weary with societal expectations, uses her wealth to establish a separatist female community, a convent of pleasure. As Tanya Wood notes, the cloister was frequently imagined as a sanctuary for upper-class women during this period.[73] This convent is full of sensual objects – fine textiles, silks, and fabrics – as well as delicious fresh food and drink, a variety of fashionable outfits, and large mirrors. In the convent, female friendship is enjoyed as amongst the greatest pleasures, but the convent is also well organized with roles for each woman and a sensibly managed and robust household system, including not the slaves of More's *Utopia* but plenty of servants to help with the efficient running of the convent. The women engage with a variety of pleasurable activities and pastimes, including writing and performing in masques and plays. Like *The Female Academy*, the utopian scenes alternate with vignettes from the outside world, which mostly exhibit male anxiety, frustration, and aggression induced by the prevention of access to these young single women. The comparison continues with the inclusion of a female mediator who appears to represent Lady Happy's interests. The men consider strategies of violence, for example setting the convent on fire or smoking the women out, and other measures, such as removing bricks from the wall and disguising themselves as women to gain entry (a suggestion that recalls in reverse women dressing up as men in Aristophanes' *The Assemblywomen* to gain entry to the Senate).

---

[73] Tanya Caroline Wood, 'Brave New Worlds? The Gender Politics of Margaret Cavendish's Primary and Secondary Realms', PhD thesis, University of Toronto, 2001, 116.

The second half of the play concerns the growing attachment between a visiting Princess and Lady Happy, whose mutual attraction, the play strongly suggests, is more than Platonic. Plays within the play are performed by the convent ladies and subject matter includes women's pervasive mistreatment by men, the oppression of marriage, and the dangers of childbirth. Happy and the Princess also perform in a pastoral scene, wherein Happy acts as a shepherdess and the Princess as a shepherd, and then in a scene where Happy plays a sea goddess and the Princess a sea god (Neptune). After some dancing, the mediator arrives and announces that there is man disguised as a woman in the convent and we discover that the Princess was actually a Prince all along. The scene ends with the Prince appearing as a groom and Happy as a bride.

Despite the ending's suggestion that the utopia may not endure into the future, *The Convent of Pleasure* appears to offer a more confident depiction of utopian sociality than *The Female Academy*. Cavendish removes the grate that provided a conduit between utopian and non-utopian spaces in *The Female Academy*, and in doing so, creates a more protected space for her community of women. The elimination of the grate is simultaneously an eradication of the possibility of the male gaze, which indeed proves a source of frustration for the men outside. No longer concerned with male encounters, as Chalmers notes, '[t]he dressing up which goes on in her "convent" and the elaborate opening of one scene into another function chiefly for the enjoyment of the participants and have no audience within the play'.[74] In this sense, it is a self-contained community with clear boundaries very much in the Morean mould.

The women's act of self-exile from the world and its social pressures is similar to Peisthetaerus and Euelpides' withdrawal from Athens in Aristophanes' *The Birds*. Happy asks, '[w]hy, what is there in the publick World that should invite me to live in it?'[75] When the Princess arrives at the Convent she says she has willingly 'quit a Court of troubles for a *Convent of Pleasure*' (228). Julie Crawford attributes this to Cavendish's royalist interests: 'Royalists' pursuit of pleasure [...] signified both commitment to the monarchy and resistance to the perceived austerities of the Puritans' interregnum'.[76] However, it is also a reproduction of a utopian trope, one not common to the city utopias of Plato, More, Bacon, or Bellamy, but more to the

---

[74] Hero Chalmers, 'The Politics of Feminine Retreat', 86.
[75] Margaret Cavendish, *The Convent of Pleasure*, ed. Sharon L. Jansen (Steilacoom, WA: Saltar's Point Press, 2016), 218. All further references are to this edition and appear in the main body of the text.
[76] Julie Crawford, 'Convents and Pleasures: Margaret Cavendish and the Drama of Property', *Renaissance Drama* 32 (2003): 177–23, 184.

body utopias of Homer, Aristophanes, the Land of Cockayne, Rabelais, and Morris, and in what Jessica Day calls the 'sextopias' of the twenty-first century, such as Katherine V. Forrest's *Daughters of an Emerald Dusk* (2005) and Jeanne G'Fellers' *No Sister of Mine* (2005).[77]

The Convent of Pleasure speaks back to More's *Utopia*, particularly on the subjects of asceticism and pleasure. The celebration of beautiful silks and costumes in the convent ('*Wee'l Cloth our selves with softest Silk, And Linnen fine as white as milk*' [221]) is justified by Happy, as she questions, '[w]hat profit or pleasure can it be to the gods to have Men or Women wear coarse Linnen or rough Woollen, or to flea their skin with Hair-cloth, or to eat or sawe thorow their flesh with Cords?' (312). This is quite different to More's utopians, who all wear 'the same sort of clothes [...] and the fashion never changes', functionality being the key consideration.[78] While More's utopians do not 'waste their time in idleness or self-indulgence, but [...] make good use of it in some congenial activity',[79] Happy claims her convent 'shall not be a Cloister of restraint, but a place for freedom, not to vex the Senses but to please them' (220).

More aligns pleasure with cerebral activity: 'the main purpose of their whole economy is to give each person as much time free from physical drudgery as the needs of the community will allow, so that he can cultivate his mind – which they regard as the secret of a happy life'.[80] But for Happy, pleasure is multisensual; it involves stimulating and appeasing multiple bodily appetites:

> *For every Sense shall pleasure take,*
> *And all our Lives shall merry make:*
> *Our Minds in full delight shall joy,*
> *Not vex'd with every idle Toy*
>
> 220–1

Delighting the mind is a sensory experience, which extends to beautiful sights ('[w]ee'l *please our Sight with Pictures rare*' (221), appealing smells ('[o]ur *Nostrils with perfumed Air*' (221), euphonious sounds ('[o]ur *Ears with sweet melodious Sound*' (221), and delectable victuals '[o]ur *Tast with sweet delicious Meat*' (221).

---

[77] Jessica Day, 'Sexual Pleasure and Utopian Desire in Twenty-First Century Fictional Forms and Cultural Practice', PhD Thesis, University of Lincoln, 2019.
[78] More, *Utopia*, 55.
[79] Ibid., 56.
[80] Ibid., 59.

Sensuality in *The Convent of Pleasure* undoubtedly extends to erotic encounters – if not as part of the convent's sexual relations in general, then at least between Happy and the Princess, who, just before embarking on their pastoral performance, '*imbrace and kiss, and hold each other in their Arms*' (235). The Princess remarks, '[t]hese my Imbraces though of a Femal kind, May be as fervent as a Masculine mind' (234). Their physical contact is perceived by Happy to contravene the boundaries of acceptable friendliness between women: 'why may not I love a Woman with the same affection I could a Man? No, no, Nature is Nature' (234). While the Princess turns out to have been a Prince all along, crucially the reader does not know this until her/his identity is exposed in the play. In the original printed copy of *The Convent of Pleasure*, Cavendish chose to position the *dramatis personae* after the end of the play, thereby preventing readers from knowing the Prince's identity until the moment of revelation within the play. This therefore works very differently to the crossdressing we see in Shakespearean comedy where audiences know that Viola is dressed as a boy in *Twelfth Night* and that Ganymede is actually Rosalind in *As You Like It*. That *The Convent of Pleasure* sustains the performance of queer desire until the end of the play, leads Emma Donoghue to describe the play as an 'extraordinarily subversive lesbian romance'.[81]

However, while Happy's utopian retreat is a space of sensual gratification, imaginative pursuit, and queer desire, the interruption of the outside world into the utopian space we saw in *The Female Academy* re-emerges in some of the scenes the ladies perform in *The Convent of Pleasure*. Like Book 1 of More's *Utopia*, which recounts the failures of the non-utopian society of the reader, these scenes in *The Convent of Pleasure* form a play within a play and function as the rationale for utopia (women are treated abominably, hence the need for a separatist female community within which they can flourish). From these scenes we learn of the oppressive nature of marriage, the miserable consequences of perpetual pregnancy, domestic violence, and child mortality. Poverty, exploitation, and injustice – so hotly at stake in Book 1 of *Utopia* – are reframed from women's perspectives. Lower-class women tell of adulterous and inebriated husbands who drink the household income and leave their wives and children starving, and a lady speaks of her husband's visits to prostitutes and his gambling away of their estate. There are complaints about female dependency, economic deprivation, and injustice, and several scenes about labour and childbirth which are strikingly graphic: '*[e]nter a Lady big with Child, groaning as in labour, and a Company of Women with her*'

---

[81] Emma Donoghue, *Passions Between Women: British Lesbian Culture 1668–1801* (New York: Harper, 1995), 230.

(231). Gweno Williams calls Cavendish's representation of childbirth 'a revolutionary moment in English dramatic writing' for 'the act of giving birth has been an offstage event, as unstageable as the other forms of bodily evacuation it so embarrassingly resembles'.[82]

Dolores Paloma highlights Cavendish's use of 'the grotesquerie of the traditional Renaissance antimasque to depict the terrors of female life: the agonies of childbirth, the abuse of husbands, the death of children, the importunities of unwanted suitors'.[83] Cavendish transforms the Socratic discourse among men, which is neatly confined to Book 1 of *Utopia*, to a female performance – within a performance – that is embedded within the centre of the utopian space. This structural rearrangement is further amplified by Cavendish's practice of genre-blurring. Cavendish employs multiple dramatic modes (masque, pastoral, city comedy, and epilogue); '[t]he colloquial style and realistic circumstantial detail of the first play-within-a-play', writes Williams, 'draws on the conventions of city comedy, whilst the pastoral in Act 4 scene I moves effectively from lyrical abstraction into rural music-making and popular dance'.[84] But this is not stylistic innovation for its own sake: '[a]s these metatheatrical interludes multiply, the audience watch the protagonists move from being passive spectators to becoming increasingly central actors, a direct reflection of the growing intensity of their courtship'.[85] Modish or generic innovation in Cavendish's work directly facilitates the testing of unfamiliar gender relations and social exchange.

Yet, this is another disappointing ending: once the Princess is discovered to be a Prince in disguise, the usually voluble Happy has only a further four, brief lines in the play and seems immediately acquiescent to marrying the Prince, this despite the Prince's troubling instruction to the Embassador: 'go from me to the Councellors of this State [...] that I ask their leave I may marry this Lady; otherwise, tell them I will have her by force of Arms' (243–4). Unsurprisingly there have been a variety of interpretations of this ending with particular attention paid to Happy's uncharacteristic quietness. Deborah Boyle decides that 'patriarchal marriage has evidently triumphed'.[86] She sees

---

[82] Gweno Williams, '"Why May Not a Lady Write a Good Play?" Plays by Early Modern Women Reassessed as Performance Texts', in *Readings in Renaissance Women's Drama: Criticism, History, and Performance 1594–1998*, ed. S. P. Cerasano and Marian Wynne-Davis (London: Routledge, 1998), 103.
[83] Dolores Paloma, 'Margaret Cavendish: Defining the Female Self', *Women's Studies* 7 (1980): 55–66, 60.
[84] Williams, '"Why May Not a Lady Write a Good Play?"', 103.
[85] Ibid.
[86] Deborah Boyle, 'Margaret Cavendish on Gender, Nature, and Freedom', *Hypatia* 28.3 (Summer 2013): 516–32, 529.

the message as 'ultimately a pessimistic one: patriarchal marriage is simply unavoidable'.[87] A different reading is offered by Paloma, who argues that '[w]hile in Shakespeare the comic error of sexual confusion is corrected and traditional social order restored, the Cavendish plays never refer back to an order that has been momentarily disturbed; instead, they open up to a new future'.[88] However, in this play, the strong implication is that the social order is in fact restored. Theodora A. Jankowski describes *The Convent of Pleasure* as a 'volatile' play, raising 'many possibilities of spiritual, emotional, and erotic unions between virgins, yet refus[ing] to commit itself as to which connections are acceptable'.[89] The play proposes that a variety of sensual pleasures are to be enjoyed at the convent, and thus its final 'recuperative gestures struggle to contain the radical issues of queer pleasure and social critique raised', Jankowski's ultimate conclusion being that the play's 'instability allows more potential for queer virginal eroticism than it forecloses'.[90]

The play moves from a utopian community of women – where female friendship, cooperation, sociability, and erotic encounters constitute the social relations of the convent – to a heteronormative reconciliation with the non-utopian, patriarchal present. However, the materiality of the utopian space offers a fascinating contribution to utopian literature and enacts a profound destabilization of both epistemological and ontological sociopolitical certainties. Horacio Sierra states, '[l]ike real-world convents, Lady Happy's commune functions more like an *other within* than a truly marginal, outsider population since it still deals with would-be suitors, disguised princes, and gossiping gentlemen'.[91] In this sense, as with *The Female Academy, The Convent of Pleasure* retains a close propinquity with the non-utopian world and is a recognizable, physical building as familiar as any other convent – from the outside at least. However, the convent is at once material and non-material: while it is imagined as a physical construction, it is simultaneously a tentative, inchoate space, whose existence is precarious. While the convent is spoken about early in the play, it is not until Act 3 that it has a dramaturgical presence and immediately it has been infiltrated: the Prince has entered disguised as a Princess. The play offers a utopian community that like dramatic performance is material but transitory.

---

[87] Ibid.
[88] Paloma, 'Margaret Cavendish: Defining the Female Self', 64.
[89] Theodora A. Jankowski, *Pure Resistance: Queer Virginity in Early Modern English Drama* (Philadelphia, PA: University of Pennsylvania Press, 2000), 184.
[90] Ibid.
[91] Horacio Sierra, 'Convents as Feminist Utopias: Margaret Cavendish's *The Convent of Pleasure* and the Potential of Closeted Dramas and Communities', *Women's Studies* 38 (2009): 647–69, 652.

Through an ephemeral performance of feminist community, the play recognizes that unlike the self-assured impermeable society of More's book, utopia is vulnerable and contingent.

Bell in Campo

The utopia in *Bell in Campo* also exists in a state of liminality but this utopia has no identifiable spatial presence and emerges instead in process and action – in the remaking of the female self, and, inter-subjectively, in the creation of a collective of female warriors. The play is in two parts, the first focused on preparations for war between the 'Kingdome of Reformation' and the 'Kingdome of Faction'.[92] Lady Victoria wishes to accompany her husband, the Lord General, to war and at first he refuses, for, he claims, 'Nature hath made women like China, or Purselyn, they must be used gently, and kept warily, or they will break and fall on Death's head' (110). But through convincing rhetoric she manages to persuade him, a change of mind that becomes a source of agitation for some gentlemen who refuse to take their wives, whilst others enthusiastically encourage theirs. However, it does not turn out as the wives had hoped: instead of staying with their husbands, they are sent to a garrison town, which is a two-day journey from their husbands. This experience of humiliation further radicalizes the women, who – inspired by Henry V-style speech-making from Lady Victoria (a rhetoric also resonant of the eloquence of Praxagora from Aristophanes' *The Assemblywomen*) – determine to learn the art of soldiery and transform themselves into the 'Noble Heroickesses' Victoria addresses them as (118). With the women's approval, Victoria becomes their 'Generalless' (120) and she draws up a disciplinary code, rules, and laws.

Like Cavendish's two other utopian plays, the utopian vignettes alternate with episodes from the non-utopian world including a focus on the lonely women left behind, two of whom, Madame Jantil and Madame Passionate, form subjects of a sub-plot; both women become rich widows and while Jantil retreats from the world to rooms next to her husband's tomb, becomes ill, and eventually dies, Passionate is wooed by an unscrupulous predator whom she marries and by whom she is treated miserably. Both cases seem to evidence the wrongs of the non-utopian gendered world where women's humanity is brutally attenuated. In contrast, the utopian scenes witness the

---

[92] Cavendish, *Bell in Campo*, in *The Convent of Pleasure and Other Plays*, ed. Anne Shaver (London: The Johns Hopkins University Press), 107–69, 107. All further references are to this edition and appear in the main body of the text.

expansion of femininity, where women un-learn their submissive, supportive roles and make themselves anew as a strong, indomitable community, capable of fighting the enemy and winning. Just after the enemy had defeated the male army and were in the process of collecting the spoils, Victoria's women warriors attacked and won, and the 'Kingdom of Faction' defeated. The play ends with the armies returning home and a large procession organized for the welcome of Victoria, who, extravagantly adorned, is carried through the streets. New laws are passed, including increased property rights and greater economic independence for women.

One of the founding rules of the women's army in *Bell in Campo* is that no men are allowed admission to their company without the permission of the Generalless. As with *The Female Academy* and *The Convent of Pleasure*, *Bell in Campo* is a separatist female utopia that reintegrates itself with the non-utopian world by the end of the play. Again, the ending has invited a variety of readings, but in this play at least, the dominant order appears to be permanently changed by the feminist utopian praxis of the female militia. Karen L. Raber views the women in Victoria's army as 'a host of married and single women, sisters, mothers, and lovers who permanently transform themselves, overwriting what men call their "nature" with custom, training, and experience'.[93] As with the other two plays, however, *Bell in Campo* is also immersed in Royalist interests: it is, as Rabey suggests, 'about the Civil War, barely bothering to provide allegorized translations'.[94] Stanton makes a strong case for resonances in the play of Queen Henrietta Maria's involvement in the civil war.[95] But as Vimala C. Pasupathi writes, royalist and feminist interests combine to produce new forms of female agency: '*Bell in Campo* is a fantasy of triumphant militarism that rewrites the outcome of England's civil wars while simultaneously authorizing women's participation in state affairs'.[96] While reimagining the civil war in favour of royalist interests, Cavendish simultaneously reshapes and widens the scripts for women.

Lady Victoria emerges as an inspirational leader delivering rousing speeches that politicize her female army of 'five or six thousand' (119). She agitates against the 'Masculine Sex' for thinking women 'unusefull' and 'troublesome' and 'only fit to breed and bring forth Children' (119). Denunciating patriarchal principles, she proclaims to her 'Noble Heroickesses' (118):

---

[93] Karen L. Raber, 'Warrior Women in the Plays of Cavendish and Killigrew', *Studies in English Literature, 1500–1900* 40.3 (2000): 413–33, 429.
[94] Ibid., 426.
[95] Stone Stanton, '"An Amazonian Heroickess"'.
[96] Vimala C. Pasupathi, 'New Model Armies: Re-contextualizing The Camp in Margaret Cavendish's *Bell in Campo*' *ELH* 78.3 (Fall 2011): 657–85, 657.

but if we were both weak and fearfull, as they imagine us to be, yet custome which is a second Nature will encourage the one and strengthen the other, and had our educations been answerable to theirs, we might have proved as good Souldiers and Privy Counsellors, Rulers and Commanders, Navigators and Architectors, and as learned Scholars both in Arts and Sciences, as men are.

119

This is not just a call for the better treatment of women but an angry railing against the historic exclusion of women from key spheres of life, the implication of which is a wholesale challenge to hegemonic gendered practices. Lady Victoria does not confine her equality claims to the intellectual and political spheres but insists on women's potential to succeed on the battlefield, 'let us practice I say, and make these Fields as Schools of Martial Arts and Sciences, so shall we become learned in their disciplines of War' (120).

None of the army is to stay in garrison towns lest they become lazy. All women who are physically able must bear arms at all times to familiarize their bodies with heavy armour and weapons, and they must train at least three times a week, if not daily. This emphasis on women's bodily potential, a self-determination rooted in corporeal power and autonomy is richly developed in a strand of twentieth- and twenty-first-century separatist-feminist utopias. The character Jael in Russ's *The Female Man* (1975) is a physically enhanced combatant, ruthless in her desire for Womanland to succeed in its war with Manland. The representation of the Amazonian women fighters of Wittig's *Les Guérillères* (1969) is a potent production of brawny physical strength interwoven with imagery of female fluids and vulvic symbolism. There is also Jackie Nixon's all-female militia in Hall's *The Carhullan Army* (2007), within which the novel's protagonist, Sister, achieves an enhanced bodily strength and ability to engage in combat that produces a profound reworking of her identity. More recent is Naomi Alderman's *The Power* (2016) where women have become physically powerful through harnessing electrical impulses from their hands. A matriarchal network of power is created and the gender order reversed.

Utopian articulations of female sociality, cooperation, and collectivism form priorities in Cavendish's plays, and are areas of commitment similarly repeated across the centuries in feminist utopian fiction. Victoria expresses appreciation of hearing the women 'speak all with one voice and Tongue, which shows [their] minds are joyned together, as in one piece, without seam or rent' (118). While the collective is a pervasive feature of many utopias from More's onwards, it is often figured as an anonymous mass, rarely stepping out of background references. Critical feminist utopias of the twentieth and twenty-first centuries combine common interest with difference and individuation and in doing so celebrate solidarity while simultaneously offering a critique of power differentials that exist within homogeneity. *Bell in Campo* marshals the potential of female collective power under the compelling control of Victoria's keen polemic; however, the presence of her acolytes – '*a number of women of all sorts*' – is 'felt' within the text: their agency has a presence, even if that agency is in accordance with Victoria's will.

This communal act of utopian self-making demands a retraining of the body and the mind. But it also involves the practice of self-mythologizing. Victoria's foundational laws and rules include the requirement that when marching 'the Souldiers shall sing in their march the heroical actions done in former times by heroical women' (124). Existing cultural and historical narratives only serve to render women as, at best, supportive actors to male protagonists and at worst disruptors of, or invisible from, male world-making. In Cavendish's play, gendered biblical truths are turned on their head – 'men are apt to corrupt the noble minds of women, and to alter their gallant, worthy, and wise resolutions, with their flattering words, and pleasing and subtil insinuations' (125) and the women participate in reimagining their history and conjuring feminist mythology through the ritualistic practices of singing and marching. This ritualistic creation of feminist folklore, as Mosher notes, 'arrests time and upsets traditional narratives, allowing Cavendish to construct her temporary utopias of liminality'.[97]

While markedly different from the other two utopian plays with its move outside of a bounded utopian space to focus instead on action, process, and physical empowerment, *Bell in Campo* nevertheless shares some core principles with *The Female Academy* and *The Convent of Pleasure*. It combines attention to micropolitical interests – marriage, childbirth and rearing, domestic affairs – with more muscular subject matter, in this case, the theatre of war. There is an amalgamation of feminine sociability, friendship, and community with critique of the political economy, property rights, and law – a separatist, feminist militia – exists within the non-utopian world with which it has several close encounters before reintegrating back into that world. While repeating the pattern of dissipating the utopia and re-assimilating the women into heteronormativity, *Bell in Campo* nevertheless closes with a more profound set of reforms of women's rights and gender equality.

---

[97] Mosher, 'Female Spectacle as Liberation in Margaret Cavendish's Plays', 9.

Utopian returns

Referring to the sixteenth- and seventeenth-century women's texts which form the subject of their book, Clare Brant and Diane Purkiss claim that many of the writings 'resist assimilation to the canon or even to the literary, acting instead as disruptive forces which expose the stories told about gender by an interpretative community willing to consult only the canonical as open to question'.[98] Something similar could be said of Cavendish's utopian plays and their relationship with the canon of utopian literature. Appreciating the distinctive contribution of Cavendish's utopian drama works to put pressure on the norms and conventions that become repeated over the course of the development of male utopian fiction. For example, the dominant literary trope of male visitors journeying to, or returning from, far-off, exotic islands, or travelling through time or space, are replaced in Cavendish's plays with temporary utopias of female community. In common with other utopian plays, Cavendish's utopian dramas replace the lengthy descriptions common to utopian prose with interchanges among characters that animate new forms of subjectivity and sociality through performative dialogue and ritualistic practices. In common with some (but not all) utopian dramas written by men, Cavendish's utopias occupy a liminal space proximate to the non-utopian world. What distinguishes Cavendish's utopian plays from male utopian drama is that the former are separatist collectives experimenting with feminist forms of organization and sociability within the non-utopian present. A further distinguishing feature is the utopias' dissipation at the close of the plays; Erin Lang Bonin states that this happens 'as if to demonstrate that culturally dominant modes of thought are dystopian for women'.[99]

Cavendish's utopian plays exploit the political opportunities generated by the Morean tradition of literary utopianism but reimagine the utopia's content and form. There are some continuities with the Old Comedy of Aristophanes, particularly in the interweaving of serious and comic, the blending of genres, and the proximity of the utopia to the non-utopian present. But *The Female Academy, The Convent of Pleasure*, and *Bell in Campo* are strikingly different, indeed patently original. The confined, 'womb-like spaces' of the first two deviate significantly from utopian convention, as Rebecca D'Monté observes: 'public/private domains are redefined to provocatively locate the genesis of

---

[98] Clare Brant and Diane Purkiss, 'Introduction: Minding the Story', in *Women, Texts and Histories 1575–1760*, ed. Clare Brant and Diane Purkiss (London and New York: Routledge, 1992), 8.

[99] Erin Lang Bonin, 'Margaret Cavendish's Dramatic Utopias and the Politics of Gender', *Studies in English Literature 1500–1900* 40.2 (2000): 339–54, 340.

intellectual creativity and right governance within such matrices'.[100] *Bell in Campo* moves out of the domestic space into the public sphere and re-appropriates hyper masculine activities for her collective of women, which Oddvar Holmesland calls a 'masculinized self-realisation'.[101] More radical than this though, the play offers a profound undermining of gendered knowledge through a fluid, ephemeral hybridization of space, gender, and language.

The innovations in the utopian genre advanced by Cavendish in her utopian plays anticipate subsequent feminist utopias that dislodge utopian expression from its patriarchal Morean roots, while staying faithful to a political desire for far-reaching change. The alternation of utopian and non-utopian scenes so prevalent in Cavendish's work are markedly unusual for an early modern utopia. However, this approach becomes a key means by which utopia in the late twentieth century is refigured as radically precarious, but politically urgent. The non-utopian scenes in Piercy's *Woman on the Edge of Time*, to take one example, offer graphic descriptions of the brutal treatment of a Mexican-American, working-class woman suffering from depression in 1970s America. That these scenes alternate throughout the novel with moments from a utopian future offers a deconstruction of the two-part Morean utopia to produce a more dynamic format. The movement back and forth creates a temporal plasticity that makes vivid the potential of historical transformation. Similarly, while it may be disappointing that Cavendish's utopias ultimately dissolve, this kind of ending also becomes more frequently deployed in modern and contemporary utopias as happy endings are increasingly read through poststructuralist theory as aligning with ideological closure.

Cavendish offers us three remarkable utopian texts, plays that like many contemporary utopias problematize and complicate Morean structures and ideologies. Female equality, independence, empowerment, and community form the primary political interests of *The Female Academy*, *The Convent of Pleasure*, and *Bell in Campo*, and these preoccupations are played out through an innovative blurring of literary and dramatic genres and modes, and a revision of utopian tropes and conventions. Taking account of these plays as part of a canon of utopian literature encourages us to think again about the narrative of the development of the literary utopia. The post-Morean formal

[100] Rebecca D'Monté, 'Mirroring Female Power: Separatist Spaces in the Plays of Margaret Cavendish, Duchess of Newcastle', in *Female Communities, 1600–1800: Literary Visions and Cultural Realities*, ed. Rebecca D'Monté and Nicole Pohl (Basingstoke: Macmillan, 2000), 106.
[101] Oddvar Holmesland, *Utopian Negotiation: Aphra Behn and Margaret Cavendish* (New York: Syracuse University Press, 2003), 53.

experimentation celebrated in modern and contemporary utopias by scholars of utopias is in fact present much earlier – in Cavendish's utopian drama – as is a feminist readjustment of the epistemological and ontological structures that underpin patriarchal thought. In place of the lengthy descriptions of other worlds found in utopian prose, Cavendish offers animated female voices – a community of women, if not physically on stage, then at least brought to life orally through group readings. Cavendish exploits drama's ephemeral, fleeting, transitory nature to create self-reflective performances of alternative gendered worlds.

4

The enhanced utopian subject

While Margaret Cavendish's work imagines an all-female community as the means to create a better world, George Bernard Shaw's utopian plays are preoccupied with the individual's capacity for contributing to the common good. For Shaw, establishing and sustaining a better world is only possible if individuals have the requisite qualities and capabilities to succeed in such a demanding endeavour. Shaw was interested in the potential of a superior human enabled by scientific enhancement. Influenced by a theory, common among socialists at the time, that eugenics offered progressive scientific opportunities to improve human beings and therefore human societies, Shaw drew on an idiosyncratic application of eugenics – Creative Evolution – to imagine an enhanced human subject, particularly by way of extending the life course and moving towards an advanced, cerebral subjectivity, unencumbered by the constraints of the fleshly body. This chapter focuses largely on Shaw's substantial utopian play, *Back to Methuselah* (1921), paying some attention to his much shorter utopian play, *Farfetched Fables* (1950), and making brief reference to *The Simpleton of the Unexpected Isles* (1934).

The theory of Creative Evolution is now deeply compromised by its association with eugenics, but the broader set of interests within which it resides – of the individual's relation to community and capacity for action – has persisted as a central concern for both the utopian artist and thinker. Shaw's acerbic critiques of capitalist organization focused particularly on its exploitation, hypocrisy, and stupidity, and these remain prescient preoccupations of utopianism. Shaw prioritized the human subject, and in particular, the undiscovered potential of human capability – as well as, crucially, the potential for individuals to undermine collective endeavour – concerns that are at the centre of his utopian vision. Instead of subordinating human consciousness to material environment, Shaw privileged the former: what qualities are needed to contribute to the making of a better society? What characteristics undermine this goal? His concern was whether one is 'a creator of social values or a parasitical consumer or destroyer of them'.[1] Whilst

---

[1] Shaw, 'Preface on Days of Judgment', in *The Simpleton of the Unexpected Isles*, in *The Simpleton, The Six, and the Millionaires: Three Plays* (London: Constable, 1936), 15.

resolutely uncompromising – and against the grain of much socialist thinking – Shaw's ideas simultaneously provide a thought-provoking supplement to the conventional utopian assumption that people who undermine the community will no longer exist in a new utopian society, or be so few in number as to be negligible, or treated with varying degrees of isolation and punishment.

The Simpleton of The Unexpected Isles is the utopian play that most exemplifies Shaw's preoccupation with individual human capacity for becoming either a 'social asset' or 'social nuisance'.[2] A play about the preconditions for utopia rather than a description of a utopia *per se*, *The Simpleton* includes what turns out to be a false utopia. The setting is a Polynesian-style idyll, where Pra, a priest, and Prola, a priestess (supranormal, orientalized figures within which Shaw's idea of the Life Force is particularly potent) initiate a eugenics experiment of polygamous family-making and the mixing of Eastern and Western genes. Perhaps surprisingly, given Shaw's subscription to eugenics, the experiment fails, and the four offspring (Maya, Vashti, Janga, and Kanchin) are deemed unproductive and lacking a moral conscience; in an unexpected day of judgement, they, along with others, whose lives, according to the play's Angel, 'have no use, no meaning, no purpose, [...] fade out'.[3] Judgement day is 'not the end of the world' says the Angel, 'but the end of its childhood and the beginning of its responsible maturity'.[4] For Shaw, utopia will not be able to function if individuals, whose actions (or inactions) threaten its success, are permitted to thrive.

While *The Simpleton* is interested in the pre-conditions for utopian citizenship rather than what a utopia might look like, the play simultaneously executes some familiar utopian tropes. Its lengthy preface – resonant of Book 1 of More's *Utopia* – spends time engaging the reader in a dialogue that makes strange the familiar, undesirable non-utopian present; Shaw's targets for the day of judgement include the man 'who cannot [...] see why he should not employ labor for profit, or buy things solely to sell them again for more [...] or speculate in currency values'.[5] While other utopias have minimized the disruptive potential of dissent in utopia, Shaw confronts it head on: 'we need a greatly increased intolerance of socially injurious conduct and an uncompromising abandonment of punishment and cruelties, together with a sufficient school inculcation of social responsibility to make every citizen conscious that if his life costs more than it is worth to the community the

---

[2] Ibid., 15.
[3] Shaw, *The Simpleton of the Unexpected Isles*, in *The Simpleton, The Six, and the Millionaires: Three Plays* (London: Constable, 1936), 69.
[4] Ibid.
[5] Shaw, 'Preface on Days of Judgment', 16.

community may painlessly extinguish it'.[6] While the effort to deal decisively with 'socially injurious conduct' by what can only mean state execution is unacceptable to most socialists and utopians, the proposal to abolish 'punishment and cruelties', so often normalized as reasonable responses to antisocial acts, even in utopian representation, is a more compelling utopian proposition. Shaw objected to what he considered to be the sadism of penal punishment – often long, slow, cruel confinements and humiliations. Shaw's preoccupation with the individual may seem to repeat bourgeois norms, but importantly his focus on the individual is not at the expense of the community; in fact, it is the opposite. The community is of primary concern: in order to build a flourishing utopian collective, the individual must contribute more than they receive in return.[7] While *The Simpleton* takes up utopian ideas and employs some familiar conventions, it does not, however, dramatize a utopian society, which, the play suggests, is to emerge after the day of judgement.

The other two plays – *Back to Methuselah* and *Farfetched Fables* – do present accounts of utopian worlds, the former offering a more extended and comprehensive vision than the latter. There are similarities between the two plays; Matthew Yde calls *Farfetched Fables* 'a sort of reworking of *Back to Methuselah*'.[8] Both include lengthy prefaces with some overlapping themes, and while *Back to Methuselah* is very long and *Farfetched Fables* very short in comparison, both are divided into sections – five parts in the case of the former and six 'fables' in the latter. *Farfetched Fables* begins in the mid-twentieth century before moving far into the future (although the exact time is unspecified); *Back to Methuselah* starts much further back in time with Adam and Eve and finishes in the year 31,920. While both explore the concepts of ageing and disembodiment, *Back to Methuselah* provides much more detail on the former, and *Farfetched Fables* is weighted towards the latter. What follows in the rest of this chapter is a consideration of these plays' distinctive contributions as utopian dramas and the implications of engaging with them as utopias. Shaw's utopian plays are characterized by an eccentric interweaving of science and fantasy in their apparently sincere proposals for Creative Evolution as utopian solution. They are unusual – as utopias – in their displacement of attention from material structures to individual human

---

[6] Ibid.
[7] This is more demanding than Marx's famous maxim: 'From each according to his ability, to each according to his needs!', which recognizes diverse human capability and modifies expectations of individual contribution accordingly. Karl Marx, 'Critique of the Gotha Programme', *The Portable Karl Marx*, ed. Eugene Kamenka (London: Penguin, 1983), 541.
[8] Matthew Yde, *Bernard Shaw and Totalitarianism: Longing for Utopia* (London: Palgrave, 2013), 185.

capacity. And they are provocative – like all the utopias discussed in this book – in their expressions as dramas rather than prose fictions.

Contexts: utopian and scientific

Given Bernard Shaw's well-known commitment to advancing philosophical, political, and aesthetic critiques of capitalism, it is not surprising that he pursued utopian themes in several of his plays or wrote full utopias.[9] Yet, it is striking that these plays emerge after the heyday of bold socialist experimentation in the utopian novel as exemplified by Edward Bellamy's *Looking Backward* (1888), William Morris' *News from Nowhere* (1890), and H. G. Wells' *A Modern Utopia* (1905). Shaw's utopian plays are conspicuous because they appeared during what Gregory Claeys has termed the second 'dystopian turn' (the first, he suggests, is the Enlightenment satire),[10] which was one expression of *fin-de-siècle* pessimism – a pessimism borne of disillusionment with an Enlightenment dependence on reason and scientific positivism. This pessimism, in turn, only strengthened in the early twentieth century, with an increasingly pervasive culture of fear, anxiety, and political uncertainty in the context of mass slaughter of World War I and the subsequent emergence of fascism in Germany, Italy, and Spain, and Stalinism in the Soviet bloc. Domination of the utopian genre by the anti-utopian and dystopian novel was vividly expressed in several popular and enduring works, including H. G. Wells' *The Time Machine* (1895), Jack London's *The Iron Heel* (1908), Yevgeny Zamyatin's *We* (1921), Aldous Huxley's *Brave New World* (1932), Katharine Burdekin's, *Swastika Night* (1937), and George Orwell's *1984* (1949).

In this context, Shaw's plays stand out as rare proposals for 'world betterment', to use his term.[11] Yet, the challenges capitalist democracies faced – such as the imperialist game playing of WWI; the Russian revolutions and revolutionary activism in Germany, Italy, and Spain; campaigns for full franchise; and an upsurge in industrial militancy leading to the 1926 general strike – were simultaneously opportunities for socialists to build and agitate. While the

---

[9] As well as the three utopian plays discussed in this chapter, many of his other plays contain utopian themes including *Man and Superman* (1903), *Major Barbara* (1905), and *Heartbreak House* (1919). Matthew Yde traces utopian longing in much of Shaw's body of work (Yde, *Bernard Shaw and Totalitarianism: Longing for Utopia* [New York: Palgrave, 2013]).
[10] Gregory Claeys, 'The Origins of Dystopia: Wells, Huxley and Orwell', in *The Cambridge Companion to Utopian Literature* (Cambridge: Cambridge University Press, 2010), 111.
[11] The first act in Shaw's *Buoyant Billions* (1948) is called 'The World Betterers'.

British left suffered splits over the question of whether to oppose the war, it was simultaneously galvanized by the events of October 1917; in Walter Kendall's words: 'Bolshevism had provided a recipe for revolution'.[12] Reading Karl Marx's *Das Kapital* (in French) in 1883 inspired Shaw,[13] but his politics were not revolutionary Marxism; along with well-known figures such as Sidney and Beatrice Webb, Emmeline Pankhurst, H. G. Wells, and Annie Besant, Shaw was an early member of the Fabian Society (established in 1884), and hence committed to a gradualist approach to socialism. However, as Stanley Weintraub observes, by the end of the first world war, Shaw 'was disillusioned about the effectiveness of Fabian permeation of political parties' and increasingly impatient with the inability of liberal democracy to facilitate justice, fairness, and fulfilment of material needs, yet alone provide a social structure that promoted full human potential.[14] Nevertheless despite this disillusionment, he remained a member of the Fabian Society and accepted the labels 'Fabian Communist and Creative Evolutionist' until the end of his life.[15]

One of the attractions of Fabianism for Shaw was its intellectualism. The Priestess, in the prologue to his play *The Simpleton*, asks, '[i]s it really kind to treat them according to their folly instead of to our wisdom?', 'them' referring to the masses.[16] Shaw's dislike of 'bottom up' approaches to socialist politics provides a context for understanding his often-cited admiration of strong leaders, such as Lenin, Stalin, Mussolini, and Hitler. He was against anti-Semitism, which he considered as 'the hatred of the lazy, ignorant, fat-headed Gentile for the pertinacious Jew who, schooled by adversity to use his brains to the utmost, outdoes him in business', and against fascism, which he viewed as 'state ownership of private finance [...] for the benefit of exploiters'.[17] However, he admired effective use of personality and leadership in the fomentation of radical political change, particularly in the context of a British parliamentary democracy that showed no signs of being able to introduce socialist transformation. The majority of the electorate, for Shaw, had so poor an understanding of politics and was up against such immense ideological misinformation that there was little hope of socialism being introduced through the ballot box. It was this perspective that moved Shaw to appreciate

---

[12] Walter Kendall, *The Revolutionary Movement in Britain in 1900–21: The Origins of British Communism* (London: Weidenfeld and Nicolson, 1969), x.
[13] Michael Holroyd, *Bernard Shaw* (London: Vintage, 1998), 79.
[14] Stanley Weintraub, 'GBS and the Despots', *The Times Literary Supplement* 22 August 2011, http://www.the-tls.co.uk/articles/public/george-bernard-shaw-and-the-despots/
[15] Shaw, 'Preface', *Farfetched Fables*, ed. Dan H. Laurence (London: Max Reinhardt, 1972), 413.
[16] Shaw, *The Simpleton of the Unexpected Isles*, in *The Simpleton, The Six, and the Millionaires: Three Plays* (London: Constable, 1936), 29.
[17] Shaw, quoted in Holroyd, *Bernard Shaw*, 543.

the October 1917 revolution, although he disliked what he perceived as a lack of importance attributed to education and the role of the intellectual by Lenin's worker bolshevism. His impatience for change, frustration with the lack of progress in the British Labour Party, respect for dynamic political personality, and distrust of the masses seem to be the context within which Shaw expressed approval of Stalinist Russia (which he visited with Nancy Astor in 1932). He valued the Soviet system for its egalitarian objectives and explained away its repression and brutalities under Stalin as a hangover from its barbarous Tsarist past, objectionable, but no worse than anything that had happened under the previous regime. Transformation of social relations had costs.

For Shaw, a commitment to the potential of human agency to transform social relations was interwoven with a subscription to the possibility of the power of Creative Evolution to enhance the human subject. Against the apparently senseless accidents of Charles Darwin's theory of natural selection in human evolution, supporters of Creative Evolution introduced agency as a mediator of biological progress: in this perspective, the human will possessed the ability to harness the Life Force and improve the human subject. While Shaw viewed Darwin's theory of natural selection as reflective of the practice of capitalist competition, he considered Creative Evolution as more in line with a socialist subscription to political agency and will.[18] A key contribution to the development of Creative Evolution as a scientific-philosophical-religious theory was Samuel Butler's vehement anti-Darwinian tract, *Luck, or Cunning?* (1887), where he proposed an opposition between the 'apostles of luck' who supported random variation (Charles Darwin, Herbert Spencer, and George Romanes) and those adherents of 'cunning' (Erasmus Darwin, Comte de Buffon, and Butler himself); for the latter, some form of design or agency was a key determiner of evolutionary progress. Influenced by Lamarck, Henri Bergson's *Creative Evolution* (1907) properly developed and established the concept – identifying *élan vital* as crucial to evolutionary development – which proved popular in the early decades of the twentieth century. Indeed, also influenced by Lamarck, but apparently not conversant with Bergson's work until 1911, Shaw was developing similar ideas of Creative Evolution in parallel, the fullest representation of which appeared in *Back to Methuselah* and its lengthy preface that was published at the same time, these ideas then being revisited thirty years later in *Farfetched Fables*.[19]

A socialist interest in the power of eugenics to imbue the human subject with greater capacity as a means of establishing a better society was

---

[18] See Paul A. Hummert, *Bernard Shaw's Marxian Romance* (Lincoln, NE: University of Nebraska Press, 1973), 138.

[19] See Michel W. Pharand, *Bernard Shaw and the French* (Gainesville, FL: University Press of Florida, 2000), 244.

undoubtedly central to Shaw's utopian imagination. A Marxist figuration of human consciousness arising from material relations, common to the utopias of the late nineteenth- and early twentieth centuries gave way, in Shaw's plays, to a more Hegelian focus on the determining power of human consciousness, intellect, and spirit, combined with a Nietzschean interest in the will. Shaw's utopian plays, along with their rather unorthodox contribution to utopian thinking, have been largely overlooked.[20] There has been very little scholarly engagement with *The Simpleton*, and even less to *Farfetched Fables*, and while more attention has been paid to *Back to Methuselah*, that focus has tended not to consider the play's significance as a utopia.[21] What follows is an unearthing of the value of Shaw's utopian plays to utopian thinking by seeking to understand the implications of the utopian depictions alongside the critiques they offer of the particular moments of their production. One of the striking contributions these plays make is the exploration they undertake of ageing and longevity; they provide a new and fertile evaluation of the capacities of the very old. For Shaw, the Life Force gained in strength and profundity in old age. His vision of very old age as having the requisite maturity to engage successfully with the complexity of the modern world brings with it some fascinating and radical insights to the identity politics of age.

The ageing question

In common with dominant narratives of ageing across historical periods, youth or youthfulness – of the body, intellect, and temperament – has usually been the ideal age phase in utopian representations. As part of this attachment to youthfulness, the experience of ageing – and interest in older utopian

---

[20] Shaw's interest in eugenics has informed a critical squeamishness towards his utopian plays. It is also apparent – as Peter Gahan observes – that there is a dominant view within Shaw Studies that Shaw's later plays (from 1920 onwards) were artistically inferior, and in particular, there has been frustration with a perceived lack of formal structuring and a move away from psychologically rounded characters in Shaw's late work. Peter Gahan, 'The Achievement of Shaw's Later Plays, 1920-1939', *Shaw: The Annual of Bernard Shaw Studies* 23 (2003): 27-35.

[21] In *The Cambridge Companion to George Bernard Shaw*, there is only one brief reference to *Farfetched Fables*, and this appears in the first chapter and is indexed (incorrectly) under the subheading 'novels/fiction'. Surprisingly, there is no reference to the play in T. F. Evans, 'The Later Shaw', in *The Cambridge Companion to George Bernard Shaw*, ed. Christopher Innes (Cambridge: Cambridge University Press, 1998). For examples of negative criticism of *Back to Methuselah*, see Margery Morgan, *The Shavian Playground* (London: Methuen, 1972), 221-2; for negative criticism of *The Simpleton of the Unexpected Isles*, see Arnold Silver, *Bernard Shaw: The Darker Side* (Redwood City, CA: Stanford University Press, 1982), 27.

citizens specifically – has often been neglected. There are very few references to old age in Tommaso Campanella's *City of the Sun* (1602) or Francis Bacon's *New Atlantis* (1627) for example, and old people are not present in the Arcadian romances of Torquato Tasso's *Aminta* (1573) or Miguel de Cervantes' *Galatea* (1585). In fact, the occasional appearance of an old character has tended to take the form of a dissenter bitterly complaining about the new progressive utopian society. Examples include Clara's grandfather, a 'grumbler', who yearns for the pre-utopian days of 'unlimited competition'[22] in Morris's *News from Nowhere*, or Severan-Severan described as 'the oldest reactionary in the world'[23] by his fellow utopians in Howard Brenton's *Greenland*. Their advanced years apparently explicate a reactionary nostalgia, itself proof that the older person is an ideological as well as physiological anachronism. Several modern dystopias evince anxiety over modernity's dislike of old people, by imagining their total removal through dystopian critique – think of Huxley's *Brave New World* (where time is up at age sixty) or William F. Nolan and George Clayton Johnson's novel *Logan's Run* (1967), and its film adaptation (directed by Michael Anderson in 1976), where one is no longer acceptable at twenty-one or thirty, respectively.

Yet, significantly, in the foundational utopian texts, old age was depicted as a stage in the life course deserving of sympathetic attention or high social status. In Plato's *Republic*, older people have intellectual, social, and political power: 'it is obvious that the elder must govern, and the younger be governed'.[24] In More's *Utopia* older utopians are respected and have social authority: the reader learns that in the countryside, each agricultural house 'accommodates at least forty adults, plus two slaves who are permanently attached to it, and is run by a reliable, elderly married couple'.[25] In the towns, the oldest male relative is in control of the household. In the communal dining hall, at the place of honour (the high table) sit 'the Styward and his wife, with two of the oldest residents', and in groups of four older and younger people alternate in seating. Old utopians are provided with the biggest and best portions and there are some special opportunities for old women: 'there's nothing to stop a woman from becoming a priest, although women aren't often chosen for the job, and only elderly widows are eligible'.[26] While much utopian literature repeats dominant age prejudices either explicitly or covertly, the vortex of the

---

[22] William Morris, *News from Nowhere* (London: Penguin, 1993), 173; 174.
[23] Howard Brenton, *Greenland* (London: Methuen Drama, 1988), 56.
[24] Plato, *The Republic*, Second Edition (revised), trans. Desmond Lee (London: Penguin, 1987), 119.
[25] Thomas More, *Utopia*, trans. Paul Turner (London: Penguin, 2003), 50.
[26] More, *Utopia*, 105.

utopian canon – More's *Utopia* and its precursor, Plato's *Republic* – respects and values older utopian citizens.

Although it is difficult to identify a coherent narrative of perceptions of old age in the early twentieth century, it is instructive to note, as Karen Chase does, that the 'elderly subject' emerges as a category of (social) science at the end of the nineteenth century, due to the development of the discipline of gerontology. Chase writes:

> Like claims of class throughout the nineteenth century, generational necessities are typically expressed as some form of 'need', pressed on a society in which resources are held to be scarce. Under these conditions, the wants of the elderly appear as excessive demand, monstrous desire, or hopeless and inconceivable fantasy that should be contained through social regulation at home or through (forced or voluntary) emigration abroad.[27]

Ageing is framed as a resource burden. Gerontologist, Thomas R. Cole, makes the point that the 'primary virtues of Victorian morality – independence, health, success' demanded 'constant control over one's body and physical energies'.[28] Cole concludes with the observation that the 'decaying body in old age, a constant reminder of the limits of physical self-control, came to signify precisely what bourgeois culture hoped to avoid: dependence, disease, failure, and sin'.[29] This is in the context of a culture dependent on material growth and economic productivity, and a concomitant rejection of bodily decay and decline. A purposeful anti-ageing discourse was thus gathering strength in the late nineteenth century, Christoph Conrad arguing that in the 1920s – precisely the moment of Shaw's *Back to Methuselah* – ageing was considered as especially 'troublesome'.[30] Part of the context for cementing associations of older age with unproductivity and economic and social dependency, are what Lagretta Tallent Lenker refers to, as the 'endless debates over old-age pensions, society's proper treatment of the elderly, and the Darwinian/Neo-Darwinian theories of evolution'.[31]

---

[27] Karen Chase, *The Victorians and Old Age* (Oxford: Oxford University Press, 2009), 6; 151.
[28] Thomas R. Cole, 'The "Enlightened" View of Aging: Victorian Morality in a New Key', in *What Does it Mean to Grow Old? Reflections from the Humanities*, ed. Thomas R. Cole and Sally A. Gadow (Durham, NC: Duke University Press, 1986), 121.
[29] Ibid.
[30] Christoph Conrad, 'Old Age in the Modern and Postmodern Western World', in *Handbook of the Humanities and Aging*, ed. Thomas R. Cole et al. (New York: Springer Publishing Company, 1992), 78–9.
[31] Lagretta Tallent Lenker, 'Why? Versus Why Not?: Potentialities of Aging in Shaw's *Back to Methuselah*', in *Aging and Identity: A Humanities Perspective*, ed. Sarah Munson Deats and Lagretta Tallent Lenker (Westport, CT and London: Praeger, 1999), 50.

A discourse of fear over the growth in the number of people age sixty-five or over in Britain intensified in the first half of the twentieth century, a period punctuated by the introduction of pensions in 1908 and the imposition of retirement in 1948.[32] The construction of ageing and the older person as problems is exemplified by Richard Titmuss and Kay Titmuss' study of the declining birth rate in the early twentieth century and the consequent increase in proportion of older people in society. They warned that Britain would soon need to prioritize 'armchairs and bedroom slippers instead of children's foods'.[33] With an expansion of the older population, they claimed that this could result in the loss of 'the mental attitude that is essential for social progress'.[34] Aptitudes vital to the advancement of society – 'intelligence, courage, power of initiative, and qualities of creative imagination' – were not 'usually [...] found in the aged'.[35] This flagrant diminishment of the older person, which was repeatedly articulated as part of normative thinking, is a crucial context for understanding the significance of Bernard Shaw's interest in ageing, and in particular, it allows us to appreciate the unconventional, indeed radically progressive, reimagining of ageing, old age, and the older subject in *Back to Methuselah* and *Farfetched Fables*.

Back to Methuselah

The first of *Back to Methuselah*'s five parts – 'In the Beginning' – is set in the Garden of Eden and is a rewriting and expansion of parts of Genesis. On encountering a dead fawn, the then-immortal Adam and Eve discover the existence of death and contemplate the lonely implications of each other's demise if one were to suffer a fatal accident. The serpent suggests they consider mortality and proposes that Adam choose 1000 as the age at which he should die, as a solution to the numbing boredom of immortality and the potential extinction of humanity if they were to suffer an accident. The serpent proposes birth as compensation for relinquishing immortality so that human life can continue from generation to generation. In a dynamic rewriting of Genesis, Adam and Eve are born of Lilith;[36] the concept of evil

---

[32] Andrew Blaikie, *Ageing and Popular Culture* (Cambridge: Cambridge University Press, 1999).
[33] Richard M. Titmuss and Kay Titmuss, *Parents Revolt: A Study of the Declining Birth-Rate in Acquisitive Societies* (London: Secker and Warburg, 1942), 46.
[34] Ibid.
[35] Ibid.
[36] Shaw, 'In the Beginning', in *Back to Methuselah* (London: Penguin, 1987), 69. All further references are to this edition and appear in the main body of the text.

exists before the forbidden-fruit episode (Eve calls death evil [66]); and Eve returns to the Garden of Eden periodically (90). After Cain (a perverse Shavian superman, a kind of dialectical provocation) has murdered Abel, instead of being cursed to wander the earth away from his parents, Cain is free to come and go wherever, whenever he chooses. These departures from scripture produced a Shavian dialectical set of tensions which were received with great pleasure. In reviews of the early productions, part one – with its 'poetry and dignity' – was the part most celebrated by theatre critics.[37] Refashioning parts of Genesis as the cornerstone of an epic, expansive utopian vision produced a creative social myth, an essential supplement, Shaw believed, to political doctrine.

Part two, titled 'The Gospel of the Brothers Barnabas', is set during the first few years after WW1 (the time Shaw was writing the play) in London. The Barnabas brothers – Franklyn (a cleric) and Conrad (a biologist) – have been developing a theory of longevity, and Conrad has published a book with their conclusions.[38] Living for 300 years would provide enough time to accrue the experience and wisdom necessary for the long-term thinking and planning essential for the creation and sustainability of a better society. Echoing the political satire of Aristophanic comedy, there are two politicians – Burge and Lubin – with obvious echoes of Liberal Party leaders and rivals, Lloyd George and Asquith (which most reviews of productions picked up on).[39] On hearing the Barnabas brothers' theory of longevity, their primary interest is its potential for aiding electioneering. Very different in form and tone from part one, part two functions in a similar way to Book 1 of More's *Utopia*: it presents a critical representation of the status quo, thereby encouraging audiences to come to their own realization of the need for fundamental change, the initial expressions of which start to become apparent in part three. The form of drawing-room comedy serves to accentuate the flaws of the characters and weakness of the social structure: people should be better and radical change is urgently needed.

Part three – 'The Thing Happens' – is set in 2170, around 250 years in the future, in the 'official parlor of the President of the British Isles'.[40] 'Short-living' –

---

[37] N.n. *Sheffield Daily Telegraph*, 6 March 1928, 7.
[38] Shaw's selection of Barnabas as the bothers' name gives 'Creative Evolution [...] added symbolic weight [...] – the historical Barnabas having been a first century missionary and a companion of Saint Paul.' Christopher Innes, 'Utopian Apocalypses: Shaw, War, and H. G. Wells', *The Annual of Bernard Shaw Studies* 23 (2003): 37–46, 42.
[39] Debenham K. Freebody's comment that the identities of Burge and Lubin were 'glaringly apparent' is typical of reviews at the time. 'Back to Methuselah: A Sombre Week of Shaw', *The Era* 27 February 1924, 18.
[40] Shaw, 'The Thing Happens', in *Back to Methuselah*, 146. All further references are to this edition and appear in the main body of the text.

which actually refers to the typical human life span of the reader or spectator – is causing immense political problems: the English are too short-lived and immature to conduct political affairs competently, and international consultants are brought in from China and Africa to help. Although also short-lived, they are more mature and thus better at managing state affairs. It transpires that there are a few people who are long-lived and have a lifespan of 300 years: the Archbishop of York and the Domestic Minister, Mrs Lutestring, who are characters from part two (the Reverend Haslam and the parlour maid), the latter of which had been the only character genuinely interested in Barnabas' theory of longevity, having closely read the book. That Shaw imbues the quiet, shy reverend and the working-class parlour maid with long life is part of his critique of class society and normative hierarchies.[41]

Part four – 'Tragedy of an Elderly Gentleman' – is set in Galway Bay in the year 3000, 830 years after part three. A visitor – a short-lived old man from the capital of Britain (now comically relocated to Baghdad) – returns to the islands of his ancestry but struggles to make sense of, and communicate with, the long-lived utopians, who now inhabit these islands. A further comical sub-plot consists of his travelling companions: the British prime minister, who is married to the old man's daughter, and the Emperor of Turania, who disguises himself and pretends to be Napoleon; they have come to consult the Oracle. At the end of the part, the short-lived old visitor wishes to stay with the long-lived utopians, and although he is warned about the life-threatening dangers of what the play calls 'discouragement' (to which I return later), he is granted permission to remain but then immediately dies.[42] This part deploys the familiar utopian trope of a visitor travelling to a utopian land, this encounter serving to produce the double effect of familiarizing the initially strange utopian ideas and simultaneously making strange – and increasingly undesirable – the familiar, non-utopian society of the spectator.

Part five – 'As Far as Thought Can Reach' – is set in the year 31,920, which is 28,920 years after part four. The long-lived community is fully established and the short-lived no longer exist. The focus of this part is on the birth of a new utopian – from an egg – who is born fully grown. The utopians are living hundreds and sometimes thousands of years now: they are potentially immortal, although a fatal accident is inevitable, the spectator is told. The utopians are also maturing much more quickly, arriving from eggs fully

---

[41] For a reading of the play as primarily about class conflict, see Fredric Jameson, 'Longevity as Class Struggle', in *Immortal Engines: Life Extension Immortality in Science Fiction and Fantasy*, ed. George Slusser et al. (Athens, GA: University of Georgia Press, 1996).
[42] Shaw, 'Tragedy of an Elderly Gentleman', in *Back to Methuselah* (London: Penguin, 1987), 19. All further references are to this edition and appear in the main body of the text.

grown, and wishing to relinquish childish play at four years of age. The scene includes two sculptors, Arjillax and Martellus, who debate the acceptability of the Ancients (the *really old* utopians) as worthy subjects for sculpture. There is also a scientist, Pygmalion, who has created two artificial humans in a lab, who are vain and violent and serve to represent the non-utopian short-lived people of Shaw's own time. The Ancients destroy them, and the part concludes with Adam reappearing in a ghostly form, followed by Eve, Cain, and Lilith, who calls upon the end of life's submission to matter – the play's ultimate utopian goal of a disembodied Life Force.

Written between 1918 and 1920 and published in 1921, *Back to Methuselah* was first performed by the New York Theatre Guild at the Old Garrick Theatre in 1922, and then in England at the Birmingham Repertory Theatre in 1923, this production transferring to the Court Theatre in London in 1924. As is evident from the above synopsis, it is a monumental play: one of the longest, epic in temporal reach, formally unusual, and titanic in ambition.[43] Shaw responded to Barry Jackson's decision to produce the play at the Birmingham Rep by asking, 'was he mad', Shaw's own passion for the play accompanied at the same time by recognition of its mammoth proportions, awkward singularity, and lack of commercial viability.[44] But after getting used to the idea of its staging, Shaw decided: '[t]he impossible had become possible. I handed over *Methuselah*'.[45] That the play itself is somehow an impossibility is peculiarly befitting of the shifting, other worldliness of the utopian vision it expresses.

Its awkward singularity is due partly to the play's blending and blurring of different forms, styles, and genres and its diverse addressees. In a press release for his publishers Constable & Co., Shaw declared that *Back to Methuselah* – which he referred to as 'his supreme exploit in dramatic literature' – would 'interest biologists, religious leaders, and lovers of the marvellous in fiction as well as lovers of the theatre'.[46] The play's comic form provided an appropriately flexible medium for a mix of philosophical treatise; drawing-room comedy, farce, and satire; political comment; scientific compendium; and fantastic and religious mythologizing. Part two – as presented by the Birmingham

---

[43] G. W. Bishop states that *Back to Methuselah* is 'possibly the longest play written outside China since the three parts of *Henry VI*'. *Barry Jackson and the London Theatre* (London: Arthur Barker, 1933), 23. The *Sheffield Daily Telegraph* claimed *Back to Methuselah* to be the longest play in the English Language (20 February 1924, 3).

[44] Shaw, quoted in H. M. Geduld, '*Back to Methuselah* and The Birmingham Repertory Company', *Modern Drama* 2.2 (1959): 115–29, 115.

[45] Shaw, quoted in Geduld, '*Back to Methuselah* and The Birmingham Repertory Company', 115.

[46] Shaw, quoted in Holroyd, *Bernard Shaw* (London: Vintage, 1998), 497.

Rep – is described by the theatre critic of the *Sheffield Daily Telegraph* as 'one of the funniest pieces that Mr. Shaw has ever written'.[47] The utopian communication of *Back to Methuselah* is couched in and contextualized by a variety of different political and aesthetic registers, allowing spectators to consider utopian ideas in manageable portions. The farcical and satirical aspects serve to interpellate a particular mode of attention, a mode encouraging laughter and mockery as much as critical thinking and utopian desire.

Many theatre reviews expressed warm enthusiasm for Shaw's 'tremendous play'.[48] The *Aberdeen Press* proclaimed 'with its Nietzschean dream of superhumanity', *Back to Methuselah* was one of the finest developments of modern evolutionary thinking that have appeared in the study or on the stage'.[49] The *Gloucester Journal* compared the play to Wagner's *Ring Cycle* saying it revealed 'all the dexterity of his brilliant intellect and caustic wit'.[50] Yet the play's temporal expansiveness, coverage of past and future human history, interweaving of different genres (or deployment of 'mixed methods' as one critic put it[51]), and bold ambition to radically rethink being human made *Back to Methuselah* difficult to grasp. While also comparing the play to Wagner and describing it as 'extraordinary drama' and 'a wonderful intellectual feat', the *Diss Express* additionally emphasizes 'the mental endurance demanded' of the work.[52] Its length and unwieldy structure also meant it was difficult to stage. Unlike the play's premiere at the Theatre Guild in New York, which produced the cycle over a period of three weeks, the Birmingham Rep followed Shaw's wishes and staged the play over four consecutive evenings with one matinée; Shaw approved as it 'preserved a sense of continuity'.[53] Shaw also suggested that the run was better received than in New York, where audiences had, he thought, been sent into a stupor.[54] But Lawrence Langner

---

[47] N.n., *Sheffield Daily Telegraph*, Saturday 6 December 1924, 4 [britishnewspaperarchive.co.uk].

[48] Ashley Dukes, 'The Stage of the Day', *Illustrated Sporting and Dramatic News*, 1 March 1924, 66. More copies of *Back to Methuselah* were sold in America than any of Shaw's other works. Max Beerbohm thought it the 'best book Shaw had written'. Shaw sent copies to many friends and acquaintances, including Lenin, who wrote comments in the margins (some approving, some disapproving). Holroyd, *Bernard Shaw*, 509.

[49] N.n. *Aberdeen Press and Journal*, Monday 14 April 1924, 3.

[50] *Gloucester Journal*, Saturday 15 September 1923, 1. Shaw had attended a performance of Wagner's *Ring* in Bayreuth in 1908 (Holroyd, *Bernard Shaw*, 359).

[51] J. M. Bulloch, 'Memories of Methuselah', *Graphic*, 1 March 1924, 10.

[52] N.n., *Diss Express*, 29 February 1924, 3. In the same review, the theatre critic states: 'it is pre-eminently a production for intellectuals, for while Shaw, as a Socialist, may make challenging claims for the rights of the ordinary person, it cannot be said that he has done anything to add to his entertainment.'

[53] G. W. Bishop, *Barry Jackson and the London Theatre* (London: Arthur Barker, 1933), 25.

[54] Eric S. Wherly, *Shaw for the Million* (London: Gulliver Books, n.d.), 84.

of the Theatre Guild (who had produced the New York production) also saw the Birmingham Rep version and found the intensity of nightly performances 'murderous'.[55] An even more intense presentation took place at the Arts Theatre in 1947, where all five playlets were performed in one day. The event started at 14:00, this being 'the only occasion that this has been done'.[56] At the Atlanta Theater production of the play in November 2000 directed by Michael Evenden, the performance was presented in two parts and the audience moved round various spaces for the five playlets.[57] A more recent production directed by Bill Largess at the Washington Stage Guild was multi-seasonal with parts one and two presented in 2014, parts three and four in 2015, and part five in 2017, the performances presented along with readings of the other parts as well as panel discussions.

As these different formats show, the play is excessive, excessive in its temporal coverage of human history (both past and future), excessive in its duration as a piece to be read or watched at the theatre, and excessive in its use of different genres, styles, and modes. Yet the excessive quality of the cycle is, I propose, part of its utopian otherness: its refusal of non-coincidence with familiar dramatic and utopian texts, modes, forms, and spectatorial experiences. That said, while much is surprising and eccentric, there is enough in the play that is familiar from other utopian texts (in both prose and drama) to provide spectatorial anchoring: critique of economic structures and political governance; imagining a post-capitalist system; radical rethinking of traditional discourses (in this case the Bible); envisaging the implications of future technological advances; and challenging conventional ideas about gender, class, and human identity more broadly.

Most profoundly and unusually for a utopian text as I have said, *Back to Methuselah* takes up the ageing question. In part three, 'The Thing Happens', the 300-year-old characters – the Archbishop and Mrs Lutestring – are vital, serious, and authoritative. The stage directions indicate that the Archbishop 'does not look a day over fifty, and is very well preserved at that; but his boyishness of manner is quite gone: he now has complete authority and self-possession' (158). We are told that Mrs Lutestring is 'in the prime of life, with elegant, tense, well held-up figure, and the walk of a goddess. Her expression and deportment are grave, swift, decisive, awful, unanswerable' (168). The 300-year-olds are represented as being in a state of extended middle age, this

---

[55] Lawrence Langner, *The Magic Curtain* (London: Harrap, 1952), 175.
[56] Raymond Mander and Joe Mitchenson, *Theatrical Companion to Shaw: A Pictorial Record of the First Performances of the Plays of George Bernard Shaw* (London: Rockliffe, 1954), 190.
[57] Dan Hulbert, 'Back-To-Back *Methuselah*', in *American Theatre* (October 2000): 11.

life phase marked as both dynamic and commanding, a combination of qualities the play considers essential for engaging with the complexities of the modern world. Part four sees a further development in longevity where a mixed age community of 'primaries' who are in their first century, 'secondaries' their second, and 'tertiaries' their third (197) have developed a utopian society that no longer recognizes gender or class divisions, private property, marriage, or the family. Much of this part consists of dialogue familiar from classic utopias where the visitor to utopia – in this case the elderly gentleman – converses with a range of primary, secondary, and tertiary utopians about the advances of the new society, advances facilitated by the extraordinary capacities bestowed by longevity.

These characters are important intermediaries in the transition period in the development of longevity and the concomitant improvement to social relations and social structures, but Shaw is most interested in the potential of extreme longevity, which is documented at the end of the cycle. The really long-lived utopians – the Ancients in the final part, 'As Far As Thought Can Reach' – have in Robert Brustein's words, a 'deeper sense of reality'.[58] Their cumulative acquirement of intellectual and spiritual engagement with the world works to perform the play's resignification of ageing as potentially progressive – as deepening, as enriching – rather than a process of decline. In place of the idea that ageing is 'pure pathology', to use a phrase Betty Friedan ascribes to a dominant strain of thinking about ageing (even within gerontology studies), Shaw's play reimagines ageing as 'a state of becoming and being, not merely as ending'.[59] The old person's value is no longer determined by economic productivity but by the accrual of experience, knowledge, maturity, sensitivity, and wisdom. For sociologist Ricca Edmondson, a key problem for older people is 'struggling to assert a commitment to meaningful citizenship in the face of a banal official language that tends to delete its expression'.[60] The utopian mode tends to remove or deprioritize economic productivity in favour of other forms of signification, contribution, and worth, which means that it provides a fertile form for reconstructing the older person as one who, through what Edmondson refers to as the ancient notion of 'cumulative value', is able to press at the limits of human possibility.[61] Shaw imbues his Ancients with an aptitude for amassing

---

[58] Robert Brustein, *The Theatre of Revolt: Studies in Modern Drama from Ibsen to Genet* (Chicago, IL: Ivan R. Dee, 1991), 201.
[59] Betty Friedan, *The Fountain of Age* (London: Jonathan Cape, 1993), 36.
[60] Ricca Edmondson, *Ageing, Insight and Wisdom: Meaning and Practice Across the Lifecourse* (Bristol: Policy Press, 2015), 16.
[61] Ibid., 38.

intellectual, spiritual, and emotional strengths. This offers an explicit counter-narrative to dominant accounts of decline. David Gutmann states: '[a]t best the aged are deemed barely capable of staving off disaster, but they are certainly not deemed capable of developing new capacities or of seeking out new challenges by their own choice'.[62] Through the advantage of longevity, the Ancients acquire an aggregation of superior qualities and an accrual of memories and different selves, producing a richly resourced utopian subject.

Shaw did not attempt to meet the theatrical challenges of presenting convincing spectacles of enhanced utopian subjectivity as expressed through old age; he wrote: 'I could not shew the life of the long livers, because, being a short liver, I could not conceive it'.[63] In his review of the Court Theatre production, Ashley Dukes describes '[t]he figures of this immense work [as] often ordinary, sometimes trivial; but the idea grows and grows until it towers above them and above us with a dizzy magnificence'.[64] The theatre critic for the *Nottingham Journal* thought that the 'very modernist setting designed by Paul Shelving made an effective background for the simple costumes of the year thirty thousand and something'.[65] Heike Hartung notes the 'problem of representing longevity in the play, which she perceives as applying to 'both the narrative and performative modes, since the difference of extreme age is expressed primarily in the descriptive mode: extended temporal dimensions have to be explained to us, they are not easily enacted'.[66] Shaw captures the Ancients' utopian otherness instead by emphasizing the uncomprehending perspectives of the young characters and short-lived spectators, who are interpellated by the play as not able to grasp or appreciate the superiority of the Ancients. The Ancients are only partially revealed, remaining strange and just out of sight or understanding. They have 'forgotten how to speak' and appear to communicate through some form of telepathy: '[a]m I wanted. I feel called', the He-Ancient asks.[67]

Utopian difference, or otherness, is expressed in the conceptual gap between the short- and long-lived, the former vulnerable, as mentioned earlier, to suffering what the play terms 'discouragement' in the presence of

---

[62] David Gutmann, *Reclaimed Powers* (New York: Basic Books, 1987), 7.
[63] Shaw, quoted in Holroyd, *Bernard Shaw*, 508.
[64] Ashley Dukes, 'The Stage of the Day', *Illustrated Sporting and Dramatic News*, 1 March 1924, 66.
[65] N.n., *Nottingham Journal*, 20 March 1928, 5.
[66] Heike Hartung, 'Longevity Narratives: Darwinism and Beyond', *Journal of Aging Studies* 47 (2018): 84–7, 87.
[67] Shaw, 'As Far As Thought Can Reach', in *Back to Methuselah*, 264; 284. All further references are to this edition and appear in the main body of the text. Communication beyond speech and text also appears in Sally Miller Gearhart's feminist utopia *The Wanderground* (1979) and Howard Brenton's *Greenland* (1988), the latter of which I discuss in Chapter 5.

the latter. An Ancient tells a youth in the final part: 'Infant: one moment of ecstasy of life as we live it would strike you dead' (253). Fredric Jameson refers to 'the terror of obliteration' that arises from the utopian encounter.[68] Utopian subjectivation requires a fundamental reconstitution of the self, which in turn, for Jameson, is a form of death wish (the death of the non-utopian self). *Back to Methuselah* seems to bear this out: encountering utopian possibility makes the non-utopian present more difficult, even unliveable in the case of the short-lived 'elderly gentleman' of part four, who, once having experienced the ways of the long-lived, now 'cannot live among people to whom nothing is real' (249). The insignificance – or lack of meaning – conventionally attributed to late life is relocated in the play to the earlier parts of the life course, and an accumulative profundity manifests in the very old. The *Nottingham Journal* observed that 'the impressive performances of the ancients, were appreciated in reverent silence'.[69] This reverence registers the gap between the bounded subject of the now and the enhanced state of a future utopian subjectivity; or, it is analogous to psychologist, Rudolf Arnheim's mapping of the late styles of artists and thinkers on to the development of civilization. He says that the early life phase 'is a state of mind in which the outer world is not yet segregated from the self'; the middle phase includes the 'conquest of reality': the exploration of the environment in order to master and control it; the late phase involves 'a world view that transcends outer appearance in search of the underlying essentials'.[70] Arnheim's description of the late styles of artists and thinkers speaks to the distinctive qualities of Shaw's Ancients, whose quests are to discover unmediated truths.

The Ancients' capacity to have a 'direct sense of life' (294), as the She-Ancient describes it, is enabled by their specific occupation of space, which they undertake freely and expansively. This directly contrasts with the progressive restrictions of space associated with dominant depictions of old age. In a discussion of the exclusionary implications of the professional mediation of old age (for example, through care work, residential homes, and other institutional forms), William F. May offers a familiar stereotype of ageing in his observation that '[t]he world at large shrinks to a single room and ultimately to a casket' and 'the psychic life of the elderly also shrinks, with an increasing preoccupation with the body and its troubles'.[71] In contrast,

---

[68] Fredric Jameson, 'The Politics of Utopia', *New Left Review* 25 (2004): 35–54, 38.
[69] N.n., *Nottingham Journal*, 20 March 1928, 5.
[70] Rudolf Arnheim, 'On the Late Style of Life and Art', *Michigan Quarterly Review* 17.2 (1978): 149–56, 151; 152.
[71] William F. May, 'The Virtues and Vices of the Elderly', in *What Does it Mean to Grow Old? Reflections from the Humanities*, 46.

Shaw's old people wander through space without restriction. They appear to live nomadically, at one point walking 'over the mountains' with friends, then – on discovering the potential power of self-improvement – walking over them alone, before concluding that the mountains 'are only the world's cast skins and decaying teeth on which we live like microbes' (294). The Ancients are not confined to domestic spaces, physical buildings, or company with each other, but instead sit or roam in the outdoors, often 'unconscious of [their] surroundings' (250). Their free movement is paralleled by a psychic depth and plasticity, an intellectual agility stretching far beyond the superficialities of youth.

The more profound engagement with the world that old age can facilitate poses an explicit Shavian counter-narrative to the hegemonic view of old age as decline and is also one that troubles the association of old age with anachrony: the idea that old age is non-synchronous with the contemporary. The older person is not *in* time, is out of date, and is *untimely*. Shaw uses this association to produce a distinctive vantage point for old age. Giorgio Agamben also makes a case for untimely figures as bearers of knowledge:

> those who are truly contemporary [...] those who truly belong to their time, are those who neither fully coincide with it nor adjust themselves to its demands. They are thus in this sense irrelevant. But precisely because of this condition, precisely through this disconnection and this anachronism, they are more capable than others of perceiving and grasping their own time.[72]

Shaw's Ancients are these untimely figures, non-coincident with the contemporary, but because of this non-contemporaneity, able to comprehend more deeply what it means to be human in the world. There are resonances of this idea, too, in the (auto)biographical articulations of Shaw himself as one both 'ahead of his time and unfashionably behind it, sometimes simultaneously'.[73]

However, while fresh in its challenge to rethinking the value of old age, Shaw's energizing reappraisal of the capacities of the old is simultaneously undermined by what appears to be a subscription to normative ideas of the ageing body – as a fundamental constraint, or even a fatal encumbrance. As

---

[72] Georgio Agamben, 'What is the Contemporary?', in *What is an Apparatus? And Other Essays*, trans. David Kishik and Stefan Pedatella (Redwood City, CA: Stanford University Press, 2009), 40.

[73] Lawrence Switzky, 'Shaw Among the Modernists', *Shaw: The Annual of Bernard Shaw Studies* 1.31 (2011): 133–48, 142.

Glenn Clifton writes: 'Shaw uses both dialogue and stage directions to manipulate the appearances of the body so that it might function as a signifier of its own meagre role as an obstruction to the evolutionary will'.[74] The utopian Ancients, in the final act, long for the day when – through the process of Creative Evolution – they will be able to shed the body and exist as pure thought. The He-Ancient exclaims: 'Look at me. This is my body, my blood, my brain; but it is not me. I am the eternal life, the perpetual resurrection' (294). A little later the She-Ancient opines: the 'trouble of the ancients' is that 'whilst we are tied to this tyrannous body we are subject to its death' (297). Cole points to a trans-historical 'tension', a fundamental conflict, 'between infinite ambitions, dreams, and desires on the one hand, and vulnerable, limited, decaying physical existence on the other – between self and body'.[75] The representation of physical decline as defective: as an attenuation of what it is to be human, precipitates, as Sally A. Gadow observes, a condition where 'the self repudiates the body to escape being contaminated by its deterioration'.[76] This informs the cultural invisibility of the ageing body, where that body serves as an observable delimitation of human potential. Shaw resolves this conflict by rejecting the body, but in the process, perpetuates official censure of the ageing fleshly body.

Yet, it is worth noting and appreciating that Shaw's vision of ageing does not attempt to mitigate bodily precarity. He could have animated his Ancients through bodily activity – created physically enhanced superhumans – which, as Moody argues, is a common response to the 'problem of late-life meaning in the modern world'.[77] The notion of 'successful ageing' (also called 'vital' or 'active ageing') first emerged as an idea in gerontology studies shortly after Shaw's death – in the 1950s – and refers to 'life satisfaction, longevity, freedom from disability, mastery and growth, active engagement with life, and independence'.[78] How to measure these states is one obvious problem with this; another is that this vision of ageing validates some forms of life – forms expressed through the fit, healthy, active body (a body that simultaneously simulates a young abled body) – and undermines others, particularly lives

---

[74] Glenn Clifton, 'An Imperfect Butlerite: Aging and Embodiment in *Back to Methuselah*', *Shaw: The Annual of Bernard Shaw Studies* 34 (2014): 108–26, 116.
[75] Thomas R. Cole, 'Introduction', in *What Does it Mean to Grow Old?* 5.
[76] Sally A. Gadow, 'Frailty and Strength: The Dialectic of Aging', in *What Does it Mean to Grow Old?* 239.
[77] Harry R. Moody, 'The Meaning of Life and the Meaning of Old Age', in *What Does it Mean to Grow Old?* 22.
[78] Moody, 'From Successful Aging to Conscious Aging', in *Successful Aging Through The Life Span: Intergenerational Issues in Health*, ed. M. Wykle et al. (New York: Springer), 59.

aligned with disabled, dependent bodies. While Shaw perpetuates a familiar rejection of the old frail body, he does not – unlike advocates of successful ageing – replace the old, infirm body with a simulation of youth. Switzky describes Shaw's Ancients as 'old, genuinely sophisticated but lacking the spark of vigor – waiting, tepidly to be reabsorbed into the "vortex" from which they originated'.[79] Brustein makes comparisons with the supposedly unattractive qualities of Shaw himself: '[t]he bodiless character of Shaw's Superman – not to mention Shaw's own vegetarianism, teetotalism, and abstention from sexual intercourse after his marriage – indicates a kind of Swiftian disgust at the human body and its functions'.[80] While Shaw perpetuates familiar Platonic and Christian notions of the body as an obstruction to the mind or soul, it is important to recognize that Shaw is no more interested in the youthful body than he is in the ageing body, and in this sense does not repeat familiar ideas of the aged *contra* youthful body as abject. For Shaw, the body in all phases of the life course was 'a bore' (298), as the sculptor, Martellus exclaims in *Back to Methuselah*.

Indeed, the body was such a bore for Shaw that disembodiment figures as utopian yearning in his drama. This is despite the Ancients' acquirement of the ability to transform their bodies through the use of creative will:

> The She-Ancient: One day, when I was tired of learning to walk forward with some of my feet and backwards with others and sideways with the rest all at once, I sat on a rock with my four chins resting on four of my palms, and four of my elbows resting on four of my knees. And suddenly it came into my mind that this monstrous machinery of heads and limbs was no more me than my statues had been me, and that it was only an automaton that I had enslaved.
>
> 296

The body – with its corporeal vulnerability and unruly desires – while a necessary conduit for human subjectivity was, for Shaw, simultaneously an impediment to the swift progression of the evolutionary Life Force. After returning to her conventional human bodily form, the She-Ancient still considers herself to be 'a slave of this slave, my body' (297). For the Ancients, the body remains a bathetic encumbrance. It is in unproductive tension with the intellect, consciousness, and the spirit, wherein the Life Force manifests.

Bernard Shaw's high valuation of old age is significant but, as I have shown, not an isolated example of utopian representation. However, his focus

---

[79] Switzky, 'Shaw Among the Modernists', 142.
[80] Brustein, *The Theatre of Revolt*, 203.

on old age as central to his utopian vision is extremely unusual.[81] *Back to Methuselah* imagines ageing and longevity as conduits through which the possibility emerges of a more advanced political subject, capable of seeing beyond short-term self-interest, with the enhanced capabilities necessary for responding to the complexities of the modern world. This unusual proposition is developed across the five playlets. The play is subtitled 'A Metabiological Pentateuch' and Shaw described the play as a bible for the modern world. The utopian societies of parts four and five emerge from the new social and political potentialities afforded by extended life, which – as well as offering the advantages of wisdom and maturity – also make possible the long-term investment in futurity and common interest central to establishing and maintaining the utopian good life. Shaw was sixty-five and ninety-four respectively when *Back to Methuselah* and *Farfetched Fables* were published, and while sixty-five might connote the beginnings of old age today, it was perceived as late life for many in the 1920s. According to a recent report published by the Resolution Foundation: 'A century ago new-borns were expected to live to 63 on average, whereas for the generation born in the last 15 years life expectancy at birth is 93, with over a third of the generation after expected to reach age 100'.[82] The inclusion of infant mortality somewhat skews these markedly different life expectancy rates, but Shaw was nevertheless considered to be old when he wrote *Back to Methuselah* and this personal experience of ageing is likely to have informed his utopian intervention into this subject.

Farfetched Fables

While the Ancients of *Back to Methuselah* yearn for disembodiment as a way of developing an ever-ageing, unbounded human consciousness uninhibited by physical form, in *Farfetched Fables* disembodiment has been realized. Written from 1949–1950, just months before his death in November 1950,

---

[81] Christopher Innes says H. G. Wells' novel *Men Like Gods* represents a utopian world that is 'almost a literal transcription of Shaw's world of A.D. 3000 in *Back to Methuselah*'. Like *Back to Methuselah*, the characters in *Men Like Gods* live extended lives without disease and with selective breeding: '[h]owever, in deliberate contrast to Shaw's "Creative Evolution," the driving force of progress in *Men Like Gods* is an ideal of "Creative Service": a communal dedication to social improvement in practical ways'. Innes, 'Utopian Apocalypses: Shaw, War, and H. G. Wells', 42.

[82] David Finch, 'Live Long and Prosper? Demographic Trends and their Implications for Living Standards', 16 January 2017, http://www.resolutionfoundation.org/publications/live-long-and-prosper-demographic-trends-and-their-implications-for-living-standards/

Farfetched Fables was the very last play Shaw wrote. It was presented privately by the Shaw Society at the Watergate Theatre, London, in September 1950, directed by Shaw himself, and publicly performed a year later at the People's Theatre in Newcastle, and has rarely been performed since. The fables begin in a public park in London in the mid-twentieth century. The scene revolves around an exchange between a young woman and man, where the latter propositions the former with marriage, but the former refuses. The horrors of the two world wars have created a hostile environment for bearing children; '[u]ntil men are wise and women civilized they had better not be born', says the woman.[83] An older man arrives, jubilantly announcing the end of the war: all the major powers have agreed to make 'atomic bomb manufacture a capital crime' (431). But like Brecht's *Mother Courage* (1941) written a decade earlier, *Farfetched Fables* is a sardonic exposure of war profiteering. Inspired by the young woman's warning that '[s]omebody will discover a poison gas lighter than air' (432), the young man (a chemist), starts to think of the money to be made by such an invention. This brief vignette combines Socratic dialogue with satire to produce a piece that contains aspects of agitprop and Brechtian epic theatre. A jarring mix of romance, satire, and tragedy produce an affective discomfort appropriate for signalling the perversity of this opportunism. The second fable continues the play's concern with the prevalence of war and is set in the War Office in London. From a conversation between the Commander-in-Chief and Lord Oldhand, it transpires that 'the South African negro Hitler, Ketchewayo the Second' bought the poison gas invented by the young man from fable one (but which was rejected by the Commander-in-Chief because of cost), and poisoned the Isle of Wight, killing much of the population (435). The rest of the scene involves the two arguing over who should take responsibility. It closes with loud sirens and the two staggering about and then dying from gas poisoning. Common to the utopian form, these two parts function as the *raison d'être* for the utopia: human society is appalling, barbarous, and self-destructive. It must transform.

The third fable is set in 'a pleasant spot in the Isle of Wight' in 'a colony of the Upper Ten' (439). It is a future utopian society, albeit one that is comically unstable. Recalling H. G. Wells' classification of people according to skills and ability in *A Modern Utopia* (1905) and Aldous Huxley's in *Brave New World* (1932), the utopian society in *Farfetched Fables* is concerned with '[c]lassifying men and women according to their abilities' (440). 'Anthropometric work is what we do here' (440), announces the matron.

---

[83] Shaw, *Farfetched Fables*, in *The Bodley Head Bernard Shaw, Collected Plays with their Prefaces* (London: Max Reinhardt The Bodley Head, 1974), 430. All further references are to this edition and appear in the main body of the text.

A girl, a gentleman, and the matron question two unexpected visitors to the island: a tourist, who has been classified as a mediocrity but thinks he is a genius, and a tramp who thinks he is good for nothing but whom the hosts think is a genius. We also learn from the gentleman that anthropometric assessment is 'compulsory for everybody. If you refuse you may be classified as irresponsible. That means that youll [sic] be enlisted in the military police or kept under tutelage in a Labor Brigade. Or you may be classed as dangerous and incorrigible, in which case youll [sic] be liquidated' (442). The comic mode provides the option to dismiss this proposition as satire; yet the play as a whole is sincere in its utopian intentions.

The fourth fable is set in the same place in the Isle of Wight although the building is now described as 'Diet Commissioners'. This scene consists entirely of a monologue spoken into a dictaphone by a commissioner. The commissioner is dictating material for a chapter of his book on human diet, entitled 'Living on Air'. He talks of a move to vegetarianism in the twentieth century, which was inspired by 'a prophet whose name has come down to us in various forms as Shelley, Shakespear, and Shavius' (445). Vegetarianism made humans 'more ferocious and dangerous than bulls' but it also led to less 'organized action of any kind' (446), which resulted in the end of war. These humans were transforming into 'supergorillas through eating grass and leaves', but while they lived much longer than meat eaters, they were still prone to disease. The assumption that all diets lead to disease and decay, we are told, was challenged by a vegetarian Russian athlete, who claimed that a diet of air, water, and physical exercise was not only possible but resulted in no disease or decay. After a general commitment by the population to this new diet, '[t]he world became a world of athletes, artists, craftsmen, physicists, and mathematicians, instead of farmers, millers, bakers, butchers, bar tenders, brewers, and distillers. Hunger and thirst [...] became a search for knowledge of nature and power over it, and desire for truth and righteousness' (448). While notably different in form from the Socratic dialogues of the other fables, this *reportage* mode, where we encounter the utopian society indirectly, recalls the framing narratives of More's text.

In the fifth fable, the scene is the same, but the building is now labelled 'Genetic Institute'. There is a return to Socratic dialogue, involving 'four persons of uncertain age, apparently in the prime of life': two men (Shamrock and Thistle), one woman (Rose) and a 'hermaphrodite', who is unnamed (449). Like the utopians in *Back to Methuselah*, this society has evolved beyond sexual intercourse to reproduce via non-viviparous means, and the pleasures of sex are replaced by the 'pursuit of knowledge and power, [which] culminate in [...] explorations and discoveries' (450). There is witty defamiliarization of the non-utopian contemporary world, which the characters read about in history books; reproduction, 'the very first business of any human society' (449) is unmentioned: 'their textbooks on physiology dont [sic] mention the reproductive organs nor hint at such a thing as sex' (450). A debate proceeds over how to improve the scientific manufacture of human beings versus the desire to evolve through the power of the creative will to a state of disembodiment.

The final fable is set in the same place but this time the building is described as 'Sixth Form School Scheduled. Historical Monument'. A civilization of superhumans called the disembodied races are discussed by students, students who themselves are atavistic throwbacks to the twentieth century: evolutionary development is not necessarily linear. The teacher tells them, '[t]he theory is that the Disembodied Races still exist as Thought Vortexes, and are penetrating our thick skulls in their continual pursuit of knowledge and power, since they need our hands and brains as tools in that pursuit' (461). As part of their journey to disembodiment, '[t]hey found they could live on air, and that eating and drinking caused diseases of which their bodies died' (461). One of the disembodied appears temporarily in comical physical form – as feathered and called Raphael. As well as invoking the judgement day angel in Shaw's earlier utopian play *The Simpleton* as Matthew Yde observes,[84] and the bird utopians of Aristophanes' *The Birds*, this character also calls to mind Raphael Hythloday, More's visitor to Utopia, and expounder of the utopian society. Like Hythloday (both earnest mediator of utopian truth and 'dispenser of nonsense' as the name translates[85]), Shaw's Raphael is at once a revelatory and comic figure.

The play's ruthless approach (liquidation) to those who refuse to contribute to the utopian community combined with some rather eccentric proposals (even by utopian standards) along with an unusual dramatic form have led to a general disregard of this play both on theatre stages and in scholarly discussion.[86] Yet *Farfetched Fables* offers an intriguing provocation to both dominant capitalist ideologies and socialist utopian thinking and is worthy of consideration. As well as presenting an acerbic critique of capitalism, imperialist war, and class society, the play also directly confronts the challenge of how a utopian society should respond to those whose actions undermine its regulations and values. As discussed earlier, Shaw was against moral

[84] Yde, *Bernard Shaw and Totalitarianism*, 191.
[85] Paul Turner, 'Introduction', *Utopia* (London: Penguin, 2003), xii.
[86] The only serious treatment of *Farfetched Fables* is by Yde, who dedicates a whole chapter to the play in his book *Bernard Shaw and Totalitarianism*. Yde's emphasis is on identifying Shaw's enthusiasm for eugenics, uncompromising attitude to dealing with counter-revolutionaries, support for hierarchical structures, and appreciation of strong leaders as informing the key ideas of *Farfetched Fables*.

condemnation of perpetrators of social harm and the cruel, often protracted punishments that inevitably ensue; instead, he understood this issue in terms of community self-defence. For a utopia to be sustained, there can be no accommodation of those whose actions threaten the community. Just as one would not hesitate to kill a cobra or tiger when threatened, the utopian society should not think twice about ridding itself of threatening members. Shaw writes, '[p]recisely the same necessity arises in the case of incorrigibly dangerous or mischievous human beings, sane or insane, hopeless idiots, or enemy soldiers'.[87] Although this has violent and tyrannous implications, it is simultaneously a rejection of the slow and subtle cruelty of the toleration of perpetrators of social harm, a tolerance, for example, that takes the form of slavery in More's *Utopia*, prison in Bellamy's *Looking Backwards*, and exile to an isolated island in Wells' *A Modern Utopia*. Shaw's proposal of capital punishment is not an acceptable utopian solution for most liberals or socialists; however, his confrontational style and exploration of uncompromising proposals through witty dialogue and shrewd critique, creates a space for debate regarding what is to be done about this troublesome issue. Shaw's approach reminds us that such thorny issues have not been satisfactorily resolved within utopian thinking.

Shaw's utopian contribution

Shaw's utopian plays are conspicuous during the early- to mid-twentieth century for their boldly imaginative investment in human agency, so very different from other examples of utopian literature of the same moment, which are mostly expressed through dystopia. Although changing, Shaw has generally been excluded from scholarly categorizations of modernism, largely due to what Switzky describes as Shaw's 'genuine singularity'.[88] In addition to the specific peculiarities of his work identified above, the dominant theme of his utopian plays – enhanced human capacities enabled through greater longevity – is also one that does not fit with modernist preoccupations. These include challenge to tradition (with which 'old' is discursively aligned), the idea that the self is continuously remade (rather than a developing aggregation), and the rejection of the belief that life has fundamental meaning. Life's meaning used to be mediated by wisdom, itself a quality

---

[87] Shaw, quoted in Alan Chappelow, *Shaw – 'The Chucker-Out': A Biographical Exposition and Critique* (New York: AMS Press, 1971), 169. Shaw prepared pre-printed postcards on many issues, which he sent out to members of the public, who had written to him asking him his thoughts of different topics.
[88] Switzky, 'Shaw Among the Modernists', 144.

aligned with elders. In the modern/Enlightenment era and especially in the modernist twentieth century with its emphasis on youth and the new, the devaluing of wisdom, as Moody observes, 'deprives old age of any particular epistemological significance'.[89] For scholars of modernism, it seems Shaw is not modernist enough; for scholars of utopias, Shaw is not utopian in the right way. By including Shaw's utopias in analyses of utopian literature and in discussions of modernism, the dominant narrative of a crisis of ambition, bold thinking, and agentic expression in the post-*fin-de-siècle* moment is put under pressure.

As discussed in Chapter 1, a dominant strain of thinking in utopian scholarship diminishes the importance of utopias expressed through fantasy, which are also, very often, body utopias. Whilst city utopias imagine better social structures, economies, and political organization, body utopias enjoy sensual gratification, escapist fantasy, or flirtations with past or mythical golden ages. Shaw's revisiting of the Creation myth and his interest in longevity and immortality are all traits common to body utopias, and to fantasy. Brustein says *Back to Methuselah* is 'seven degrees removed from the real world' where 'insoluble dilemmas can be resolved in wishful fantasies'.[90] Dan Hulbert describes the play as a 'fantasia on cosmic themes'.[91] The drama contains fantastical elements of body utopias in representing a newly fashioned human subject, unrealistic dramatic leaps in age attainment and a sincere desire to abandon the unwieldy human body. Yet, Shaw's utopian plays also include characteristics of the city utopia. The plays are concerned with human effort, self-determination, and social and political organization. Human agency, effort, and will to improve are precisely what is distinctive about Lamarckian-inspired Creative Evolution (as opposed to the 'series of blind accidents' of Neo-Darwinian natural selection).[92] For Shaw, significant changes from one generation to the next were possible if human will expressed itself sufficiently. As Piers J. Hale states, '[e]ventually, the build-up of this "life force" and creative desire to change would be irresistible', Shaw thought, 'and a child would finally be born without relapse with a fully inherited acquired aptitude'.[93] Human effort culminates in a post-capitalist society in *Back to Methuselah*, where the institutions of religion and marriage

---

[89] Moody, 'The Meaning of Life and the Meaning of Old Age', 32.
[90] Brustein, *The Theatre of Revolt*, 195.
[91] Dan Hulbert, 'Back-To-Back *Methuselah*', *American Theatre* (October 2000): 11.
[92] Julie Sparks, 'The Evolution of Human Virtue: Precedents for Shaw's "World Betterer" in the Utopias of Bellamy, Morris, and Bulwer-Lytton', in *Shaw and Other Matters*, ed. Susan Rusinko (Selinsgrove, PA: Susquehanna University Press, 1998), 63.
[93] Piers J. Hale, 'Of Mice and Men: Evolution and the Socialist Utopia. William Morris, H.G. Wells, and George Bernard Shaw', *Journal of the History of Biology* 43.1 (2010): 17–66, 53.

no longer exist. These structural changes are precisely the kinds of utopian re-organization expected in city utopias.

Notwithstanding the play's interweaving of unusual ideas about longevity, the play is more conventionally utopian in its marshalling of hope as the harbinger of progressive change. However, what makes this noticeably different from most other utopias similarly dependent on hope, is its focus on the individual person as the primary site of change. The idea that humans can learn to live peacefully, ethically, and sociably – given the right material conditions – dominates most city utopias: remove poverty, property, and economic competition, and the substantial causes of misery and crime are, as a result, eliminated. But instead of focusing on material structures in this way, Shaw concentrates on radically refashioning the human subject; this, according to Julia Sparks, is 'the two-part inadequacy in the human species that makes it incapable of establishing the socialist utopia: lack of political capacity, which would point out "how to do it" and lack of "magnanimity", which would make us "really want" to live there'.[94] Human agency is considered by utopian scholars to be a key element of authentic utopias: body utopias are often dismissed where nature or the gods provide the good life without human intervention. The idiosyncrasy of the idea of willed longevity and its investment in a more idealist than materialist school of philosophy provides a stimulating supplement to the more familiar utopian socialist focus on material structures as the route to revolutionary transformation.

It is also striking that Shaw's fantastical elements – such as living several hundred or thousands of years – are newly resonant in the contemporary moment. *Back to Methuselah* sincerely assumes that longevity is a scientific possibility and while this may have seemed fantastical to many in 1921 (particularly because the characters simply willed it), the attainment of a significantly longer life span is less farfetched today. The subject of longevity is peculiarly resonant in the twenty-first century, when ageing and longevity are among the most conspicuous of social changes of our age. Ageing and death have remained perplexing issues for scientists. Georges Minois asks, '[h]ow is it that cells, which are potentially immortal, end by weakening and dying through non-generation?'[95] While Shaw got some of the science wrong, he correctly predicted the likelihood of significant leaps in age attainment. A recent *Guardian* article with the headline: '[a]geing process may be reversible, say scientists', which covers scientists' findings in recent experiments with gene therapy and mice, says: '[t]he scientists are not claiming that ageing can

---

[94] Sparks, 'The Evolution of Human Virtue', 77.
[95] Georges Minois, *History of Old Age: From Antiquity to the Renaissance* (Oxford: Polity Press, 1989), 1.

be eliminated, but say that in the foreseeable future treatments designed to slow the ticking of this internal clock could increase life expectancy'.[96] Shaw exploited the lack of scientific knowledge of the causes of ageing and death, and combined scientific possibility with a supranormal investment in the idea of Creative Evolution. In some ways, the play proposes a high-tech, futuristic vision of human being – as opposed to an impossible fantasy of magic and the supernatural. Even the bizarre elements – such as humans being born from eggs – have been proposed in utopian science fiction, such as Huxley's *Brave New World* (1932) and Marge Piercy's, *Woman on the Edge of Time* (1976), as plausible scientific possibility (fetuses are grown outside the womb in breeders.) The prospect of humans reproducing via non-viviparous means is certainly within reach, as a *Guardian* article, which discusses the recent success of lambs being developed in artificial wombs, evidences.[97]

Notwithstanding scholarly underestimation of plausible scientific speculation in Shaw's plays, undoubtedly his drama contains elements of fantasy, particularly the inclusion of the disembodied races in *Farfetched Fables*. But as I argued in Chapter 1, the sf/fantasy binary, which has poorly served fantasy, particularly in terms of its capacity to generate utopian critique, is a reductive structure that places limits on utopian expression. Shaw's interweaving of sf and fantasy in his utopian visions helps to break down this dualistic paradigm. His interweaving of science and fantasy to create an enhanced human who is a product of both, works to destabilize this binaristic form of categorization. A further destabilization is Shaw's expansive use of time: both back to Biblical beginnings as well as substantially forwards, to far beyond Shaw's own moment. This lack of temporal restraint, its unbounded movement between the pre-modern era of the body utopia and the far-flung future of the thirty-second century further works to dissolve the integuments of these restrictive taxonomic approaches. Shaw's plays help us to appreciate the generative interplay of fantasy, sf, supernatural, and political in the service of utopian critique.

The extraordinary features of Shaw's utopian plays – both dramatic and utopian – have been submerged, not permitted to shape the way we understand utopianism or early twentieth-century drama. Sincere engagement with these plays as utopias means pressing at the edges of utopian taxonomies. These

[96] Hannah Devlin, 'Ageing Process May be Reversible, Scientists Claim', 15 December 2016, https://www.theguardian.com/science/2016/dec/15/ageing-process-may-be-reversible-scientists-claim
[97] Aarathi Prasad, 'How artificial wombs will change our ideas of gender, family and equality', *The Guardian* 1 May 2017, https://www.theguardian.com/commentisfree/2017/may/01/artificial-womb-gender-family-equality-lamb

genre blurring, eccentric, and ambitious plays combine with an audacious idea of human capacity and social possibility not in tune with scholarly discussions of writing of the time. The aesthetic strategies of Shaw's work – the blending of styles, the deliberate dissonance of sincerity with satire, the mix of the earnest and ironic – provide an exhilarating provocation for the spectator. The individual is the site of interest in Shaw's utopias, which is unusual in utopian literature. But as I have demonstrated, there is also a deeply focused and thoughtful attention to ageing, the potential of the ageing person, and the power and social possibilities of longevity more generally, which offer exciting and meaningful stimulations, and which reverberate newly in the twenty-first century. The plays clearly propose that the prospect of long life help humans to think more expansively and profoundly about how to develop and sustain better lives and a better world. Utopian literature has been at the forefront of providing radical new ways of thinking differently about identities, particularly classed, gendered, raced, and sexual identities. Shaw's utopian dramas extend this to age, particularly to old age, and in the process, offer a rare utopian vision of the value of old age, and a radical denunciation of a deep-rooted normalization of gerontophobia.

5

Utopia and the triumph of ordinary life

As established in Chapter 4, George Bernard Shaw imagined his utopians as ancient, wise, mature, and superior: as superhumans intellectually and spiritually enhanced through longevity enabled by Creative Evolution. Shaw's was a very different conception from the utopianism discussed in this chapter, which is much less remarkable. Ordinary life, recognition of the human body (in all its fleshly awkwardness), the importance of feelings and sensations, and slow, uneventful participation in the world form the substance of utopian living examined in Chapter 5. The focus several decades after Shaw – during the height of Thatcherism – is on the plays of Howard Brenton. In contrast to Shaw, Brenton pictured the utopian citizen as commonplace and childlike, engaged in everyday practices and simple forms of living. Thirty-two years after writing the third play in his utopian trilogy, *Greenland*, Brenton reflects, 'I was trying to dramatize what I call the triumph of ordinary life'.[1] Indebted to William Morris' *News from Nowhere*, Brenton's utopian vision additionally conjoins his long-term interest in the ideas of the Situationist International and particularly Guy Debord's concept of the 'Society of the Spectacle' with, as Brenton puts it, an attempt to 'dramatize the peace you imagine lying behind your anger and frustration and feelings of twistedness about the world'.[2]

This chapter examines what Brenton retrospectively called his trilogy of utopian plays: *Sore Throats* (1978), *Bloody Poetry* (1984), and *Greenland* (1988), performed together as the 'Three Plays for Utopia' season of 1988 at the Royal Court Theatre and directed by Max Stafford-Clark. The plays benefit from being considered together, as *Sore Throats* is not a utopia but a dark portrayal of the aftereffects of a bad marriage. Brenton explains:

> My instinct was that if you are going to show people moving towards a transformation into citizens of Utopia or, in *Sore Throats*, a Utopian state of mind, you have to show them first at their vilest and their most unhappy. A playwright who shirks from writing about people at their

---

[1] Howard Brenton, Skype interview with author, 15 June 2020.
[2] Ibid.

worst, will not be believed when trying to write about them at their best. The three characters in *Sore Throats* set out on a crazy voyage in the play's second act. I finally imagined where to in the new play of this season, *Greenland*.[3]

Notwithstanding the cruelty and violence of *Sore Throats*, the play nevertheless traces a wilful and wanton disconnection with conventional life, a disconnection that expresses a deep desire for something other than what is. The second play in the trilogy, *Bloody Poetry*, examines the endeavours by bohemian circle, Lord Byron, Mary Shelley, Percy Bysshe Shelley, Clare Clairemont, and Harriet Westbrook to practise utopian forms of living. While the play is not a utopia *per se*, it is certainly utop*ian* in its evaluation of this group's engagement in prefigurative utopian practice, a way of being in the world that transgresses regulatory parameters. However, *Greenland* – in its dramatization of a utopian world 700 years in the future – is a fully-formed utopia: it both simulates the two-part structure of Thomas More's *Utopia* moving from the non-utopian contemporary society marked by poverty, discrimination, and oppression to a utopian world free from these. It follows through the threads of interest from *Sore Throats* and *Bloody Poetry* in liberating desire, selfhood, and sociality from the determinations of capitalism. My aim in this chapter then is to establish the ways in which Brenton's utopian trilogy draws on ideas developed by Debord and the Situationist International to suggest how an authentic, ordinary life – beyond capitalist social relations – might be experienced.

A storm of a bad time

Like Bernard Shaw, Brenton is known for being a socialist, and for his socialist politics constituting a crucial informant of his playwriting. Brenton is often located in the context of a generation of socialist playwrights, which include David Edgar, Trevor Griffiths, Edward Bond, and several times collaborator David Hare, a grouping whom, as Richard Boon observes, 'shared a belief and determination that political debate is the proper stuff of the modern British theatre, Fringe or established'.[4] Often narrated as a male cohort, I would add Caryl Churchill and Timberlake Wertenbaker to this group to provide a fuller picture of this generational composition. Again, like Shaw, Brenton has been incredibly prolific, writing more than fifty plays across seven decades,

[3] Brenton, 'On Writing the Utopian Plays', in *Greenland* (London: Methuen, 1988), 3.
[4] Richard Boon, *Brenton: The Playwright* (London: Methuen, 1991), 1.

and employing a diversity of forms, styles, topics, and themes, moving from the fringe in the late 1960s and early 1970s to frequenting the main stages of such venues as the National Theatre and the Royal Court, as well as numerous subsidized theatres across the UK. His larger-scale plays for the main stages in the mid-to-late 1970s were informed by Brechtian epic theatre and directly confronted political subject matter. With a few notable exceptions – including *Greenland* – the 1980s saw him move to smaller-scale productions, and more reflective, private subject matter.

The broader theatrical context for Brenton's utopian trilogy is noticeable for a dearth of utopian drama. There are a few plays that have utopian interests but not many. Examples include Arnold Wesker's *I'm Talking About Jerusalem* (1960), which is the third play in the Wesker trilogy (the first two being *Chicken Soup with Barley* [1956] and *Roots* [1958]). It engages with the pursuit of socialist ideas, as Ada and her husband Dave move from London to a remote part of Norfolk where they attempt to establish a better integration of work, home life, and nature. Arthur Miller's comic play, *The Creation of the World and other Business* (1973), evokes Shaw's *Back to Methuselah* in its retelling of biblical scenes from Genesis. Several of Caryl Churchill's plays contain utopian moments or impulses – for example, *Light Shining in Buckinghamshire* (1976), *Vinegar Tom* (1975), *Fen* (1983), and *Mad Forest* (1990) – where utopian longing for radical systemic change drives the dramatic narratives. Tony Kushner's epic *Angels in America* (1991) – with part one set during the Reagan years during the AIDS crisis and part two continuing into the 1990s – contains scenes fuelled by both anger and hope, utopianism present in an ambivalent, dialectical interplay.

The decade within which Brenton's three utopian plays were staged – 1978–1988 – is known for its increasing levels of privatization, contraction of the state, hostility to the Arts, and attacks on civil society and the labour and trades union movement. As I have noted elsewhere, this is a story of traditional forms of resistance and opposition being defeated by an aggressive neoliberalism, which bankrupts human cultures and economies through the processes of globalization, consumerism, and marketization.[5] The rapid liberalization of capital during the 1980s was neatly illustrated by the 'big bang' – the deregulation of the financial markets – in 1986, which was a further rebalancing of the political economy in favour of finance. Transformation of the political idiom was a key element to the success of the

---

[5] Siân Adiseshiah, '"The Times" of Caryl Churchill's Theatre', in *The Theatre of Caryl Churchill*, ed. R. Darren Gobert (London: Bloomsbury, 2014), 214–24; Siân Adiseshiah, *Churchill's Socialism: Political Resistance in the Plays of Caryl Churchill* (Newcastle: Cambridge Scholars Publishing, 2009).

political and economic vision of Thatcherism. The move away in mainstream politics from negotiating the political world through social democratic categories, which brought with it a retreat from the language of social class, was helped by 'the highly successful Thatcherite endeavour to Americanise people's conception of the working-class', as observed by David Edgar.[6]

This decade also saw substantial cuts to the arts, which had a particularly devasting impact on left theatre. In response to the socialist theatre collective CAST's (Cartoon Archetypical Slogan Theatre) cut in funding, co-founder, Roland Muldoon attributed this to their being 'too dangerous'.[7] John McGrath of 7:84 England and Scotland claimed that by the end of the 1980s, alternative theatre 'was effectively shut down in England'.[8] Out of a 'Theatre in Crisis' conference at Goldsmith's College in 1988 emerged a declaration signed by several playwrights (including Brenton), actors, and directors, condemning the cuts in funding, claiming theatre as a basic cultural right, which should be accessible to all, and calling for the theatre to be funded by public money.[9] The political and economic hostility of this period for left theatre prompted a general shift from subject matter focused on the public sphere to an interest in private settings, a tendency towards less explicitly political subject matter, or a move towards biting satire as exemplified by Brenton and Hare's *Pravda* (1985), a lampooning of mainstream journalism, and Churchill's *Serious Money* (1987), a coruscating invective on the stock markets in the City of London and the perverse celebration of greed this unleashed. As Brenton retrospectively observed in relation to *Greenland*, 'it was a storm of a bad time to put a utopian play on'.[10]

Society of the spectacle

Brenton's general move from agit-prop and large-scale epic theatre towards smaller productions with more local or personal focuses belies both his enduring interest in Brechtian theatre and a lasting engagement with the

---

[6] David Edgar, *The Second Time as Farce* (London: Lawrence and Wishart, 1988), 124.
[7] Roland Muldoon, 'Interview', in *Fringe First: Pioneers of Fringe Theatre on Record*, ed. Roland Reese (London: Oberon Books, 1992), 75.
[8] John McGrath, *The Bone Won't Break* (London: Methuen, 1990), 30.
[9] The declaration was signed by Howard Brenton, Caryl Churchill, Max Stafford-Clark, David Edgar, Trevor Griffiths, Peter Hall, John McGrath, Harold Pinter, Sheila Hancock, Verity Lambert, Jane Lapotaire, Juliet Stevenson, Jonathan Pryce, Janet Suzman, Timberlake Wertenbaker, and Arnold Wesker. See D. Keith Peacock, *Thatcher's Theatre* (London: Greenwood, 1999), 57.
[10] Brenton, Skype interview with author, 15 June 2020.

theory and practice of the French countercultural movement, the Situationist International, and Debord's *Society of the Spectacle* (1967) in particular. Brenton acknowledges the influence of this Debordian concept on *Greenland* and notes that he 'still think[s] that the Society of the Spectacle analysis (the Situationists) is true and truer and that public life is actually nothing to do with how people actually live: it's about how they must pretend to live'.[11] Brenton explains Debord's concept as follows:

> the state runs a spectacle, which is like a printed circuit board – that is, the way you speak, the way debates are conducted, the way news is put out, the way you can think something and cannot think something, the span of time you have to say something, the length of lessons, the syllabus in schools. All of it is like a printed circuit board, so that things will run in an orderly way. The state puts up a show, a spectacle, in which you say, 'I am a ...; I am a ...' But in actual fact, no one lives in the spectacle. It's like a giant projection which dictates the way which, if you're going to be understood or make your way in the world, you've got to follow.[12]

This cleavage between official life (within which we are obligated to participate if we are to survive) and authentic life (what we really are, how we really live) Debord frames in terms of time. How people really live 'has no relation to the society's official version of irreversible time, and conflicts with the pseudo-cyclical rhythm of that time's consumable by-products' (irreversible because it refers to expropriated time – time based on commodity production – pseudo-cyclical because it follows a repetitious pattern of day/night, work/rest). Authentic life then for Debord is a 'disconnected everyday life', which is 'without language, concepts, and without critical access to its own past, which has nowhere been recorded. Uncommunicated, misunderstood and forgotten, it is smothered by the spectacle's false memory of the unmemorable'.[13] It is this 'disconnected everyday life' that Brenton traces in his utopian trilogy, and which *Greenland* seeks to enable and liberate in a post-capitalist social formation, an authentic life outside of the Spectacle.

For the Situationists everyday life had been diminished to a mere representation of experience, with social relations and consciousness determined by the Spectacle – the accumulation of images from the mass

---

[11] Ibid.
[12] Brenton, 'Interview', in *Making Plays: Interviews with Contemporary British Dramatists and Directors*, ed. Duncan Wu (Basingstoke: Palgrave Macmillan, 2000), 22.
[13] Guy Debord, *The Society of the Spectacle*, trans. Ken Knabb (London: Rebel Press, 1983), 90.

media. Although also suspicious of the theatre, as Cathy Turner has suggested, the Situationists themselves in fact focused on the 'dramaturgy of the city', using a form of 'relational or "porous" dramaturgy' to destabilize the Spectacle of the city.[14] The Spectacle controls human relations and consciousness, causing the experience of life to move from an authentic encounter to a representational experience, concealing the division between original and copy. Agitating for a revolutionary transformation in the experience of everyday life, the Situationists understood such a transformation as enabling an abundant passionate life through participation in intentionally designed ephemeral moments. The key Situationist idea of the Spectacle arose in the context of the ascendancy of television as a new media during the 1950s and 1960s, although Debord dates the ascendancy of the Spectacle from the 1920s with the emergence of a consumer culture along with the rise of marketing and advertising. The idea of the Spectacle builds on the Marxist theory of commodity fetishism to describe interrelational subjectivity as operational via a reification of commodities: 'the spectacle', Debord exclaims, 'is not a collection of images; it is a social relation between people that is mediated by images'.[15] This reification, which is transmitted through the mass media, technological platforms, and other cultural signifying practices, constitutes people's official experience of life. Debord describes the Spectacle as 'the *materialization* of ideology brought about by the concrete success of an autonomised system of economic production – which virtually identifies social reality with an ideology that has remoulded all reality in its own image'.[16] Constant reproduction of reality or the ongoing perpetuation of official life – constituted by a commercial imaginary – forms the material context of a pervasive experience of alienation, which cuts across social class.

A primary Situationist strategy for countering the Spectacle was the construction of 'situations', which often took the form of inverting the capitalist organization of the urban space, a space based on maximizing productivity and facilitating the flow of capital, by proposing a ludic expansion of life. Such an expansion involved disrupting the consumer spectacle precipitating a momentary blurring of the division between performance, situation, and life, which aimed to jolt onlookers into a heightened state of consciousness. For Situationists, the relentless encounter with official life subject to the Spectacle constituted an experience of endurance, suffered rather than chosen, foisted by the penetration of the

---

[14] Cathy Turner, *Dramaturgy and Architecture: Theatre, Utopia and the Built Environment* (Basingstoke: Palgrave, 2015), 22.
[15] Guy Debord, *The Society of the Spectacle*, 7.
[16] Ibid., 116.

market rather than freely determined or created. Importantly, the Situationist construction of the situation was at once a rejection of life determined by the Spectacle as well as an anticipatory projection of the liberated potentiality of life beyond capitalist social relations.

The Situationists' Manifesto argued that the expansion of automation would inevitably result in less time spent working, and a concomitant centring of play and of living a 'life freely constructed'.[17] While emphasizing the 'value of play' and equating 'playful creativity' with 'freedom for each and all', actually what the Manifesto seems to urge is not so much a decrease in time spent working and an increase in free time but a move beyond 'the old division between imposed work and passive leisure',[18] and towards what Sam Cooper describes as 'the ludic and free construction of a life not separated into work time and leisure time'.[19] This is an image of unalienated relationality born from the reproduction of the means to live without recourse to the commodity. The resulting creation of new modes of subjectivity not determined by the Spectacle enables more integrated and vital ways of being in the world: '[a]s opposed to spectacle, Situationist culture, when put into practice, will introduce total participation. [...] [I]t will involve direct organization of the lived moment'.[20] The Situationist agitation for full participation is a rejection of the non-participative, or passive, life of consumption we all live under the Spectacle.

Additional twin Situationist concepts of relevance are: *récupération*, which refers to the now very familiar notion of bourgeois co-option, or neutralization, of politically radical ideas, and its opposite, *détournement*, which the Situationists described as, 'the reuse of pre-existing artistic elements in a new ensemble', the reconfiguration of which forms a radical repurposing.[21] Situationists must make art at the same time as recognizing that capital uses that art as part of its Spectacle; in this way, as Cooper notes, '*[r]écupération* makes the Situationist project necessary and impossible'.[22] From the French 'to divert' or 'to hijack', *détournement* refers to the activity of re-arranging past

---

[17] N.n., Situationist International, '"Situationists": International Manifesto', 1960, in *Programs and Manifestoes on 20th Century Architecture*, ed. Ulrich Conrads (Cambridge, MA: MIT Press, 1990), 172.
[18] Ibid.
[19] Sam Cooper, '"Enemies of Utopia for the Sake of its Realisation": Futurism, Surrealism, Situationism and the Problem of Utopia', in *Utopia: The Avant-Garde, Modernism and (Im)possible Life*, ed. David Ayers et. al. (Berlin: De Gruyter, 2015), 25.
[20] N.n., '"Situationists": International Manifesto', 173.
[21] N.n., Situationist International, 'Détournement as Negation and Prelude', *Internationale Situationist* #3 (1959), in *The Situationist International Anthology: Revised and Expanded Edition*, ed. and trans. Ken Knapp (Berkeley, CA: Bureau of Public Secrets, 2006), 67.
[22] Sam Cooper, 'Enemies of Utopia for the Sake of its Realisation', 28.

manifestations of human practice. An early phase of *détournement* is present in the work of writer, Isidore Ducasse, who experimented with creative forms of plagiarism. Picasso, Georges Braque, and the Dadaists developed this further as 'collage' and 'photomontage'. For Debord, *détournement* offered political potential of huge significance, largely due to its exploitation of the paradox of creativity which, under the Spectacle, is original and privately owned by the individual, the protection of which is guaranteed by intellectual property rights; yet at the same time creative expression is fundamentally and necessarily plagiaristic in its remodelling of existing material and ideational content. An explicitly plagiaristic and misappropriating practice, *détournement* involved the rereading of an existing aspect, providing it with fresh meanings, while simultaneously destabilizing its original meaning; in this way the practice of *détournement* is at once a creative anticipation of a situation beyond the Spectacle and an exposure of the fictions of individual originality and genius under the Spectacle.

It will be apparent by now how Situationist theory and practice lend themselves to the utopian project of both imagining a better world beyond the prevailing socio-economic structure and simultaneously critiquing that structure. The Situationist construction of situations, which aim to invert the appearance of capitalist forms is simultaneously a prefigurative utopian practice, an anticipatory exercise operating within, against, and beyond the Spectacle. Understanding the ways in which utopian desire and politics are operational in Brenton's utopian drama is dependent on an appreciation of how Situationist ideas permeate all three plays. Figuring ideology in terms of the Spectacle is deeply embedded in the work, and the plays stage various examples of life under, and resistance to, the Spectacle. The creation of situations and inclusion of illustrations of *détournement* are key methods Brenton uses in the construction of his utopian trilogy.

The utopia will not be dramatized

The challenge of using drama, theatre, and performance to create a utopian world is expressed acutely in Brenton's reflections on writing these three plays, and *Greenland* in particular: '[t]hroughout the eighties I had been wrestling with the notion of writing a Utopian play, a version of William Morris's *News from Nowhere*. Several attempts at doing so had broken down – I was building up a "bottom drawer" of half-completed Utopias'.[23] In an

---

[23] Brenton, 'Writing in Thatcherland: Five of My Plays', in *Hot Irons: Diaries, Essays, Journalism* (London: Nick Hern, 1995), 35.

earlier interview with *Plays and Players* in 1988, Brenton noted: '[a]fter *The Romans in Britain* I tried to write a play of William Morris's *News from Nowhere*. I burnt it. So I tried an account of several days in the distant future and burnt that too'.[24] Such a dramatic method for discarding his utopian plays is symptomatic of Brenton's anxieties about writing a utopia.[25] In fact, it took around ten years for his utopian play to materialize. Deciding on a name, too, seemed insurmountable. He said in an interview with *New Theatre Quarterly* in 1987: 'I'm writing a new play which has been through two titles so far, *Heaven Made* and *Diving for Pearls* – and is at the moment called *All Tomorrow's Parties*'.[26] The play appeared finally as *Greenland*. The strain of settling on a title is an additional indicator of the unease involved in the act of crafting a utopian play.

As I hope is evident from this book thus far, the small number of fully-formed utopias in dramatic form has meant an absence of a tradition of generic conventions and tropes for utopian drama. *Greenland*'s intertextual encounter with fictional utopias is primarily a dialogue with utopias imagined in prose fiction: *News from Nowhere* is clearly an influence; More's *Utopia* is echoed in *Greenland*'s two-part non-utopia/utopia structure; Ursula Le Guin's post-gendered world in *The Left Hand of Darkness* (1969) reverberates in Brenton's; as does Sally Miller Gearhart's foray into telepathy in *The Wanderground* (1979). Brenton's utopian plays have features in common with those of Aristophanes, Cavendish, and Bernard Shaw, but the commonalities lie more in their shared idiosyncrasies, eccentricities, and a kind of *comic* acknowledgement of the non-translatability of utopia – from a concept/nowhere/desire – to an aesthetic form, particularly a dramatic one. Indeed, despite Brenton's evident struggle with writing a utopian play, he also recognizes theatre's distinctive potential: '[t]he powerful advantage of our theatrical tradition is that it is profoundly comic. Serious matters can be tackled in the theatre by mucking about and having some fun with what is meant to be unstageable'.[27] An advantage of drama, Brenton says, 'for doing a Utopia, [is] because it is just one evening, and doesn't have the (element of) "Holy Writ" a book has. *In a way*, it doesn't matter if it's nonsense ... You try to "write the spaces", to invite people to say "Yes we could live like that", or

---

[24] Brenton, 'Brenton's Erehwon', interview with Robert Gore-Langton, *Plays and Players* (April 1988): 10–11, 10.
[25] Brenton's burning of his utopias is reminiscent of the women's frequent burning of their 'feminaries' (the foundational cultural texts of the utopia) in Monique Wittig, *Les Guérillères* (London: Picador, 1972), 11.
[26] Brenton, 'The Red Theatre under the Bed', *New Theatre Quarterly* 3 (1987): 195–206, 201.
[27] Brenton, 'Preface', in *Howard Brenton Plays 2* (London: Methuen, 2013), xv.

"No we couldn't" ... It's a way of moving political thought in an audience, hopefully.'[28] It is to Brenton's trilogy that the next section now turns, focusing specifically on the ways in which the plays' dramaturgical attempts to approach utopia can be usefully read through the lens of Situationist theory and practice.

'You're a dirty old slut': sex, violence, and *Sore Throats*

Sore Throats was first performed by the Royal Shakespeare Company at the Warehouse Theatre, London in 1979. Directed by Barry Kyle, its three characters – Judy, Jack, and Sally – were performed by Paola Dionisotti, Malcolm Storry, and Ruby Wax respectively. This work was not initially conceived as the opener of a trilogy of utopian plays; Brenton began to gather the three into a utopian grouping after he wrote *Bloody Poetry*: 'the real conscious decision was to move on to *Greenland*. To begin *Greenland* was to say, "[t]his *is* a trilogy, this is a three-arch play." The other two were, in a way, about defeat'.[29] Despite the fact that Brenton did not imagine *Sore Throats* as the first play in a utopian trilogy when he wrote it, it works well as an exemplification of the alienation from which we want to escape. Subtitled 'an intimate play in two acts', *Sore Throats* makes defeat felt through its dramatization of bad feelings constituted by the constraints of heteronormative sexual relations under the Spectacle.

These bad feelings are encountered with most intensity by the audience as onstage, graphic, and repeated acts of domestic violence. Jack (a police officer) has left Judy (housewife) for a younger woman. The entire play takes place in one room in Judy's unfurnished flat. Jack arrives, wanting to claim half the money from the sale of their former, shared house in order to fund a new life for him and his girlfriend, Celia: '[t]here's a job in Canada. The Royal Canadian Mounted Police'.[30] It is not long before he becomes violent: '*He turns away. He argues with himself. He turns back and hits her in the mouth*' (351). We discover from Judy that this was a regular occurrence during their marriage: '[m]ost blows were to the face. Though, three times in the sixties, you hit me in the breast' (353). He repeatedly demands the money and

---

[28] Brenton quoted in Richard Boon, 'Retreating to the Future: Brenton in the Eighties', *Modern Drama* 33.1 (1990): 30–41, 39.
[29] Brenton, 'Interview', in *Making Plays*, 31–2.
[30] Brenton, *Sore Throats*, *Plays 1* (London: Methuen, 1986), 351. All further references are to this edition and appear in the main body of the text.

threatens to 'beat it out of' her (354), which is immediately followed through: 'Jack *hits* Judy *with a straight right to the head*. *She gasps*' (354), and very soon after this, '[*h*]*olding her by the ankle he kicks her in the stomach*' (354), and then '[*h*]*e kicks her in the stomach again*. *She screams*' (355), and quickly after this, [*h*]*e steps on her head*. *She screams*' (355), and '[*h*]*e stamps on her arm*. *She yells then weeps*' (356). Jack plays the classic role of violent partner in his victim blaming, '[w]hy did you always let me hit you?' (353) and his simultaneous expression of shame, 'I'm sorry' (356), coupled with a displacement of blame, '[t]here's got to be something getting at me! Making me do –' (356).

John Coldstream of the *Daily Telegraph* described the play as involving 'some of the nastiest domestic violence written for the stage'[31] and for this reason it is not surprising that, as Michael Coveney of the *Financial Times* noted, 'Brenton was attacked by feminists' (although Coveney himself found this attack an 'incredible' response to a 'deeply moral, beautifully written play'[32]). Jim Hiley of *Listener* referred to the 'prolonged, hideous first act assault on Judy by Jack' and reflects, '[i]t's not that Brenton deploys this violence gratuitously, but it demands some sort of answer or response, which he fails to provide'.[33] That this violence does not receive an ethically satisfying response within the space of *Sore Throats* makes its location as the opener in a trilogy more significant. However, given that many spectators would not have encountered the trilogy *as a trilogy*, or at least not within a timespan that encourages an appreciation of the subsequent corrections to the violence of *Sore Throats*, the visceral, close-up, performance of male assault on a female body, is ethically troubling. It is also troubling that the play is not focused on finding fresh ways of critiquing domestic violence; instead, domestic violence is viscerally rendered as a potent example, metaphor even, of bad feeling.

The focus on intimacy in *Sore Throats* enables Brenton to demonstrate the corruption of human feeling in an intensely affective way. The alienation of all human life under the Spectacle turns, in this play, on the degradation of the female body. This is, as I have said, Brenton showing humans at their worst. The corruption, or brutalization of human inter-connection, is, at the

---

[31] John Coldstream, Review of *Sore Throats*, *Daily Telegraph*, 27 April 1988, in Reviews of *Sore Throats*, in *London Theatre Record* 22 April – 5 May 1988, 536.
[32] Michael Coveney, Review of *Sore Throats*, *Financial Times* 26 April 1988, in Reviews of *Sore Throats*, in *London Theatre Record*, 535.
[33] Jim Hiley, Review of *Sore Throats*, *Listener*, 5 May 1988, in Reviews of *Sore Throats*, in *London Theatre Record*, 535.

same time, expressive of a craving for the experience of authentic life outside of the Spectacle. Desire for something 'real' permeates the play:

> **Judy**   Oh, that's the real you, that's the real heart of you. Your shying away. You look away. You never actually say what you want to say. Never actually put your hand in the fire. Always at the last second you shy away.
>
> 344

A few lines later, Judy asks, '[w]hy did you never let me see your private parts?' (344). Jack signals the truth of Judy's question when he admits, '[w]hen I first saw her. Celia. You know – naked. I cried. [...] I was helpless, my hands. I faltered. Felt ashamed. I. So real, she was the real world' (345). This exchange suggests the body, nakedness, and sex constitute profoundly real experiential phenomena potentially in excess or transgressive of the Spectacle's circuit board; '[y]ou've got to be free. Or you've got to feel free. That you do things freely. Or one thing, the best thing. Love', Jack says (346). The first act is littered with barbed but intimate verbal fencing, both combative and confessional, aggressive and intimate.

The play shifts in tone towards the end of the first act and in act 2, where a third character, Sally, a young estate agent looking for a room to rent, arrives and moves in with Judy. Unlike the famous door-slamming departure of Nora in Ibsen's *A Doll's House* (1879), who exits to gain knowledge of herself and the world, Judy's quest for self-realization takes place in one room with her new flatmate. Like Nora though, Judy seeks transformation:

> I want a good time.
> *Wait.*
> I want to change myself.
> *Wait.*
> Skin inside?
> Eh?
> Hanging down me, on their little tubes, all the bags and things, kidneys, liver. Precious things, heart. The real me, exposed.
>
> 364

Authentic life is located in the nakedness, sex, blood, guts, and organs of the body, a bareness that is vulnerable, defenceless, and exposed, but which is potentially the site of genuine feeling. Judy completes her speech by saying, '[w]ell if I can't do that the least I want is a good fuck'; Sally's rejoinder: 'Don't we all' is followed by the stage direction '[t]*hey laugh*' (365).

Plenty of fucks are precisely what Judy and Sally get during the second act, but mostly it seems, with adolescent boys in 'terylene trousers. Two-tone plims. Marks and Sparks boy briefs', who receive '[a] five pound note. A free bath. [Their] first fuck' (366). Sex with fourteen-year-old boys in this act, like the inclusion of domestic violence, in act 1, does not address child abuse but functions rather to demonstrate bad attempts at self-liberation. The abjection of mature female sexuality provides the context within which Judy tries to experiment sexually; 'you're a dirty old slut' (365), Sally replies to Judy who has just said she's playing sardines with a teenage boy, 'Sardines? Who's going to crawl into your tin? Ugh, squeeze up to you in rancid oil'; Judy retorts, '[y]ou're no teeny-bopper tiddler', to which Sally replies, 'I know I know, when you're twenty-four – you start to give off that fishy smell of the older woman' (367). If an authentic life is evidenced by genuine (sexual) feeling, a fleshly reality, that reality is experienced as a 'fishy smell' by Sally and Judy in a sexual-social dynamic determined by the Spectacle.

Other attempts by the women to pursue their 'experiment in living' (368) – the pleasures of drinking, the thrill of inessential shopping, a refusal of domestic order – seem equally unable to facilitate their access to an authentic life. While clearly a darkly comic satire on their clumsy efforts to feel something real, the play, however, is completely sympathetic to their desire for experiences beyond conventional life. 'I'll not go back to that front room' (376), Judy says, referring to her previous existence as a bored, middle-class housewife married to Jack:

> In the back of my mind, like a ghost, I am still there. Drinking coffee, listening to the rain drip in the hedge.
>
> I don't know where, but I saw a picture. People, leaning out of their windows, of English houses. Their souls floating away out of their mouths. Their real selves, flying away.
>
> 376

This poetic image of the loss of self – an escaping self, airborne, fleeing – is more poignant for its contrast to the language of obscenity the women have normalized; '[y]es I have become foul mouthed. It's an experiment in consciousness raising. Or lowering. So fuck yourself', Judy says to Jack early in act 1. The swearing, obscenities, vulgarity, mess, blood, indiscriminate consumption, and dodgy sex are bold, but blundering bids to discover a different relationality with the world, to encounter life more authentically.

With the failure of these experiments, Judy proposes to ratchet up the intensity of bare living: '[b]urn what's left of the money, and steal if we have to. Nail the door up if we have to. Block the windows with bricks. Move. Sleep in the open. Sell ourselves. Get guns. Kill, if we have to' (376). This plan to escape social regulation is expressive of a thwarted utopian desire, the distortions of which are brought into relief by interruption of a more familiar utopian vision – '[s]ee a country, the other side of the wall. Sweet fields, rivers, forests. All you have to do is knock a few bricks out, wriggle through a hole onto the grass' (378). Jack returns towards the end, seeking a share of the money, with a carrycot and a long, emotional story of Celia giving birth at a roadside in Canada after their car had crashed, only for Judy to discover a brick in place of a baby under the blanket of the carrycot. The final image of the play is the three characters looking at a pile of torn money, Judy striking a match, and declaring: 'I am going to be fucked, happy and free' (390). Describing his intentions, Brenton explains, '[a]t the end of *Sore Throats*, I wanted to say, "What would they do without money?" [...] The play asks, how can she be "fucked, happy and free"? So it's more of an open-ended one, perhaps. It has a comic structure'.[34] Judy's wilful destruction of the very thing that provides her with the means to survive under the Spectacle serves as an essential condition for freedom, at the same time as ushering in a life of misery and impoverishment. In this way, it is an example of Debordian *détournement*, a performative inversion of money, the ultimate symbol of value.

While it is tempting to read *Sore Throats* as staging a particularly dispiriting scene from the grim dystopian reality of contemporary life under the Spectacle, the play, at the same time, includes a utopian drive that presses up against the edges of social confinement. Brenton describes a production 'in, of all places, St. Louis, Missouri: 75% Catholic; gate to the "Red Neck South"! It was done in a studio there, and it drew large black audiences, most of them women. It turned out they have 20,000 members of the Battered Wives Association, and they really got a hold of the play! To them, it was a comedy. It's a ferocious play, and they roared with laughter'.[35] 'The author's tone', is not, as Kimball King claims, 'despairing throughout'.[36] Judy and Sally's manipulation of misogynist tropes – their witchy, predatory sexual exploits and gleeful transgression of the conventions and codes of middle-class femininity – offers an energizing, if objectionable, counter to the Spectacle. *Sore Throats* critiques the effects of psycho-sexual alienation under the

---

[34] Brenton, 'Interview', in *Making Plays*, 31.
[35] Brenton, quoted in Janelle Reinelt, 'Selected Affinities: Bertolt Brecht and Howard Brenton', in *Howard Brenton: A Casebook*, ed. Ann Wilson (New York and London: Garland, 1992), 53.
[36] Kimball King, 'Howard Brenton's Utopia Plays', in *Howard Brenton: A Casebook*, ed. Ann Wilson (New York and London: Garland, 1992), 21.

Spectacle but registers as malign the bungling attempts by Judy at experiencing authentic life; as Boon observes, Judy 'can only create a new self from parts of her old, damaged, socialized self, and the contradiction comes close to destroying her'.[37] However, that a different, healthier, more integrated self is possible, an unalienated self not twisted or fragmented by commodity fetishism, is never in doubt in the play.

'[W]e will invent a new society and a new human nature': prefigurative utopian experiments and *Bloody Poetry*

A continuing interest in a Situationist-inspired conception of the self – an authentic, free self, unbound from the ties of capitalist conformity – is the site of utopian liberation and the central preoccupation of Brenton's 1984 play, *Bloody Poetry*, which focuses on the radical circle of romantic writers and poets Mary Shelley, Percy Bysshe Shelley, Claire Clairemont, and Lord Byron. Commissioned by Foco Novo Theatre Company, the play premiered at the Haymarket Theatre, Leicester, 1 October 1984, and, was revived in 1988, at the Royal Court along with *Sore Throats* and *Greenland* as part of a season of utopian plays. Brenton describes *Bloody Poetry* as offering 'a way of broaching the subject [of utopia], for the quartet are determined to invent a new way of living, free of sexual repression'.[38] Thus also like *Sore Throats*, a mode of sociality unfettered by the distortions of capital is considered by the play to take its most visceral form in an unlocking of the body and through an unshackled sexual practice.

The life of Brenton's romantic circle attempted to move beyond the transgression of regulatory regimes to reproducing social relations outside of social regulation. The circle, deemed seditious and depraved, were in effect exiled from England for periods of time, and the play takes place 'between the summers of 1816 and 1822'.[39] In contrast to the claustrophobic one-room set of *Sore Throats*, the action in *Bloody Poetry* moves across 'Switzerland, England and Italy' (8). The characters' self-conscious endeavour to live a free life is a prefigurative utopian performance both inspirational and devastating, inspirational for its audacious refusal of conventional social models of

---

[37] Boon, 'Retreating to the Future: Brenton in the Eighties', *Modern Drama* 33.1 (1990): 30–41, 37.
[38] Brenton, 'Writing in Thatcherland: Five of My Plays', in *Hot Irons: Diaries, Essays, Journalism* (London: Nick Hern, 1995), 35.
[39] Brenton, *Bloody Poetry* (London: Methuen, 1988), 8. All further references are to this edition and appear in the main body of the text.

behaviour and courageous rewriting of the rules of psycho-sexual relations, but devasting in the grim consequences of emotional anguish and destructive neglect of others, particularly children. As Brenton observes, this circle makes a 'terrible mess of it. Some found the "morality" of the play bewildering. I was not concerned with saying whether these people were "good" or "bad", I wanted to salute their Utopian aspirations for which, in different ways, they gave their lives. It is a celebration of a magnificent failure'.[40]

A 'magnificent failure' might equally describe the 1984–5 miners' strike which started on 6 March 1984, seven months before the first performance of *Bloody Poetry*. It is striking that the play's engagement with its Thatcherite political context – exemplified by the miners' iconic class struggle – is both to move back in time and to a utopian elsewhere. The political awkwardness of this apparent neglect of the strike is recognized in the play itself. As the characters, in Italy, are pursuing experimental forms of living, back in England in St. Peter's Field, Manchester, the Peterloo massacre – a notoriously brutal example of state violence – is being viciously played out; '[a]nd where was I, the poet?' Shelley asks, '[i]mpotent in Italy, in the sun' (70). The play thus registers the incongruities of the pursuit of aesthetic innovation and experimental forms of sociality with practical, class struggle, and leaves open the question of the potential of art to effect political change. Near the end of the play, there is the tragic death of Mary and Shelley's daughter and the horror of the Peterloo massacre, which are put in tension with Shelley's production of his poem, 'The Mask of Anarchy': '[t]he great revolutionary, English poem – unpublishable! Bury it in your daughter's coffin, poet', Mary exclaims. That audiences of *Bloody Poetry* can appreciate the afterlife of the 'The Mask of Anarchy', establishes its lasting, symbolic power with its deeply stirring lines, much quoted within the socialist movement:

> Rise like Lions after slumber
> In unvanquishable number –
> Shake your chains to earth like dew
> Which in sleep had fallen on you –
> Ye are many – they are few.
>
> 78

Yet, the play leaves suspended – as unresolved – the degree to which aesthetic practice contributes to political change, the very relevance of this verse across two hundred years exposing both its power to speak to political struggle as well as its failure to be superseded by its victory.

---

[40] Brenton, 'Writing in Thatcherland', 35.

This is a juxtaposition of what Jennifer Burwell frames as the utopian and critical impulses, the former of which she sees as generating a 'self-contained and inaccessible ideal "elsewhere" where social contradiction has always already been resolved', and the latter, which she views as limiting 'themselves to a negative hermeneutics of exposure'.[41] The tension of this relation forms a central lens through which the dynamic of *Bloody Poetry* works. It drives a dialectical movement (started in *Sore Throats*) of working within, against, and beyond capitalist social relations. There are clear continuities both backwards to *Sore Throats* and forwards to *Greenland*: Claire's declaration early in the play – 'I'm going to be loved, happy and free' (14) repeats Judy's final line of the first play (but replaces 'fucked' with 'loved'). Elsewhere in *Bloody Poetry*, with metadramatic clarity, Claire announces: '[a]ll of us will become magnificent. The men and women of the future will thank us. We are their great experiment. We will find out how to live and love, without fear' (12). The last line especially anticipates the essence of the Greenlanders from the later play. Representing utopian felt experience as living without fear is one of the primary achievements of *Greenland*, and significantly while the utopians in *Bloody Poetry* are extraordinary, the Greenlanders are very ordinary.

The extraordinary magnificence of this circle within the context of a bleak, oppressive England of both the early nineteenth and late twentieth centuries forms a key problematic of the play. Socialist-feminist historian, Sheila Rowbotham asks '[w]hen we glimpse freedom and equality are we to relegate it to the future or try and live differently? If we seek to live the future in the present what are the traps which will distort and deform our vision?'[42] Living as if in the future is both an impossible, but essential prerequisite for this circle's ability to persist as themselves, as it were. As Duncan Wu observes, 'though deeply flawed, Brenton asks us to value them for their attachment to ideals which were impossible to reconcile with the reality of their lives. They were adventurers, and their example is a promise of new realms to be discovered'.[43] Their prefigurative, anticipatory utopian interaction with the world is simultaneously an overture of faith in a liberated future as well as a peculiarly bruising act of self-harm both to themselves and each other.

The 'little band of atheistical perverts, free-lovers, [and] poeticals' (9) as Byron describes his circle, practise freedom through a potent mix of radical poetics, unconstrained sexual expression, and (particularly in the case of

---

[41] Jennifer Burwell, *Notes on Nowhere: Feminism, Utopian Logic, and Social Transformation* (London: University of Minnesota Press, 1997), ix.

[42] Sheila Rowbotham, 'Hopes, Dreams and Dirty Nappies', *Marxism Today* (December 1984): 8–12, 9.

[43] Duncan Wu, *Making Plays: Interviews with Contemporary British Dramatists and their Directors* (Basingstoke: Palgrave Macmillan, 2000), 14.

Byron) excessive indulgence in alcohol and drugs; '[a] library, bedroom and bar-room on wheels. What more could a poet desire?' (10), exclaims Mary with reference to Byron's customerized coach. When the quartet meet, Byron states exuberantly, 'we will summer together! [...] we will all go communist. We are upper class renegades, we can afford it. [...] Plans, plans, of changing the world, of ripping human nature apart, love and summer' (34). Byron is sleeping with Claire, has had a scandalous affair with his half-sister, Augusta, and also with others (both 'boys' and women) while also giving Mary a *sexual look*' (18); meanwhile Shelley, who has deserted his first young wife Harriet Westbrook (who drowns herself and appears as a ghost in the play) is in a triangular, polyamorous relationship with Mary and Claire (which prompts Mary to refer to 'the higgledy-piggledy jumble, tumbled confusion of the state of our affections' [24]), and Shelley is, at the same time, wooing Jane Williams, his boatsman's wife. Mary is the character who most often acknowledges the tragic irony of trying to be free in an unfree world:

> Let us play at gods and goddesses, moving in brilliant light on a beach by a lake, in dresses of white silk flowing about limbs, we statues. But we must not forget that statues – do not eat, they do not have bank accounts overdrawn by thousands of pounds, they do not – *With a glance at Bysshe.* – have lungs of mucus and blood, they do not – *She looks at Claire, pauses.* – have women's wombs.
>
>   13

The circle's attempts to convert utopian desires into a material practice in the here and now come up hard against the meanness of their social and material circumstances. The limitations of 'free love' are borne out in the explicit suffering experienced by all the play's women: Harriet, Claire, and Mary. Shelley's abandonment of Harriet leads to her suicide, and both Claire and Mary have few legal rights as mothers, and both lose children. Claire suffers Byron's cruelty and Mary expresses unease over Claire's relationship with Shelley ('[y]ou deny you still sleep with him?' [24]). All the circle takes pleasure in negating what Shelley calls 'man-made tyranny [...] Love is the very essence of liberty – we constrain it by the feudal savagery called the institution of marriage' (41). However, the consequences of their transgressions are felt unevenly across the group, and take a particularly hard toll on the women.

Brenton's interest in the 'felt self' – a Situationist self, liberated from the Spectacle –makes itself present in objectiveless, violent, and self-destructive acts in *Sore Throats*; in *Bloody Poetry*, the pursuit of an authentic life is a conscious politics, a deliberate coarticulation of utopian practice, self-liberation, and an antagonistic relationship with the public sphere. These characters engage in a kind of Situationist-inspired direct action similar to what has been practised by later social movements and radical environmentalist activists, who, in their antagonist approach, as Alberto Melucci observes, 'embody goals and forms of action that are not negotiable with the existing arrangement of social power and with the forms of political hegemony exercised by dominant interests'.[44] The circle is not interested in strategizing for a deferred or modified form of liberation and social justice; 'the world is yet to be made', says Claire, 'we are changeable, we will invent a new society and a new human nature' (42).

However, their refusal to negotiate with the prevailing social structure, and instead to 'follow [their] natures' (42) as Shelley says, affords only partial and temporary experiences of emancipation. Byron asks Shelley if he has had male lovers to which the latter responds, '[n]ot my nature' (42). Byron retorts:

> Y'bloody hypocrite! Where is your legal wife? In England! The two women you are with, Mary y'call your wife, Claire y'friend – concubines, sir! Y'mistresses, sir! All your idealism, revolution in society, revolution in the personal life, all trumpery! The practice of it, sir, the practice doth make us dirty, doth make all naked and bleeding and real!
>
> 43

Non-marital sex is legible only as shameful beyond the safety of the circle, and however much they reject 'English bourgeois morality' (48), it nevertheless places limits on their ability to live as themselves. Their attempts to be faithful to an authentic self are ultimately compromised: '[w]e haunt ourselves', says Shelley, 'with the ghosts of what we could be, if we were truly free!' (40). The circle's efforts to live wholly and authentically produces a form of sociality both dynamic and jubilant in its stretching beyond the confines of permissibility, but the consequences are severe: mental anguish, loneliness, lost children, and suicides.

Brenton says of the circle: '[t]hey belong to us. They suffered exile from a reactionary, mean England, of which ours in the 1980s is an echo. They were defeated, they also behaved, at times, abominably to each other. But I wrote *Bloody Poetry* to celebrate and to salute them. Whether they really failed in their "Utopian dreams" is not yet resolved'.[45] The characters are trapped in a social formation within which they failed to survive; however, as Brenton observes, '*Bloody Poetry* looks like a tragedy, but then they became Byron and

---

[44] Alberto Melucci, *Challenging Codes: Collective Action in the Information Age* (Cambridge: Cambridge University Press, 1996), 39.
[45] Brenton, 'On Writing the Utopian Plays', 3.

Shelley after they were both dead'.[46] Mary Shelley is at least as significant a figure, her omission in Brenton's claim ironically echoing the gender politics of the circle. Brenton's fear that '[t]he rush to easy moral judgement is a danger in the play'[47] may be true, but the striking unevenness in gendered experiences of the quartet constitutes a central difficulty in the play's articulation of the appeal of 'sexual liberation' within a heteropatriarchal social arrangement. More broadly we can see *Sore Throats* and *Bloody Poetry* working dialectically to put in tension the endemic cruelty of life under the Spectacle and prefigurative utopian interruptions of that life, interruptions that endeavour to engender unalienated forms of sexual sociality and ways of being in the world. The confrontation of these incompatibles leaves the group crushed: the play ends with Shelley drowned and the group defeated. Byron's final lines – 'Burn him! Burn him! Burn him! Burn us all! A great big, bloody, beautiful fire!' (80) – resonate with the final image of *Sore Throats* (Judy about to burn a pile of money) – and reflects the zenith of this collision, the conflagration of which marks an appropriately dramatic moment in this dialectical process.

The triumph of ordinary life: *Greenland*

Confrontation between micro utopian performatives and the broader repressive arrangement of social power in *Bloody Poetry* enacts a dialectical movement that enables the production of Brenton's final play in the trilogy, *Greenland*, which, unlike the first two plays is a fully-formed utopia. First performed at the Royal Court on 1 June 1988 and directed by Simon Curtis, *Greenland* is divided into two acts. The first takes place on 11 June 1987, the day of the general election when Margaret Thatcher won a third term in office. The second act is set in the future utopian world of Greenland. Brenton states: '[i]n *Greenland* I come clean. Over half the play is set seven hundred years in the future. I have tried to dramatize how I hope my children, or my children's children's children, will live and think. The "Greenlanders" in the play are strange, and their sense of humour is disturbing, but I would love to meet them'.[48] As an explanation for including the first non-utopian act, Brenton refers to the importance of representing people at their most undignified in order to be able to depict with credibility characters who lead happy, self-respecting, and satisfied lives.

---

[46] Brenton, 'Interview', in *Making Plays*, 32.
[47] Ibid., 29.
[48] Brenton, 'On Writing the Utopian Plays', 3.

A pilot for *Greenland* was 'Questions in Paradise: A short story', which Brenton published in the *Guardian* newspaper a few weeks before the opening performance of *Greenland*. The short story explores in miniature some of the same ideas but through a conversation between a male narrator (who seems to be a version of Brenton), a character similar to the utopian young nurse named Palace in *Greenland*, and the historian or 'specialist', Severan Severan, a grumbling malcontent who yearns for the pain of the non-utopian past. The short story distils what is explored more expansively in the play; we read of an 'incredible development' in scientific advancement in the utopia that manifests in phenomena, whose value is illegible from within the non-utopian Spectacle: 'hologram nail varnish ... kites flown everywhere, made not of cloth but of coloured gases, caught in some kind of magnetic molecular field' but not 'an everyday, practical technology, eg the combustion engine'.[49] Concern for the environment is prioritized explicitly in 'Questions in Paradise': '[t]his is a scientific culture [...] which knows how to make plutonium deposits safe, but is bewildered by the idea of car engine. Indeed, the point of a car, let alone an aeroplane. Nearly every Greenlander I met had travelled, very far, but very slowly, taking years to drift from place to place, even continent to continent'.[50] Gone is the capitalist imperative of speedy movement of capital and labour. Equally absent is a conception of history based on conflict, violence, and struggle: 'when I asked a Greenlander about "her history, the last seven hundred years," she showed me her painted finger nails. And why they were so beautiful. Her gesture meaning "well, we've got this far..."'[51] A life undetermined by the Spectacle is no longer meaningful through familiar narratological frames. In Greenland, '"Ordinary life" triumphed and woke up to produce an extra-ordinary world'.[52]

Representing the utopian world of Greenland within the form of a play posed specific challenges. Brenton's efforts to discover a method for writing his utopia was simultaneously reflective of an appreciation of the various aspects that make writing a utopian play difficult: the common equation of drama with conflict; the absence of a dramatic tradition of utopias; and the scenographic limitations of the stage as a site for signifying a transformed world. However, Brenton's approach manifests an exercise in the Situationist practice of *détournement*. Generic structures and tropes associated with particular reception histories and meanings are spliced together and repositioned in new contexts. Such a manoeuvre enables both a subversion

---

[49] Brenton, 'Questions in Paradise: A Short Story', *Guardian*, 22 April 1988, 23.
[50] Ibid.
[51] Ibid.
[52] Ibid.

and critique of the kinds of life narratives determined by generic categorization under the Spectacle, as well as proffering signs of what life might be like beyond it.

As I have argued in an earlier journal article on *Greenland*, the play's form is constituted by a manipulation and blurring of genres, and as such makes for a potentially dislocating spectating experience.[53] *Greenland* resembles More's *Utopia*, in its two-act structure, the first act echoing *Utopia*'s Book 1 with its depiction of the unappealing non-utopian (dystopian even) world, which functions to provide the argument for the need for utopia; the second act, in a similar way to More's Book 2, relocates the reader/spectator to a strange, utopian space. *Greenland*'s form and title situate it in the tradition of stage comedy. The first satirical act is resonant of Jacobean city comedy, the second of pastoral, green-world comedy. This is a genre blurring not untypical of Brenton; reflecting on the contrast in tone of acts 1 and 2 of his play, *The Romans in Britain* (1980), Brenton describes its dramatic shape as 'perverse, for it goes from "dark" to "light", with a first half that is violent, dynamic and tragic, while the second half is elegiac, still and flooded with an hysterical, light-hearted, comic spirit.'[54] A similar structural 'perversity' is present in *Greenland*. After a long time searching for a suitable dramatic form for this play, Brenton eventually found inspiration in Shakespearean romantic comedies, such as *As You Like It* and *A Midsummer Night's Dream*, where 'people like us, with all our hates, confusions and contemporary troubles hanging from them like rags, get lost in a "magic wood," a new, alternative reality'.[55] This is quite different to the comedy of act 1, which instead grounds the dirty, immoral, competitive, and exploitative London of the non-utopian 1980s in seventeenth-century city comedy of the Ben Jonson or Thomas Middleton variety. *Greenland*'s amalgamation of the conventionally discrete genres of city and green-world comedies within the same play leads to some estranging effects, particularly in relation to the question of closure: for example, the city comedy reassurances of justice, retribution, and atonement are denied, but so too are the green-world comedy comforts of romantic union and re-assimilation with the social order.

Greenland is an act of Situationist *détournement* in its use and refunctioning of existing cultural forms – such as green-world comedy – for utopian purposes. Northrop Frye describes Shakespearean comedy as 'the drama of the green world, its plot being assimilated to the ritual themes of the triumph

---

[53] Siân Adiseshiah, "'I just die for some authority!'": Barriers to Utopia in Howard Brenton's *Greenland*', *Comparative Drama* 46.1 (Spring 2012): 41–55.
[54] Brenton, 'Preface', in *Howard Brenton Plays 2*, viii.
[55] Ibid., xv.

of life and love over the waste land'.[56] Andrew Stott speaks of green worlds as 'wish fulfilment locations, always rural, often enchanted, in which the normal business of the town is suspended and the pleasurable pastimes of holiday prevail'.[57] These worlds are spaces of 'love, leisure, levelled social hierarchy, and play ... in which solutions to urban problems can be worked through'.[58] Importantly, as Stott notes, '[i]mmersion in the green world is immeasurably healing, but always temporary; holiday is defined only as such because it must be distinguished from the everyday world'.[59] Green worlds have much in common with utopias, but a crucial difference is that the experience of them is transitory. Participation in rule-bending activities in the Arcadian retreat (Bakhtinian carnival, disguised identities, transgendering, subversion of conventions) comes to an end and the audience encounters a restoration of the social order, which usually takes the form of a return to the city. In an act of *détournement*, *Greenland* does not follow the logic of the genre by depicting the utopian world of peace and freedom as a *temporary* ludic space from which citizens are returned restored and refreshed to conventional society; the utopia instead demands attention as the post-capitalist alternative future. *Greenland* reworks the genre expectations of green-world comedy and moves audiences to rethink what are usually assumed to be structural givens.

It is noteworthy that *Greenland* was not received particularly well by several theatre critics. In fact, Brenton observes, '[i]t was greeted, on its first production, with incomprehension. I wanted to stage a world in which Shelley, Byron, Mary and Claire would be happy to live ... I know that this play was a reckless undertaking. Gentleness and peace are not meant to make good drama. The mental agony of *The Genius*, the death and defeat of *Bloody Poetry*, the dystopia of *Thirteenth Night* were praised, while the sly, quiet contentment and weird utterances of "The Greenlanders" were derided by the critics'.[60] The Royal Court designer, Paul Brown's hyper real set, which in act 2 comprised real soil, trees, water, and wooden boards – a literal green land – provided an appropriate space for *Greenland*'s mix, as Patricia Troxel's observes, of 'natural philosophy, pseudo-mythology, and simple existence not political or economic struggle'.[61] With the play's endeavour to articulate what

---

[56] Northrop Frye, *Anatomy of Criticism: Four Essays* (Princeton, NJ: Princeton University Press, 1957), 182.
[57] Andrew Stott, *Comedy* (London: Routledge, 2004), 29–30.
[58] Ibid, 30.
[59] Ibid.
[60] Brenton, 'Writing in Thatcherland', 35.
[61] Patricia Troxel, 'Haunting Ourselves: History and Utopia in Howard Brenton's *Bloody Poetry* and *Greenland*', in *Text and Representation*, ed. Karelisa Hartigan (New York and London: University of America Press, 1990), 100.

significance and value might look like outside of the Spectacle, the triumph of ordinary life – as the core idea of the utopia of act 2 – struggled to signify effectively as either triumph or ordinary.

In act 1, audiences are presented with a condensation of political, economic, and social life almost a decade through the Thatcher period. The class spectrum runs from a Peer of the Realm – Paul, Lord Ludlow (resonant of Lord Lucan, a British peer who famously disappeared in the 1970s after being suspected of murder) – to an unemployed alcoholic – Brian – both of whom are selfish, unhappy, and violent. Both characters treat women badly (Paul beats up his wife in act 1 and kills Siu in act 2; Brian exploits his sister's hospitality in act 1, and rapes Annette in act 2) and both appear to be motivated by self-loathing. Another pair of characters, mother and daughter, Betty and Judy, are similarly opposites and echoes of each other: Betty (resonant of reactionary social campaigner, Mary Whitehouse) is a deeply conservative, evangelical Christian focused on policing sexual propriety, whereas Judy is a sexually confident lesbian actor in a Situationist-style street theatre group (and bears the same name of the protagonist in *Sore Throats*). The other key character, Joan, is a soft-left Labour candidate for parliament (called 'looney left' [27] by the right). The aggressive circulation of bad attachments in *Sore Throats* is similarly felt in *Greenland*, but this time considered from a panoramic perspective; the lone domestic room of the first play is replaced with several locations in London, and the play traverses – at rapid speed – through a range of class encounters and social scenarios.

Act 1 shows intense feelings of alienation and disconnectedness as a result of the distorted interactions humans from all classes are forced to have with each other within a society determined by the penetration of the market into all its aspects. While the play offers numerous examples of harm characters do to, or receive from, each other, all express desire for something else. Betty yearns for a moral society; Judy craves a socially just, sexually liberated world, observing, '[w]e all want a new world. That has ... Light. That's human, and decent, and ... Clean? We both want ... A new Jerusalem?' (24). The aristocrat, Paul, a heavy drinker, unable to take pleasure from his material wealth ('I have forty suits in my dressing room. They are of silk or wool. [...] Life should be so ... good!' [19]) and fearful of losing it from gambling or increased taxes from a Labour government, is in 'in hell' (19), and, in an echo of Jack from *Sore Throats*, expresses this through violence towards his wife, Milly: '[h]*e punches her in a kidney. She doubles and falls*' (19). Milly wants 'to be back in the early seventies, in a secret Chelsea garden. [...] Drinking wine. Giggling. Feeling naked in a short skirt, my legs long and golden. And a handsome young aristocrat, leaning over me, helplessly in love' (19). Brian stumbles through the streets of South London, getting increasingly inebriated on cheap lager and '*having a football fantasy*': 'N' a long cross, deep from deep mid-field! And the striker! Runs thirty fuckin' yards! Into the box! And with his noddle, bang!' (29). The Labour Party candidate, Joan, channels her yearning for a better, fairer world into a practical attempt to effect political change; however, she fails to win her seat and Labour does not win the general election.

Bad feelings circulate in act 1 and characters express deep unhappiness and self-dislike. Paul's wife, Milly, says 'I just don't want to be who I am' (22):

If I were not me, what would I ...
... wear?
What would I know? What would I think?
What would be the colour of my hair?
How would I ...
Move? Smile? Turn ...
Where would I live?
Who ...
would I love?

23

Milly's desire to be different is paralleled by Judy's search for a lost, authentic self: 'Mum, we must find our real selves' (24). The play notes a range of resistances to, and coping mechanisms with, life under the Spectacle, such as the various forms of alcoholic or violently escapist actions we see from Paul and Brian, as well as the activism of Betty's anti-pornography campaign and Judy's radical feminist theatre group, and Joan's electioneering for the Labour Party. None is effective, and the play deduces that systemic change is the only meaningful response to the deep despondency and dysfunctionality that characterizes contemporary sociopolitical life.

Systemic transformation occurs between acts 1 and 2, and 700 years separates the two societies. Like Brenton's short story, the utopian world of Greenland combines a mix of high and low technologies both to undermine the assumption of a linear narrative of technological progress, and to underline the importance of environmental sustainability. The prehistoric and futuristic are juxtaposed in the first stage direction and lines of dialogue of act 2: '*They are swathed in oilskin cloaks. DRAW holds a large, asymmetrical umbrella above them*' (32). Draw asks A'bet: 'Do y'get anything?' She replies, 'Oh he's in luck. And alive' (32). Combining the attire of primitive humans with an advanced mode of communication (telepathy) that recalls Shaw's Ancients from *Back to Methuselah* brings asynchronous technologies into simultaneity, the encounter of which is both comical and estranging. The Greenlanders' choice to focus on developing confident selves, social connectedness, and public intimacy, and not to (re)invent the combustion engine, run cars, or foster high fashion registers as political intention the Greenlanders' refusal to evolve along familiar historical trajectories.

In contrast to the competitive fast-paced 1980s of act 1, with its continual deferral of life, the utopian world of act 2 puts forward an alternative narrative of slowness and a conscious participation of the Greenlanders in their present moment. This is expressed partly through investment in the aesthetics of the carnivalesque; yet *Greenland*'s act of *détournement* transforms temporary participation in carnival into a permanent mode of living (un)structured by the (i)logic of carnival. Bakhtin's idea of the language of the marketplace – the idiom of the plebeian classes, a language reflective of sexuality, the body, and bodily functions – is exemplified by the Greenlander, Jace. Evocative of the unalienated craft work so valued in Morris' *News from Nowhere* and celebrated by the Situationists, Jace is a jeweller, and spends much of his time carefully carving beautiful gems and stones from rocks with his lathe. Resonant of the utopian visitor to Earth, Janet Evason, from Joanna Russ' *The Female Man* (1975) who is sent because she can be spared, Jace is similarly unremarkable: 'If you're lost', Jace says to Joan, 'don't think I can find you for you. Sorry. Your bad luck hitting me. I not got much up top' (34). Joan becomes increasingly disgusted at Jace's frequent, but unconscious, acts of scratching his crotch; 'look could you, do you think you could please stop doing that?' (46). Jace's alignment with his body is reiterated in various actions, such as squatting on his haunches and standing on one leg, which are repeated throughout the act and continually infuriate Joan.

This staging of simple uninhibited bodily actions ('*Jace still balanced on one leg, is now picking his nose*' [47]) is part of Brenton's interest in staging ordinary life. The bodily – as disgusting – still retains this connotation through the privileging of Joan's perspective; however, this baseness is interwoven with simple acts of kindness ('*He lifts his cloak. She hesitates, then snuggles beneath it. He puts his arm around her*' [34]) and an unfathomable, but remarkable skill and proficiency: '[h]e said [the stone] was cut in seven dimensions, I looked at it. And God or the Devil or something help me, it was. And, worse for me, just for a second I saw how it was done ... I was terrified. I found tears streaming down my face' (47). In this way the play registers the extraordinary capabilities of human communities afforded by a utopian society – outside of the Spectacle – but insists on the value of ordinary life: slow craft, pleasure in the seasons, a cuddle with a friend, and a diminishment of self-regard, or what we might consider an absence of the Rousseauian notion of *amour propre*.

For the eighteenth-century philosopher, Jean-Jacques Rousseau, the origins of illegitimate rule were in the replacement of *amour de soi* – an instinctive self-protective disposition marshalled by early humans to enable the reproduction of the essentials of life in primitive society – with *amour propre*. The latter, emerging with the development of civil society was conceived by Rousseau as a form of self-regard, which was easily distorted by the competitive individualism of capitalist society and expressed through vanity, a desire to be superior to others and to be esteemed and admired. In Book 2 of the *The Social Contract*, Rousseau proclaims, '[w]hoever ventures on the enterprise of setting up a people must be ready, shall we say, to change human nature, to transform each individual, who by himself is entirely complete and solitary, into a part of a much greater whole from which that same individual will then receive, in a sense, his life and his being'.[62] This is part of Rousseau's theory of the General Will, which is not especially relevant to *Greenland*, but the play's displacement or diffusion of an individualism determined by a prideful *amour propre* as essential components of a free life outside of the Spectacle is important to the play's utopian reformulation of sociality in Greenland.

Brenton succeeds in making visible a figuration of subjectivity that retains both the appeal of another (that out-of-reach attractiveness beheld by someone else) and the solidarity of the collective – the warm, support of the group with common interests. Troxel notes of *Greenland*: 'the utopian future offers a world of multiplicity and fecundity, but it also demythologizes the value of the individual. [...] Greenlanders [...] become selves within a greater social self'.[63] There is a shifting subjectivity in the play that is difficult to account for within current discursive formulations. The following exchange occurs when the utopian characters, A'Bet and Draw, discover the alcoholic Brian lying unconscious:

A'bet He's violent.
Draw Good reason to leave him alone. He'll be flying, through something personal ...
A'bet I don't think this one knows how t'do that.
A pause.
We'll get him into the boat, and back to the house. And advice.
DRAW, in sudden agreement.
Draw Yes, we're right

32

---

[62] Jean-Jacques Rousseau, *The Social Contract* (London: Penguin, 1968), 84.
[63] Troxel, 'Haunting Ourselves', 101.

The odd shift in pronoun in Draw's '*we're* right' after proposing precisely the opposite course of action to A'bet, loosens the sovereignty of individualism (the simple mapping of notions of individuality onto individual bodies). A nourishing tenderness is produced through an effortless intimacy of fluid selves, and at the same time, this is a mode of social relations that avoids a simple conflation or homogeneity of subjectivities.

The disentanglement in *Greenland* of separate bodies, fictions of individualism, and the notion of discrete, bounded selves provides a basis for a new appreciation of ordinary life outside of the Spectacle. Unfixing subjectivity in this way disperses egotistical self-regard across a community of selves; without the driver of *amour propre*, Greenlanders are not in need of constant validation by others. Brenton says of them, '[t]hey were, that is they are, and will be ... very disturbing people to meet. [I]t is very frightening to meet someone who has no fear'.[64] Act 2 has dissolved recognizable structures and practices of identification, dissembling old coordinates of identity in the process. The process of subjectivization that occurs in Greenland is a kind of symbiotic attunement. Alternative forms of sociality are enabled through a fomentive reimagining of identity.

Conclusion

The following exchange between Joan and Bill takes place in act 1 of *Greenland*:

> **Joan** Do you have a crystal clear idea of what a just, democratic socialist England would be like? A communist England?
> **Bill** Hey now ...
> **Joan** No! Really like. To breathe in. Go through a door in. Get on a bus in, if buses there will be. Do you have any idea?
> **Bill** No. 'Course I don't.
> **Joan** Nor do I.
> **Bill** Babbling of Utopia?
> **Joan** Yes. I am.
> **Bill** A communist society would be made by its citizens. It would be up to them if they had buses. Or doors, come to that.
> **Joan** So by definition Utopia cannot be described.
> **Bill** Did Marx?

---

[64] Brenton, 'Questions in Paradise: A Short Story', 23.

Joan William Morris tried.
Bill Oh yeah. Endless country dancing with the sun out all the time.
Joan People want to know what we want, Bill. On the doorstep. And we can't describe it. Only flat, lead phrases ... Dignity of working people ... Right to work ... Healthcare, pensions, decent life ... blah, blah. I mean what, what life?

28–9

This scene animates the difficultly with which the play wrestles: how to describe a post-capitalist society using language and conceptual tools conditioned within capitalism; how to produce a vision of utopia that centres the collective but is the product of an individual imagination. 'I once had an argument with an audience after a play', Brenton reported: '"We know what you hate, why not show us what you love," they said. My pompous retort is that I show people in struggle, and in staging defeats there is always the ghost of achievements'.[65] However, Brenton remained alert to the political limitations of a critique that does not simultaneously propose political alternatives. Rowbotham lamented the left's neglect of this: 'the effort to get anywhere becomes a ritual without meaning unless there is a conception of where you are going or at least the reason for travel. And this is the light which in modern times both Marxism and Labourism have not tended.'[66] The political imperative for socialists to contribute alternative visions eventually led to Brenton relenting. While the dramaturgy of *Greenland* rises to the challenge of this, it is simultaneously interwoven with acknowledgement that the project of attempting to stage a utopia is an impossibility – albeit an impossibility that is generative in its attempt.

In contrast to Bernard Shaw's disembodied utopianism and an enhanced version of human, Brenton centres the human body and ordinary life in his trilogy as the key sites through which his utopian imagination is expressed. The plays' focus on embodiment affords particular attention to the viscerality of felt experience, which in turn is peculiarly able to signal the cruelty of life under the Spectacle and to indicate what life might feel like in the absence of such cruelty. The brutal and brutalizing effects of the Spectacle are dramatized palpably in *Sore Throats*. Located deep within the belly of the beast, the action of the play anticipates the 'in-yer-face' theatre of the 1990s, but its violent, sex-smeared scenes simultaneously contain unmistakable, albeit misdirected, longings for something altogether different. The utopian romantic circle of

---

[65] Brenton, quoted in Robert Gore-Langton, 'Brenton's Erehwon', *Plays and Players*, April 1988, 10–11, 10.
[66] Rowbotham, 'Hopes, Dreams and Dirty Nappies', 9.

Bloody Poetry attempts a prefigurative utopian practice, forging cracks in the mantle of capitalism to create enclaves for utopian experimentation. The characters in this play come up against the inevitable limitations of structural containment: no systemic change means no lasting utopian alternative. The implication is that without a revolutionary transformation of social, political, and economic life utopian interventions within the here and now will never be more than contained, muted, or distorted, and will inevitably dissipate. Hence the annunciation in the third play of the trilogy of a holistic utopia, a new society unencumbered by existing structural parameters. As part of marking the radical systemic alterity of *Greenland*, it is relocated far into the future, but life in this new world is not offered in futuristic sf images. It is instead remarkably ordinary. Its lack of the spectacular is the point.

6

Utopian conversations

My analysis of Brenton's utopian trilogy in Chapter 5 identified the work's utopian vision as influenced by the revolution of everyday life *apropos* the ideas of Guy Debord and the Situationist International: on the imperative to puncture the capitalist hegemony of the Spectacle to enable a flourishing of an embodied, authentic life based on meaningful connections with others. Brenton pursued these ideas through a dialectical interaction of separate forms: a challenge to the prevailing system (informed by a distorted utopian longing) in *Sore Throats*, utopian activity within the confines of political reality in *Bloody Poetry*, and a utopian form of life flourishing beyond the system in *Greenland*. Utopian drama from the late twentieth and twenty-first centuries retains a similar commitment to alternative forms of living, or, to frame this in more contemporary terms, the twin desire to produce counter narratives to the stifling effects of capitalist realism and engage in a radical process of systemic dismantling. But there are notable differences. Contemporary theatre no longer appears obligated to *represent* utopia, instead experimenting with staging performative exchanges about utopian possibility that redeploy language, meaning, perspective, and subjectivity as utopian counter-narratives to the fatalism of current political discourse. Concomitantly, recent utopian drama has combined what were disaggregated in Brenton's trilogy as single works – utopian expression within, against, and beyond the capitalist present. In this way, utopia is relocated at once to the within, marshalled against, and located to a point beyond the systemic status quo. Utopia in the examples discussed in this final chapter becomes a contemporary practice, an historical invention, and a strategy for a revolutionary politics.

This book has demonstrated that theatrical treatments of utopia on stage have been rare occurrences historically. Remarkably rich and intriguing as these plays are, they have appeared, variously, as satirical (Aristophanes' *The Birds* and *The Assembly Women*), not performed in their own time and possibly intended as page plays (Cavendish's trilogy), as eccentric, unwieldy, or baffling (Shaw's *Back to Methuselah* and *Farfetched Fables*), or peculiarly self-conscious, defensive even (Brenton's *Greenland*). However, I would like to suggest in this final chapter that this might be changing in the present period. Contemporary utopian theatre is freeing itself from this kind of idiosyncratic incongruity, and this seems linked to a number of factors – a liberation from feeling obligated to depict a utopian society, an interest on the part of both dramatic and postdramatic theatre in a post-ironic sincerity of intersubjective connection,[1] the transformative cultural politics in recent years framed by movements like Black Lives Matter, Decolonise the University, Me Too, Trans rights, and so on, and the interpellating politics engendered by the climate emergency that demand more than dystopian critique or modest reform.

The move from *representing* utopia towards a spectator-performer encounter with its *co-creation* – utopia conceived as wresting open the future as already scripted – has something in common with Tom Moylan's concept of the critical utopia. As discussed earlier in this book, Moylan developed this concept to make sense of the resurrection of utopian writing witnessed in the 1970s, which moved away from the static, blueprint visions of early utopias to representing utopia as provisional, inchoate, fluid, flawed, and dynamic. A sf-utopian exploitation of the space-time relation finds a place in some of these contemporary plays too, its imaginative capabilities used as a route out of the reality principle, a way to mitigate the fatalistic assumptions of the ideological present.

An affective symptom of this fatalism – a cloying pessimism or false hope disregardful of the grim realities of human society – is observable in the exponential growth of dystopian cultural forms within the mainstream, which shows no sign of weakening. I acknowledged in the Introduction that there are contemporary examples of dystopia that sustain both political critique and (a precarious) utopian hope, but the genre in general terms, as Raffaella Baccolini has observed, has been excessively commodified and appropriated in the twenty-first century.[2] The prevailing fashion for dystopia has meant its imbrication in the occlusion of political struggle and a premature foreclosure of hope. In response to dystopia's saturation of contemporary culture, I had assumed utopia on the contemporary stage would be difficult to unearth: that it would need coaxing out of its hiding places in critical dystopian or post-apocalyptic plays or performances, or be confined to micro-utopian moments, images, aspects of scenography, or lilts of the voice. While it would be untrue to say utopian plays are in abundance,

---

[1] For a full discussion of the new sincerity in contemporary theatre, see Siân Adiseshiah, 'Spectatorship and the New (Critical) Sincerity: The Case of Forced Entertainment's *Tomorrow's Parties*', *Contemporary Drama in English* 4.1 (May 2016): 180–95.

[2] Raffaella Baccolini, '"Hope isn't stupid": The Appropriation of Dystopia', *mediAzioni* 27 (2020): http://www.mediazioni.sitlec.unibo.it/index.php/no-27-2020/120-dossier-the-domestication-of-utopia/402-hope-isnt-stupid-the-appropriation-of-dystopia.html

there are some powerful theatrical examples of utopia interrupting dystopia's stranglehold on the present worthy of consideration. Claire MacDonald's *Utopia: Three Plays for a Postdramatic Theatre* (written and performed during the period 1987 to 2008), Mojisola Adebayo's *STARS* (2018), and African American writer Cesi Davidson's playlet, 'Voice Lessons: Wishes to the Outside', which appears in her collection *Articulation: Short Plays to Nourish the Mind and Soul* (2019), are significant examples and form the case studies for this chapter. Other contemporary work usefully described as utopian includes Uninvited Guest's performance piece from 2006, *It is Like It Ought to Be: A Pastoral*, the theatre of Suspect Culture (as eloquently exemplified by Dan Rebellato[3]), Joel Horwood's play *This Changes Everything* (2015), and the work of the playwright and theatre maker, Andy Smith. Smith's most recent project is called 'Plays for the People' (2021), plays written to be read by spectator performers – groups of friends meeting in person or online – and designed to be followed by a discussion of the issues contained therein and the experience of participation.[4]

These works, to varying degrees, are striking for their engagement with the postdramatic in their use of non-mimetic performance.[5] In a move that parallels the utopian novel's rejuvenation in the 1970s as the critical utopia, utopian plays have broken from their confinement within a generically conventionalized representative model to emerge as a fresh mix of text-based drama with postdramatic aesthetics. Not without some irony, utopia is worked through in plays that might be called postdramatic, but which also are productively likened to the originary *literary* utopia of More's, which saw the subsequent centralizing of the dialogical mode of the conversation as a vehicle for utopian ideas. In a special issue on utopia in the journal *Theater* in 1995, Cheryl Faver describes her idea of what drama in a utopian society would be like:

> Most important, the new drama would be constructed around *the conversation* instead of the debate. In a debate, there is a central point of

---

[3] Dan Rebellato, '"And I Will Reach Out My Hand with a Kind of Infinite Slowness and Say the Perfect Thing": The Utopian Theatre of Suspect Culture', *Contemporary Theatre Review* 13.1 (2003): 61–81.
[4] Andy Smith, 'Plays for the People' currently includes two plays: *The Actions* (created in collaboration with director, Sam Pritchard) and *The Rule of Six*: https://www.andysmiththeatre.com/plays-for-the-people
[5] The example that does not do this – Joel Horwood's *This Changes Everything* (2015) – is also the play that most lacks utopian desire. While more of an attack on specific forms of utopianism than utopianism per se, it nevertheless expends more of its energies critiquing a well-worn narrative of island utopia politics than expressing utopian desire for an alternative society.

focus, an organizing principle to which everyone – spectator and participant – must adhere. In a conversation, there is the freedom to wander, to change one's mind, and to explore new subjects endlessly.[6]

The full freedom of conversation might only be possible in a post-capitalist utopia, and, for sure, the limitations on what is conversationally possible within the ideological present are tussled with by the utopian plays considered here. But Mick Short's description of drama as the exemplar of the conversational genre as it is 'most like naturally occurring conversation' is fully mined for its utopian potential in the examples I discuss.[7] Anne Ubersfeld's claim that 'theatrical discourse is by nature an enquiry into the status of speech: who is speaking to whom, and under what conditions one can speak' helps us see how theatre offers a distinctive opportunity to test the dialogic possibilities of the fictional utopia.[8]

Morean dialogics

It is useful to consider Thomas More's *Utopia* as a dialogic form to appreciate the significance of contemporary utopian drama's use of dialogics. Underpinned by its debt to the Socratic method, *Utopia*'s formal distinctiveness is its dialogic and dialectical structure. Book 1 stages a conversation using direct speech between More himself, his friend and Antwerp magistrate, Peter Gilles, and the fictional traveller to Utopia, Raphael Hythloday. Raphael reports a discussion he had with the Archbishop of Canterbury, a lawyer, and a group of obsequious courtiers. In its satirical critique of the non-utopian world of its author, Book 1 produces, what Robert M. Philmus calls the dialectical model: 'it necessarily defines itself, at least implicitly, against a status quo'.[9] Philmus draws from Kenneth Burke's proposition that the model of utopia can be understood in terms of the 'dialectical' and the 'ultimate', the latter describing utopian representation that proposes itself as superior to the here and now.[10] Following this formulation,

---

[6] Cheryl Faver, 'Refracted, Distracted, and Hopeful', *Theater* 26. 1–2 (1995): 139–55, 149.
[7] Mick Short, *Exploring the Language of Poems, Plays and Prose* (London and New York: Longman, 1996), 168.
[8] Anne Ubersfeld, *Reading Theatre* (Toronto, ON: University of Toronto Press, 1999), 168.
[9] Robert M. Philmus, 'The Language of Utopia', *Studies in the Literary Imagination* 6 (1973): 61–78, 62.
[10] Philmus references Kenneth Burke, *A Grammar of Motives and A Rhetoric of Motives*, (Cleveland, OH: Meridian Books/World, 1962).

Utopia's Book 2 is the 'ultimate'; it consists of Raphael conveying to More and Peter Gilles a detailed account of the superior society. For Philmus, the relation between the 'dialectical' and the 'ultimate' informs the ideological perspective of the utopia – 'which is satirical to the extent that "dialectical" outweigh "ultimate" considerations, visionary to the extent that the reverse is true'.[11] While Philmus deems Plato's *Republic* as mostly visionary due to its suppression of dialectical elements, he considers *Utopia*'s dependence on the dynamic of the differences between the 'dialectical' Book 1 and the 'ultimate' Book 2 that form the work's structuring device, as resulting in 'an equilibrium of visionary and satiric impulses'.[12]

So, the dialogic in *Utopia* is considered in this formulation to be held in productive tension by the two-part structure of contrasts, which Philmus claims, 'resists efforts to isolate Utopia as an ideal in itself'.[13] I am not so sure. While there are textual complications in *Utopia* (multiple framings, paratexts, and jokes) that bring into question the sincerity of the text's utopian intentions, Book 1's satire is a critique of the non-utopian world to which the utopia of Book 2 is a solution. In this way, the two books work together as a collaboration: Book 2 is the synthesis of the dialectical antagonism we see in Book 1 between those defending the status quo and Raphael's questioning of it. Furthermore, although Book 2 is an extension of the same scene of conversation as Book 1 (continuing with Raphael's direct speech), it is notable that the whole of Book 2 is a single-voiced monologue, the reader only reminded of the presence of listeners at the very end when the voice changes to More's: '[w]hile Raphael was telling us all this, I kept thinking of various objections'.[14] Thus, while on the one hand *Utopia* contains a dialogic and dialectical structure, that process is played out within the containment of a predetermined and tightly prescribed model. Hence, *Utopia* (and many utopias that follow) is distinctive for its dialogic structure, but this does not mean the text contains any presence of undecidability of outcome attributable to the text's format as a conversation. The conversation is, after all, a frame for Raphael's extended monologue. Utopia in More's book thus appears as predetermined and knowable. If there is undecidability, it is produced through the satirical aspects of the paratexts, the inclusion of jokes, and the ironic naming of people, places, and geographical features.

---

[11] Philmus, 'The Language of Utopia', 62.
[12] Ibid.
[13] Ibid.
[14] Thomas More, *Utopia*, trans. Paul Turner (London: Penguin, 2003), 113.

Dialogics and undecidability

By contrast, some aspect of undecidability forms part of the dialogic structure of the plays I discuss in this chapter. This is an undecidability – not born of a postmodern critique of truth claims – but understood instead as an attempt to break a linear continuity of past, present, and future, a continuity that forecloses the future as an evolution of what is already known (as opposed to a disruption of the known). Marc Augé explains the political passivity of populations in terms of their understanding of the status quo as 'impassable, immovable. It is what it is, and what it is comes from the past, the solidified past that dictates the words used [...] to say everything that can be said about the future. Outside the extremist parties [...] evocation of the past almost always precedes invocation of the future, conceived broadly as a simple extension of the past'.[15] The undecidability of contemporary utopian dramatic conversations plays out in the scene of the present and functions to keep the possibility of an unknowable future open. This is facilitated by the collaborative materiality of theatre – theatre as an interdependently relational practice – as well as the unknowability of outcome that characterizes genuinely collaborative creative work. Departing from the singular vision of classic utopias (the monologue within a dialogic frame which is the case in More's *Utopia*), utopia in these contemporary plays is articulated through two or more voices where the dialogic exchange is intrinsic to the enablement of utopian contemplation.

Utopian pessimism

A co-founder of Leeds-based experimental theatre company, Impact Theatre Co-operative (1979–1986), Claire MacDonald, continued a longstanding preoccupation with the imaginative potential of writing, language, text, sound, time, space, and performance in her utopian trilogy: *Utopia: Three Plays for a Postdramatic Theatre*. Utopian possibility has underpinned her approach for many years: 'the task of artistic practice', MacDonald states, 'is to create impossible worlds and see what might happen in them'.[16] The first play in the trilogy – *An Imitation of Life* – was created collaboratively by MacDonald with Pete Brooks, and commissioned and performed at the Bush

---

[15] Marc Augé, *The Future*, trans. John Howe (London: Verso, 2015), 12.
[16] Claire MacDonald, 'Written Worlds', in *Utopia: Three Plays for a Postdramatic Theatre* (Bristol: Intellect, 2015), xiii.

Theatre, London, in January 1987. With a character list of two, 'Man' was played by Tony Guilfoyle and 'Woman' by Jan Pearson. The second play, *Storm from Paradise*, was performed just over a year later in May 1988 at Lancaster University Playroom with the same character and cast list as *An Imitation of Life*. The final play, *Correspondence*, produced ten years later, was a commission by the Menagerie Theatre, Cambridge, and first performed there in 2008 with Jerry Killick playing Man and Stefanie Mueller playing Woman. The production then toured in the UK with the same cast, and later on with Cathy Naden as Woman.

The three plays spanned a twenty-year period: two were performed in the late 1980s and the third in the twenty-first century. MacDonald chose to publish them together under the title *Utopia* to signal their mutual interest in 'ideas about imaginary places and spaces, one of which is of course the theatre itself'.[17] All three plays stage 'a rhetorical conversation' between two people, a man and a woman, and there are no prescribed settings: in *An Imitation of Life*, 'the speakers sat on the chairs and talked. Occasionally they got up and changed places, walked, circled, embraced, fought. Almost nothing else happened'.[18] *Storm from Paradise* 'is a conversation in a room, anywhere, any time'; and *Correspondence* 'has almost no stage directions, and it describes its own context as it proceeds'.[19] MacDonald's introduction is replete with references to utopian ways of thinking and making; the reader learns that the plays are 'grounded in theatre as a space in which imaginative geographies are assembled and dismantled'.[20] This assembling and dismantling is a processual rearrangement of the architecture of perspective, a shifting of viewer positionality, relationality, and intersubjective experience. MacDonald was interested in 'how language itself could stand in the place of objects and settings to create rich, experientially full, imaginary stage worlds that related to contemporary ideas and debates'.[21] She speaks of wanting to propose 'alternative realities' and to deal with 'hope, desire, foolishness and failure'.[22] The question, 'To whom does the power to imagine belong?' underpins the desire of the work, whose imaginative energy uses the theatre space as an exploratory landscape, rather than a space of dramatic encounter.[23] Theatre here is 'a place for proposing extraordinary visual worlds in which ordinary

[17] Ibid., xiv.
[18] Ibid., xi.
[19] Ibid.
[20] Ibid., xiv.
[21] Ibid., xvii.
[22] Ibid., xiv.
[23] Ibid., xviii.

rules of engagement might be suspended, revealing, perhaps, alternate states'.[24] This speaks to Diana Knight's insight, in her book on Barthes and utopia, that the theatre is 'a sort of laboratory for constructing the liberated social space of utopia'.[25]

MacDonald thinks of the trilogy as 'dialogues, conversations and [...] as essays'.[26] In an exchange with the writer, Lenora Champagne, MacDonald says:

> one of the things I was trying to do in these plays was to find a means through dialogue in which I could create chamber pieces. The idea of the essay was crucial there, thinking about 'essay' etymologically, as a kind of 'attempt', as well, that was also there. The idea that a play could be a conversation, an essay, an attempt to do something, not using dramatic but literary or philosophical forms, like Socratic dialogues, they take the form of a dialogic reflection on being.[27]

More's *Utopia* is also an essay of sorts, an essay, – the French 'essayer' – to attempt, to try, to trial – marks a willed commitment to do something. 'To do' is the ultimate action verb, a performative form that precipitates or accounts for the accomplishment of a thing, this endeavour *to do something*: a hope-bearing act of faith in a future not yet decided. In 'Essay as Form', Theodor Adorno writes that the essay 'does not permit its domain to be prescribed. Instead of achieving something scientifically, or creating something artistically, the effort of the essay reflects a childlike freedom that catches fire, without scruple, on what others have already done'.[28] He considers '[l]uck and play' as essential to the essay, which 'does not begin with Adam and Eve but with what it wants to discuss; it says what is at issue and stops where it feels complete – not where nothing is left to say'.[29] MacDonald's trilogy includes some of the features Adorno attributes to the essay. The plays exhibit a ludic freedom that ranges over what others have done. These are effortful theatre pieces where the determination of the attempt is an observable part of their purpose. Yet, despite their negation of prescribed structures (they try to begin with what they want to discuss), originary narratives (Man/Woman – Adam/Eve) are the congealed forms, a stubborn resistance with which the plays wrestle.

---

[24] Ibid., xix.
[25] Diana Knight, *Barthes and Utopia: Space, Travel, Writing* (Oxford: Clarendon Press, 1997), 22.
[26] Claire MacDonald, 'Written Worlds', xiv.
[27] Ibid., 71.
[28] Theodor W. Adorno, 'The Essay as Form', *New German Critique* 32 (Spring–Summer, 1984): 151–71, 152.
[29] Ibid.

These forms align with the organising principle of the debate to which Faver counters the utopian conversation. There is an oscillation between the radical provisionality of the playworlds, illustrated by the contingency of the world suggested in *Correspondence* ('Woman: Remind me. Man: What do you mean? Woman: Just ... remind me where we are. Man: We're travelling. Woman: How? Man: By train'[30]) and the sticky residue of heteropatriarchal white normativity. MacDonald describes her trilogy as 'written worlds composed of tricky narrative sparring, each speaker's contingent subjectivity framed by the speech of the other'.[31] The utopian potential for alternative figurations of subjectivity is placed alongside more familiar narrating positions. In this way, MacDonald's *Utopia* (unlike More's) retains the suggestion of undecidability of outcome of a radically dialogic piece, even if it simultaneously acknowledges its pre-scriptedness.

There is a refusal to reproduce the familiar narratives of the prevailing system in this utopian trilogy, but as I have noted the plays are caught within the constraints of a sociopolitical exchange haunted by the most familiar of intractable structures. White heteronormative coupledom forms the trilogy's central social unit, and the plays' attempts to re-script relationality bump up against that structural limit. In the published collection of the trilogy, there is a letter from MacDonald's walking companion and theatre scholar, Deirdre Heddon, who compares the scene of *Correspondence* to 'the space of a convivial walk':

> both are journeys, in which relations unfold and extend and anything could happen. Indeed, it's this 'anything' that the woman in the train carriage seems to hold out for. But what's striking is that she recognizes how difficult it is to bring that 'anything' into this particular space, because the space itself – the carriage of the train – is scored with familiar lines: a man, a woman, war, threat, murder, sex. The man says it's a classic situation. She says it's a cliché.[32]

In this way, the plays hold in balance the utopian unpredictability of unknown futures and familiar social formats that keep things in place. Hope – not as uncritical optimism – but as commitment, a radical act of labour, a willed

---

[30] MacDonald, *Correspondence*, in *Utopia: Three Plays for a Postdramatic Theatre* (Bristol: Intellect, 2015), 54. All further references are to this edition and appear in the main body of the text.

[31] MacDonald, 'Written Worlds', xvii.

[32] Deirdre Heddon, Letter to Claire MacDonald 30 September 2013, in Claire MacDonald, *Utopia: Three Plays for a Postdramatic Theatre* (Bristol: Intellect, 2015), 47.

political agency – permits the utopian dynamic at play. It is an ambivalent hope, a precarious hope, hope against hope – but hope nonetheless.

Despite the political weight of these plays' efforts to see differently, textual conditions constrain the terrain of what is possible to say, the creation of new worlds articulated as a fragile process. MacDonald says of the second play in the trilogy, *Storm from Paradise*, that it stages 'imaginative failure'.[33] The heteropatriarchal frame is difficult to escape, the following exchange from *Correspondence* making this especially visible:

> **Man** They're old friends, lovers.
> **Woman** No, not necessarily, I mean, I don't think you even have to set that up, they are just there. Just *there* on the train. Together.
> **Man** So you want nothing to happen. They are just there.
> **Woman** Telling stories, or not even stories, just reminiscing.
> **Man** It isn't threatening?
> **Woman** Why do you bring that into it? I didn't say *anything* about that, no, no that's something entirely different . . .
> **Man** . . . conflict, drama. It's not just two people talking.
>
> 61

The woman attempts to generate a form of storytelling beyond the logic of patriarchal narratology, but her co-creator is not similarly minded. Nor does he understand the woman's belief in the possibility of a social encounter underdetermined by conflict. The idea that drama must involve conflict is an understanding shown to be interlocked with patriarchal expectations of narration. Tension over the question of whether drama must meet patriarchal expectations of conflict produces the very conflict from which the woman seeks to be liberated.

These plays strive to change the conversation, drawing explicitly on utopian thinking as a methodology. However, the 'imaginative, hopeful and decisive' qualities of the founders of the Dartington utopian community in Totnes (founders who inspired parts of the trilogy) compete with the aggressive hold of the 'conflict between man and woman'.[34] For these reasons, I am describing MacDonald's trilogy an example of 'pessimistic utopia'. Søren Baggesen draws on Ernst Bloch's notion of latency (the hidden historical possibilities of what could have happened) and its relationship with the actual tendencies of history, the dialectics of which make possible the

---

[33] MacDonald, 'Written Worlds', xxvi.
[34] MacDonald, 'Written Worlds', xxiv.

prospect of utopian hope for the not yet here of what is latent. Baggesen translates Bloch as follows:

> History would not work without the space of possibilities generated by the whole dialectics [*Wechselverhältnisses*] of tendency and latency in the world – a space of possibilities [*Möglichkeitsraum*] at once refracted [*gebrochenen*] and objective and object-like [*object-objekthaften*]. In all of which, it is as possibility, not as actuality, that latency is to be valued: just as in it there is no decided, hence resigned [*resignierenden*] pessimism, but only a militant one, with world-changing humanity in the front line of the historical process.[35]

The 'resigned pessimism' Bloch refers to is fatalistic: the bleak future is already decided in its foreclosure; whereas 'militant pessimism' acknowledges the hostility of actual tendencies but equally commits to the future as not yet decided – as radically open, or what Augé describes as 'opening onto the radically new'.[36] Baggesen calls this 'utopian pessimism' and deploys it as a way of making sense of the ambiguous utopian politics of Ursula Le Guin's 1972 novel, *The Word for World is Forest*. It chimes with Tim Etchells' description of MacDonald's *Utopia* collection as giving 'a taste of the rigorous work of imagining we are all capable of, of the value of that work that navigates but does not accept the landscaped garden we are offered, off the peg'.[37]

Black skin, white forms

A second example comes from the African American writer, Cesi Davidson. A prolific playwright, Davidson has written and produced more than 200 short plays since her first in 2009, some performed in off-off-Broadway theatres, and some as part of free dramatic readings at public libraries in Harlem, New York City. Many of her plays, are 'wildly imaginative' to quote Zachary Sklar, a screenwriter and author of the Foreword to Davidson's 2019 collection of plays, *Articulation: Short Plays to Nourish the Mind and Soul*.[38]

---

[35] Ernst Bloch, *Experimentum Mundi*, quoted in Søren Baggesen, 'Utopian and Dystopian Pessimism: Le Guin's *The Word for World is Forest* and Tiptree's "We Who Stole the Dream"', *Science Fiction Studies* 14 (1987): 34–43, 36.
[36] Augé, *The Future*, 6.
[37] Tim Etchells, 'You Did Not Know Who You Were', in Claire MacDonald, *Utopia: Three Plays for a Postdramatic Theatre* (Bristol: Intellect, 2015), 6.
[38] Zachary Sklar, 'Foreword', Cesi Davidson, *Articulation: Short Plays to Nourish the Mind & Soul* (Seattle, WA: Aqueduct Press, 2019), iii.

Much of her work presses at the edges of possibility, exploiting what she refers to as the 'pure freedom' the play affords.[39] She rewrites nursery rhymes and draws on fantasy, includes speaking animals as characters (for example, talking birds in 'A Girl & Her Bird' and a gender fluid rabbit in 'Veronica Bunny Read Her Text Messages'); she experiments with bizarre settings (such as a full-term pregnant stomach in 'Linea Negra'), and the personification of vegetables: the characters Judy and Lenora are radishes in 'Temporary Associations'.

While many of Davidson's plays contain a utopian impulse in their use of non-realism, sf, and fantasy as a means to encourage both non-normative perspectives on this world and conceptions of alternative worlds, one play in particular – 'Voice Lessons' with the subtitle 'Wishes to the Outside' – explicitly takes on the form of a utopia. With a reminder of Brecht, the play begins with a synopsis:

> 'Voice Lessons' is the story of two celestial beings named HE and SHE who reside in a Caribbean utopia somewhere between heaven and earth. In exchange for the privilege of remaining together for eternity, they perform time-travel missions. Their responsibility is to collect lessons from the experiences of Africans in the diaspora that can help relieve the current suffering of the people. Once collected, they disperse the lessons as intentions that people feel as 'inspiration'.[40]

The character list indicates that He is a 'handsome Black man' and She, a 'beautiful Black woman', and the setting is '[a] hilltop in a Caribbean utopia. There is a coconut tree full of coconuts' (103). The play is at once recognizable in its utopian references – an island utopia in the Americas (like More's *Utopia*) – and like MacDonald's trilogy (and Shaw's *Back to Methuselah*), it evokes Genesis in its focus on a lone heterosexual couple and a tree with tempting fruits (or nuts), although it complicates this trope by making the couple Black. The play's re-racing of these white narratives is, in part, a comical gesture: the comedy is produced through the constraints of inherited structures – the incongruity of the relation between a model of utopian encounter coded as white (the island utopia) and utopian protagonists raced as Black. This is interlaced with an additional complicating narrative that works as a double reminder of the colonial origins of the utopian tradition of island utopias (in More's *Utopia*, King Utopos imposed his utopia on the

---

[39] Cesi Davidson, 'Introduction', *Articulation*, 2.
[40] Davidson, 'Voice Lessons', in *Articulation*, 103. All further references are to this edition and appear in the main body of the text.

indigenous islanders of Abraxa) and the violent history of enslavement and dispossession that frames Black Caribbean identity.

The play begins in comic conversational mode: the utopian couple re-enacts a familiar gendered scene where She wants He to get her a coconut from high up the tree ('no, me say me wan de one en de top . . . de one close to de sky' [104]), but he offers her one that is in much easier reach ('Woman, why ya need trouble me so' [104]). The play offers no serious attempt to register utopia as alternative in any way. In fact, the opposite is the case: the laughs are generated from the familiarity of what seems like an intractable gendered dynamic. While the relationship is affectionate and warm (*'She strokes His Face.* [. . .] *She and He embrace'* [106]), its heteronormative futurism ('[*i*]*n exchange for the privilege of remaining together for eternity, they perform time-travel missions'* [103]) retains romantic heterosexual coupledom as the privileged site of solidarity, care, and love. However, instead of reproducing the patriarchal lesson against insubordination familiar from the biblical narrative – Adam and Eve (encouraged by Eve) eat from the tree of knowledge, gain an awareness of evil, and, as a result, shamefully fall from innocence – in 'Voice Lessons', He and She both eat from the coconut tree, but with a superhuman consciousness-raising altruism redistribute the knowledge and lessons of historical actions and experiences, as a utopian method. The formation of a utopian vantage point from which to perceive our capitalist present and its histories, enables a critique not compromised – at least in narrative terms – by sharing a fictional world with its object of scrutiny.

This has affinities with the critical utopias of the 1970s, where utopian characters time travel to other temporalities, including the non-utopian present of the writer.[41] Reversing the conventional utopian structure where the visitor from the non-utopian world travels to utopia to learn about the better society afforded a more dynamic encounter between the seemingly impassable capitalist present and an articulation beyond political entrenchment. After the comic opening, the couple sit down and begin to chant: '*[a]s the chanting becomes more intense, the tree magically disappears and the hilltop becomes an abyss. She and He time-travel to a woodland area between two farms in northern Virginia, 1858. He and She have become people in the time period – enslaved Africans'* (106). The romantic exchanges in the play's opening are transposed onto this historical setting with She waiting for He in a pre-arranged clandestine meeting: 'I need to fix myself pretty' (106). The lovers

---

[41] In Marge Piercy's *Woman on the Edge of Time*, the utopian character Luciente appears first in the novel as a time travelling visitor to 1970s New York. Similarly, in Joanna Russ' *The Female Man*, the utopian character Janet crosses time to visit non-utopian 1970s New York.

meet in a deeply familiar romantic scene. He presents a gift of fern-dyed cloth to She, saying, '[d]ying and printing remind me of home' (108), diasporic connections instantly forged through this reference to home and its associated experiences of dispossession. This reminder of brutal displacement foreshadows the ending of the scene where slave catchers and dogs arrive, '*He and She run in opposite directions. [. . .] Sounds of slave catchers beating He. He screams from agony and pain. Sounds of dogs biting and chewing on His flesh. Wails of She as she watches the beating in the distance and hears the sound of His voice*' (108–9).

There are two further time travelling scenes: the first in a contemporary kindergarten where '*He and She are inhabited by the spirits of five-year-old children*' (109) and the second a psychiatric ward where the adult version of He from the previous scene visits the adult version of She, whose '*face is deformed from assaults and burns*' (113). The creative, joyful energy of the kindergarten scene, where She makes up songs and dances and He writes a story about a dragon with five heads, is superseded in the psychiatric ward by aching melancholy. 'I had a voice once', says She, '[a]n outside voice that other people could hear. Now I only have an inside voice. . .' (113). Her experience of psychic breakdown is intertwined with physical wounding. '*She reenacts a beating disfiguring her face*', the stage directions read, and She says: 'I can't feel my legs anymore. . . Not my face . . . Don't beat my face' (113). Through the continuing impact of the slavers beating and burning of She's body, this scene positions the present epoch – our present – as determined by, and in a continuum with, the necropolitical logic of historical dispossession, enslavement, and colonialism.

The voice lesson from this last instance of time travel is '[s]hare your inside with the outside' (116). Exteriorizing subjective experiences of injustice, brutality, and oppression works to form a historical materiality with which there must be a reckoning. Once He and She have returned to the utopian island, the stage directions read: '*Stars appear all around He and She. They gather the stars which represent intentions that will become inspiration and put them in the knapsack. They hold the knapsack together and cast the stars out on the people*' (116). In this way, historical lessons of dispossession are collectively shared, and morph into inspiration – a stimulus to collective action.

'Voice Lessons' experiments with the classic model of the island utopia and the dialogic form as a means to facilitate a counter narrative to the existing ideological frame. While MacDonald's utopian experiments attempt to forge paths out of the frame (although struggle to escape prescribed lines of flight), the position from which 'Voice Lessons' speaks is located beyond the systemic break. This enables Davidson both to make visible the colonial inheritances of utopian forms and to displace white occupation of the primary speaking positions within utopian dialogics. The play does not concern itself with dramatizing utopian forms of life (beyond the bond of heterosexual monogamy); it uses utopian structures as a means of escaping the historical limitations of the present, and of resisting subsumption by the ongoing impacts of slavery, what James Baldwin calls 'one of the most obscene adventures in the history of mankind'.[42] Talking about ritual, Augé says: 'people want to act on the future, but a future conceived and desired as identical to the past'.[43] 'Voice Lessons' disrupts the continuity between past, present, and future through staging conversations from within different points in history as well as across historical moments. It utilizes a utopian not yet/not here as an outside position from which to make political interventions into the past and present.

'Me, We' in the chillout space

A third, quite different example is Mojisola Adebayo's play, *STARS*. Adebayo is a Black South Londoner – 'London born, Nigerian/Danish', as she describes herself on her Queen Mary University of London staff profile.[44] She is a playwright, director, producer, performer, and facilitator, and prioritizes working with people who are 'young, Black, Asian, D/deaf, disabled, HIV+, homeless, slum dwellers, living under occupation, incarcerated, in children's homes, affected by the criminal justice system, female survivors of gender based violence, elders'.[45] She has worked extensively with the late Brazilian theatre practitioner, Augusto Boal, and is trained in the Theatre of the Oppressed. The published script of *STARS* notes that the play is '[d]edicated to all us survivors', an indication of its concern (like Davidson's 'Voice Lessons') with the ongoing traumatic effects of brutalizing experiences and histories.[46] *STARS* was developed during a residency in 2016 with Idle Women – an arts and social justice project that seeks to create 'vibrant and adventurous spaces with and for all women'.[47] It was first performed as a

---

[42] James Baldwin, 'Of the Sorrow Songs: The Cross of Redemption,' in *The Picador Book of Blues and Jazz*, ed. James Campbell (London: Picador, 1996), 329.
[43] Augé, *The Future*, 9.
[44] Mojisola Adebayo, staff profile (performance page), Queen Mary University of London, https://www.qmul.ac.uk/sed/staff/adebayom.html
[45] Adebayo, staff profile (public engagement page), Queen Mary University of London, https://www.qmul.ac.uk/sed/staff/adebayom.html
[46] Adebayo, *STARS*, in *Mojisola Adebayo: Plays Two*, intr. Lynette Goddard (London: Oberon Books, 2019), 187. All further references are to this edition and appear in the main body of the text.
[47] Idle Women website, https://idlewomen.org/about/

staged reading at Ovalhouse Theatre downstairs in June 2018, and as work-in-progress at the Unity Theatre, Liverpool, in November 2019 as part of Homotopia Festival (the UK's longest running LGBTQIA arts and culture festival). It is due to be performed at the Ovalhouse (now the Brixton House) in 2022 (having been postponed more than once due to the Covid-19 global pandemic).[48]

Adebayo plays a character called 'Mrs', an old (80+) woman in search of her first orgasm, a search that culminates in a trip to outer space. She also plays several other characters: Mrs' GP, an 11-year-old neighbour (Mary), her late husband as both young and old (Terry/Mr), a male admirer from church (Chris), church elders, European scholars, her mother and father, a laundrette worker with whom she had a sexual encounter (Shelley), a friend who is intersex (Maxi), Maxi's mum, Maxi's partner (Barry the butcher), and a doctor. The play is a collaboration with DJ DeboA of Mix 'n' Sync. Adebayo's brother, Debo Adebayo, plays Mrs' DJ son, and along with live DJing, the play includes projected animation sequences. An extract of *STARS* is included in Isabel Waidner's 2018 collection, *Liberating the Canon: An Anthology of Innovative Literature* which seeks to capture 'the contemporary emergence of nonconforming and radically innovative literatures in the UK and beyond'.[49] It seeks to bring together 'intersectionality and literary innovation' and does so with a not-for-profit publisher as part of an attempt to gain the widest possible readership.[50] *STARS* is striking for its centring of issues of access: there is frequent use of voiceover (to the animation sequences) and subtitles, an onstage BSL interpreter, and the creative team listed in the published play also includes arts access workers, D/deaf community consultants, FGM consultancy, and an intersex community consultant. The politics of the play – its desire for sexual, social, and political emancipation, its privileging of marginalized histories and voices – is scored into the materiality of its production. As Lynette Goddard writes in her introduction to Adebayo's *Plays Two*, the work 'bridge[s] gaps between art and activism, community and professional theatre, blackness, disability and queerness'.[51]

---

[48] I am very grateful to Mojisola Adebayo for generously lending me a video recording of a performance of *STARS*. The recording captures the performance of the play after only three days' rehearsal, and the published script has changed since then.

[49] Isabel Waidner, 'Liberating the Canon: Intersectionality and Innovation in Literature', in *Liberating the Canon: An Anthology of Innovative Literature*, ed. Isabel Waidner (Manchester: Dostoyevsky Wannabe Publishing, 2018), 7.

[50] Ibid.

[51] Lynette Goddard, 'Introduction', *Mojisola Adebayo: Plays Two* (London: Oberon Books, 2019), 14.

STARS replaces the central dialogics of the other plays discussed in this chapter (heteronormative coupledom in MacDonald's trilogy and Davidson's 'Voices Lessons') with an intergenerational and intercultural exchange between a very old woman and a girl, Mary, 'of African descent' (197) – actually Maryam, but she calls herself Mary to reduce instances of Islamophobia. Mary has undergone female genital mutilation, struggles to urinate painlessly, and visits her neighbour Mrs' house to use her toilet. The particularity of each character's individual personal history under heteropatriarchy (a lifetime's experience of the banality of sexist marriage and denial of sexual pleasure for Mrs and the violence of FGM for Mary) produces an irreducible singularity of experience, this irreducibility oscillating in productive tension with waves of intersubjective connectedness and shared feeling. Adebayo's playing of both Mrs and Mary makes the two inextricably entangled with modes of subjectivity figured beyond straight correspondence between single, discrete bodies and distinct selfhoods. In a later scene, this break in connection between body and self undergoes a further mutation; the stage directions read: '*MRS playing MARY playing MARY'S MOTHER*' (220). Discussing the effects of Adebayo's 2011 play *Moj of the Antarctic*, Deirdre Osborne observes, '[f]rom a single source is created many tributaries. The self-knowledge obtained from the 'I'-monologic and the 'I'-polyphonic produces a self as correlated with other(s') meanings'.[52] *STARS* produces a dynamic plurality of figurations of subjectivity and social relationality in ways that reject a constraining individual/collective formulation. The conversation in this play is not just diversified within existing epistemological terrain but begins to express differently articulated forms of human relationality that indicate routes out of prevailing ideological norms.

Adebayo describes theatre as:

> the art of human relationships in space – in the now, it is the art of being human on planet earth – together, it is the art of dialogue in the sense of working things out with one another (with or without words), it is the art of *ubuntu* – to quote the Southern African philosophy of humanity, empathy, understanding and compassion which broadly means, I am me through you and you are you through me or to quote Muhammed Ali: 'Me, We'.[53]

---

[52] Deirdre Osborne, 'Skin Deep, a Self-Revealing Act: Monologue, Monodrama, and Mixedness in the Work of SuAndi and Mojisola Adebayo', *Journal of Contemporary Drama in English* 1.1 (2013): 54–69, 57.

[53] Adebayo, Interview, in *Theatre in Times of Crisis: 20 Scenes for the Stage in Troubled Times*, ed. Dom O'Hanlon (London: Bloomsbury, 2020), 3.

This realignment of bodies and selves and the consequent complication of the play's dialogics is further modulated in *STARS* by the effects of a solo performer playing multiple roles. The continuity of Adebayo's bodily presence on stage – Adebayo as the physical conduit for multiple voices of diverse ages, genders, classes, and ethnicities – also resonates with the play as a concept album for the stage. *New Yorker* journalist, Doreen St. Félix, describes the concept album as 'an extravagant obfuscation of what we imagine as the artist's "self"'.[54] It is possible to read the multiple performances in *STARS*, on some level, as obfuscations of Adebayo, but this only adds to the numerous and shifting traces of subjectivity in process in the play. Osborne states '[f]or black writers, the "I am" of the *cogito* philosophies is not a certain foundation, for, both as citizens and artists, it is fraught with the legacies of "you are".'[55] The play's repeated process of creating and dissolving the first-person speaking position as Adebayo moves, for example, from Mrs with a 'South East London accent' to the GP's 'white English RP' (193) to Mary's 'RP English but as a second language, with a faint memory of somewhere in Africa – non-specific' (197) to Terry's 'white, cockney, Jack-the-Lad' accent (226) via several other voices and accents evades the freight of subject/object positioning and produces surprising intersubjective encounters in the process.

A further wrinkle in the philosophical assumptions of *STARS* is its Afrofuturist framing. An aesthetic movement that melds past, present, and future temporalities, political and cultural histories with futuristic technologies, from Black, African diasporic perspectives, Afrofuturism produces what Alex Zamalin in *Black Utopia* describes as 'texts that both revise history and imagine impossible trajectories of black freedom'.[56] The play opens with a ritual: the male performer is dressed, as the stage directions note, in '*robes and a hat that resonate with the culture of Dogon, Mali, as do all the visual elements of the show*' (191). '*The female performer*' we are told '*represents the Nommo – an African androgynous anthro-amphibian space traveller*' (191). These '*extraterrestrial Afro-hermaphrodite anthro-amphibian migrants*' (212) are Harawayan Afro-cyborgs – gender fluid, human/animal blurrings, with shifting, utopian forms of subjectivity, who travel through time and space. Mrs is also a Harawayan cyborg: as an orphan (a 'throwaway baby of a runaway English wife and a black American G.I.' [224]), she resides outside of oedipal symbiosis; like the cyborg, she 'does not dream of

---

[54] Doreen St Félix, 'The Otherworldly Concept Albums of Janelle Monáe', *The New Yorker* 1 March 2018 https://www.newyorker.com/culture/culture-desk/the-otherworldly-concept-albums-of-janelle-monae
[55] Osborne, 'Skin Deep, a Self-Revealing Act', 56.
[56] Alex Zamalin, *Black Utopia: The History of an Idea from Black Nationalism to Afrofuturism* (New York: Columbia University Press, 2019), 10.

community on the model of the organic family', and yet is 'needy for connection'.⁵⁷ The significant bond in the play is between Mrs and Mary, whose difference from Mrs is underscored by her age, culture, and nationality. *STARS*' displacement of the heterosexual romantic union centred in the other plays discussed in this chapter suggests a queering of family with Mary presenting a foil to the white heteronormative child imagined in the reproductive futurism critiqued by queer theorist Lee Edelman.⁵⁸ This representation chimes with a 'politics of regenerative cyborgs' where '[b]onds of affinity, solidarity, and kin-making replace those of blood, property, and nation', a praxis for which eco-communist utopian collective Out of the Woods strives.⁵⁹

The conversation in *STARS* is further enriched by the participative presence of music. The play has the intriguing subtitle *A Concept Album for the Stage*, and it makes its intervention through multiple means with music forming a central element of its aesthetics and intervening as participant in the conversation. Musicologist Lori Burns defines the concept album as one that 'sustains a central message or advances the narrative of a subject through the intersections of lyrical, musical, and visual content'.⁶⁰ The title of the play – *STARS* – seems explicitly to riff on the tradition of Afrofuturist concept albums.⁶¹ The pre-show music of *STARS* is 'Space is the Place' by Sun Ra. The Sun Ra Arkestra, an American Jazz group formed in the mid-50s, has retrospectively been called a pioneer of Afrofuturism. Adebayo's placing of Sun Ra's 'Space is the Place' as the framing track signals its centrality to the politics and pleasures of *STARS*. The song is repeated towards the end of the show – this time, a version by the Jonzun Crew, an American electro funk-hip hop group from the 1980s influenced by sf Afrofuturist themes from bands like George Clinton's Parliament-Funkadelic (a Funkadelic track is played in *STARS*), and Sun Ra.

Sun Ra personifies the, at times, eccentric ungainliness of utopian interventions. In a paralleling of diasporic deferrals to Africa, Ra claimed Saturn as home. The strangeness of this self-performance is an essential part of its strategic appeal, the impossibility of the claim loosening the hold of a

---

[57] Donna Haraway, *A Cyborg Manifesto: Science, Technology, and Socialist-Feminism in the Late Twentieth Century* (Minneapolis, MN: University of Minnesota Press, 2016), 9.
[58] See Lee Edelman, *No Future: Queer Theory and the Death Drive* (Durham, NC: Duke University Press, 2004).
[59] Out of the Woods Collective, *Hope Against Hope: Writers on Ecological Crisis* (New York: Commons Notions, 2020), 61.
[60] Lori Burns', 'The Concept Album as Visual-Sonic-Textual Spectacle: The Transmedial Storyworld of Coldplay's *Mylo Xyloto*', *IASPM Journal 6: 2* (2016), 91–116, 95.
[61] I am grateful to David Bell who shared useful thoughts and references with me on Afrofuturism and the concept album.

debilitating realism. Space is figured as a politically fertile trope, and for Ra, 'space music is the key to understanding the meaning of the impossible'.[62] The lyrics of 'Space is the Place' allude to ways in which space provides an imaginative apparatus for utopian experimentation. A free place, without limits, where all human life has value and can take different forms: space here is a somewhere/nowhere of emancipation. Jazz writer and musician, John Corbett, notes that 'Ra called for listeners to do the impossible, to make manifest a fantastic journey, a highly politized, poetical trip into unknown worlds'.[63] Adebayo threads through *STARS*' dramaturgy a Ra-inspired rhetoric of space as an enabler of utopian thinking and practice, and as pivotal to the kaleidoscopic range of subjectivities through which its dialogics are constituted.

The music in *STARS* plays continuously throughout the performance. The playlist combines Afrofuturist, sf, and space themes, through a mix of club genres, mostly electronic, some of which emerge from Electro-Funk – the precursor to British Hip Hop, House, and Techno, and what was a new wave of Black music imported on New York labels that hit the British club scene in the early 1980s. DJ and producer, Greg Wilson, observes that 'there was no set template for this new Dance direction, it just went wherever it went and took you grooving along with it. It was all about stretching the boundaries that had begun to stifle black music'.[64] The music functions both as an interwoven sign system in *STARS* and as raconteur in the various conversations in the piece. The playlist – as actant, narrator, storyteller – weaves in and out of different relational positions *apropos* Mrs and the other characters: at times acting as energizing force as Mrs gets up and dances a little, sometimes as framer of the conversation as quiet background music, and, on occasions, as an interlocutor.

The highly idiosyncratic selection of music in *STARS* moves beyond the purely illustrative in contributing an esoteric sample of underground electronic music that is itself associated with the experimental avant-garde and subcultural club and rave scenes. For example, the Bearcubs track '3am' played in the second half of the show is described by *Covert Magazine* as containing 'Bladerunner-esque blissed out beats', this track playing through

---

[62] Sun Ra, quoted in Graham Lock, *Blutopia: Visions of the Future and Revisions of the Past in the Work of Sun Ra, Duke Ellington, and Anthony Braxton* (Durham, NC: Duke University Press 2000), 33.

[63] John Corbett, 'Anthony Braxton's Bildungsmusik: Thoughts on Composition 171', in *Mixtery: A Festschrift for Antony Braxton*, ed. Graham Lock (Exeter: Stride, 1995), 185.

[64] Greg Wilson, 'Electro-Funk – What did it all mean? Dance Culture's Missing Link', *ElectroFunk Roots* November 2003, https://www.electrofunkroots.co.uk/articles/what.html

the animation of a recurring dream of Mrs' with DJ son's voiceover and subtitles including direct quotations from the film, *Blade Runner*.[65] The Italian electronic auteur, Lorenzo Senni has a track included on the playlist called 'Elegant and Never Tiring'. Senni is described by music journalist, Chal Ravens, as an 'arch conceptualist' with a 'penchant for deconstruction'.[66] Seven Davis Junior's 'Sunday Morning' is played towards the end of the performance, which, as Philip Sherburne writes, puts Davis's voice 'center stage: "Bet you never had a love like this before", he sings in a loop, and it's not just the lyrics that do the talking; it's his playful voice, swooping and diving, the very embodiment of joy at its most seductive'.[67] The penultimate track is Floating Points' 'Peroration Six', which Marcus J. Moore describes as 'the edgiest' of *Elaenia*'s (the album from which it is from) compositions: 'while the rest of the album is largely unrestrained, this track fuses electro-jazz and rock in a combustible burst of seething intensity'.[68]

DJ son's live on stage playing of these tracks constitutes a crucial component of the performance, providing an affective richness to the multiple ways in which meaning and feeling are produced and experienced. As I have noted elsewhere, music – through its constitutive elements of rhythm, tone, intonation, and sound – has no direct signified or referent, this affording a semantic freedom that equally applies to utopia (itself detached from a referent).[69] Writing in his book on Bloch's musical philosophy, Benjamin Korstevdt likens music to utopia because they are both 'always "noch nicht", phenomenologically always in a state of becoming, the coming moment crowding in as the present moment recedes into immediate memory'.[70] Adebayo says that *STARS* 'transforms into a club night'.[71] The pure joy of dancing (with or without drugs) – at an underground club or rave, the latter unlicensed irregular spaces (both often grassroots and anti-establishment) – compounds this intensity, generating something akin to Jill Dolan's notion of

---

[65] Baz Jobson, 'Bearcubs – 3am – Cadence Sampler', http://www.covertmag.com/2012/06/bearcubs-3am-cadence-sampler/ 4 June 2012.
[66] Chal Ravens, Review of Lorenzo Senni, 'Sacco Matto', *Pitchfork News* 29 April 2020, https://pitchfork.com/reviews/albums/lorenzo-senni-scacco-matto/
[67] Philip Sherburne, Review of Seven Davis Jr. 'Universes', *Pitchfork News* 16 July 2015, https://pitchfork.com/reviews/albums/20756-universes/
[68] Marcus J. Moore, Review of Floating Points, 'Peroration Six', *Pitchfork News* 5 November 2015 https://pitchfork.com/reviews/tracks/17800-floating-points-peroration-six/
[69] Siân Adiseshiah, '"We Said We Wouldn't Look Back": Utopia and the Backward Glance in Dorothy Reynolds and Julian Slade's *Salad Days*', *Studies in Musical Theatre* 5.2 (2001): 149–61.
[70] Benjamin Korstevdt, *Listening for Utopia in Ernst Bloch's Musical Philosophy* (Cambridge: Cambridge University Press, 2010), 56.
[71] Mojisola Adebayo, staff profile (research page), Queen Mary University of London, https://www.qmul.ac.uk/sed/staff/adebayom.html

utopian performatives, which 'describe small but profound moments in which performance calls the attention of the audience in a way that lifts everyone slightly above the present, into a hopeful feeling of what the world might be like if every moment of our lives were as emotionally voluminous, generous, aesthetically striking, and intersubjectively intense'.[72]

The music selection in the playlist evokes the 'PLUR' ethos of the rave scene, an acronym standing for peace, love, unity, and respect.[73] By themselves these ethical codes are not necessarily utopian, and, as several scholars have argued, in many ways rave culture produced alternative bubbles that were variously escapist, politically apathetic, or actually quite simulative of the mainstream.[74] At the same time, PLUR values pushed back against competitive individualism, and, expressed a celebration of being together in solidaristic ways. These values thus enabled unorthodox possibilities for playing out different versions of self and other. Tammy L. Anderson and Philip R. Kavanaugh make the observation that '[r]avers danced individually, but in unison with others around them', this embodying the 'values of independence and connection', and that the sociality of communal friendship and proxemic intimacy replaced the more familiar 'sexual courting and conquest' common to mainstream socializing.[75] This alternative value system informed a semi-autonomous field of expression for ravers, which, as sociologists Sarah Riley, Christine Griffin, and Yvette Moray claim, helped 'to create (temporary pockets of) sovereignty over their own existence' as a form of political practice 'aloof from institutions of governance'.[76]

---

[72] Jill Dolan, *Utopia in Performance: Finding Hope at the Theatre* (Ann Arbor, MI: University of Michigan Press, 2005), 5.
[73] For a fuller discussion of the context for PLUR, see Scott Hutson, 'The Rave: Spiritual Healing in Modern Western Subcultures', *Anthropological Quarterly* 73.1 (2000): 35–49; Simon Reynolds, *Generation Ecstasy: Into the World of Techno and Rave Culture* (New York: Routledge, 1999); Melanie Takashi and Tim Olaveson, 'Music, Dance and Raving Bodies: Raving as Spirituality in the Central Canadian Rave Scene', *Journal of Ritual Studies* 17.2 (2003): 72–96.
[74] See Hutson, 'The Rave: Spiritual Healing in Modern Western Subcultures'; Christina Goulding and Avi Shankar, 'Age is Just a Number: Rave Culture and the Cognitively Young "Thirty Something"', *European Journal of Marketing* 38 (2004): 641–58; Sarah Thornton, *Club Cultures: Music, Media, and Subcultural Capital* (London: Wesleyan University Press, 1996).
[75] Tammy L. Anderson and Philip R. Kavanaugh, 'A "Rave" Review: Conceptual Interests and Analytical Shifts in Research on Rave Culture', *Sociology Compass* 1/2 (2007): 499–519, 503.
[76] Sarah C. E. Riley, Christine Griffin, and Yvette Morey, 'The Case for "Everyday Politics": Evaluating Neo-tribal Theory as a Way to Understand Alternative Forms of Political Participation, Using Electronic Dance Music Culture as an Example', *Sociology* 44.2 (2010): 345–63, 358.

Close attention to the sonics of *STARS* is important, as recognition of the music's situatedness enables a deeper appreciation of the play's conjoining of experimental aesthetics with radical politics. Much of the music DJ son plays is mellow with mid-or down-tempo beats, the kind of ambient vibes associated with the chillout spaces of clubs or raves, prevalent on the electronic dance music scene in the 1980s and 1990s. Chillout rooms were attempts to provide safe spaces which supported sociality (solidaristic connections and regroupings) and aloneness (solo relaxation, reflection, and imaginative interaction with the music). Music journalist, Joe Muggs, describes these spaces as 'intergalactic portals where one could, if one wanted, drift on hyperspatial currents of sound for sweet eternities', the 'abstracted space music' played here having 'powerful solvent properties'.[77] The aesthetics of *STARS* are thus crafted with intricate care, the subversive potential of electronic dance music culture harnessed for its ability to interpose an affective psychostimulant within the dialogics of the conversation, the rules of which are loosened with a disregard for grammatical propriety in a bid to forge paths out of systemic circumscription. Subject positions in the play's conversation are liquescent, producing a nimble and responsive form of solidarity, or what Kodwo Eshun calls '*flui*darity'.[78]

While *STARS* experiments with the political potential of 'me, we', it is cautious of eclipsing individual difference. Alice Rayner claims, 'we' does not need to be a synthesis of identities, it can offer a rhetorical intervention – 'an invitation to join in a collective enterprise directed toward a community that is yet-to-be'.[79] Its usage does not inevitably operate on an exclusionary basis nor demand a 'prior self-similarity between members of a group'.[80] It can instead operate as a rhetorical solicitation. Rayner describes 'we' as 'the most radical "shifter" of English grammar' due to the endless possibilities for its appropriation and mutation.[81] On the other hand, indigenous Canadian writer and theorist, Leanne Betasamosake Simpson's emphasis on the interconnectedness of ourselves to others (both past and present) is closer to the ways in which 'me, we' plays out in *STARS*. Simpson refers to the Nishnaabeg word 'kobade', which she describes as a 'a link in the chain between generations, between nations, between states of being, between individuals'.[82] She refers to 'an ecology of

---

[77] Joe Muggs, 'Return to the chill-out room: when did ambient music last have it so good?', *Fact* 9 October 2014, https://www.factmag.com/2014/10/09/ambient-2014-round-up-joe-muggs/

[78] Kodwo Eshun, *More Brilliant than the Sun: Adventures in Sonic Fiction* (London: Quartet Books, 1998), 003.

[79] Alice Rayner, 'The Audience: Subjectivity, Community and the Ethics of Listening', *Journal of Dramatic Theory and Criticism* 7.2 (Spring 1993): 3–23, 11.

[80] Ibid.

[81] Ibid., 12.

[82] Leanne Betasamosake Simpson, *As We Have Always Done: Indigenous Freedom Through Radical Resistance* (Minneapolis and London: University of Minnesota Press, 2017), 8.

intimacy', 'a web of connections to each other, to the plant nations, the animal nations, the rivers and lakes, the cosmos'.[83] Yet, the openness of connection in *STARS* – the mutability of subject positions as they shift and spark – is matched by a sensitivity to the fragility of the felt self:

> **Mrs** [*to her son*]   No, no you don't understand, Mary came to me, Mary revealed it all, and she made me think about everything I've denied in my life and then she just disappeared as if she was never there, as if she was just a story in *The Mirror* and then last night I had a dream about an eclipse and I heard your voice and now I think she might be dead and she was my sun, my son, she was my reason for getting up in the morning.
>
> 223

Mrs' self moves and adapts as it conjoins and coalesces with other castings of personhood, but her expression of pain at the loss of Mary is both a retention of some aspect of ipseity and a registration of the profound interdependence and reciprocity of human subjectivity. In this way, the play's 'me,we' dialogics offer both a dissolution of dominant fictions of subjectivity and recognition of the affective implications of singular personhood.

Conclusion

These examples all use the mode of the conversation as a way of making possible a route to a future with meanings that are not yet known. The plays use dialogic structures in exploratory efforts to signal alternative forms of being human, the struggle to achieve this comprising a central component of each work. MacDonald's trilogy moulds and manipulates language – uses it like clay or plasticine – to make different shapes, to exploit its mutability. But like these materials, language/discourse/conversation are technologies situated within this historical context and subject to its heteropatriarchal rules. The trilogy's arduous endeavour to compose alternative lines of flight is a powerfully rendered failure of creative praxis – but it is politically galvanizing and hope forging nonetheless.

Davidson's 'Voice Lessons' displaces the whiteness of the utopian conversation, casting a Black Caribbean couple in the central dialogue. Dialogue itself comes under scrutiny as the play is on some level about articulation (as its name suggests), and particularly the struggle to voice the pain of living a

---

[83] Ibid.

racialized life with its brutalizing histories. There are multiple conversations between the beautiful utopians He and She, enslaved Africans in a romantic relationship, children playing in a kindergarten, and a psychiatric patient and her male lover with whom she is unable to speak. The temporal plasticity of 'Voice Lessons' puts several historical moments into critical dialogue from the perspective of the utopian future, which in turn offers a conceit by which the play is able both to critique past histories and the prevailing system, as well as wrench open space for marking the possibility of a different future. The play is at the same time ghosted by the colonial underpinnings of the island utopia, which works both to undermine the (racial and gendered) exclusiveness of this utopian form as well as to exploit its imaginative affordances.

Adebayo's *STARS* rewrites the dialogics of the utopian conversation by breaking free of sexist and colonial structures and producing alternative notations of subjectivity and radical forms of social relationality. Cross-generational female sexual autonomy, desire, and pleasure form the personal-political kernel through which a much broader set of political desires are marshalled. As a collaborative piece with a live DJ, the play interposes the participatory presence of the DJ and his playlist into the conversation, which expands and diversifies its scope and resonances. The central encounter between youth and old age is enhanced by involvement of other generational cohorts: contemporary young audiences are interpellated by the play's transformation into a club night, and there is a simultaneous invitation to Gen Xers, who were young during the height of the electronic dance music scene. The play invokes the political potential of the electronic dance music scene – and particularly the chillout room – drawing on both the experimentation of its sonics and its alternative value system. The political efficacy of the play is produced in part through what Simpson calls 'constellations of coresistance': *STARS* creates alternative notations of subjectivity and intersubjective experience in a utopian dialogical performance.[84]

All three plays participate in a refutation of what Kodwo refers to as 'compulsory pessimism', the fatalistic notion that 'because social relations in capitalism are bleak this sets the parameters of our thought', making thought 'hemmed in, and locked, at a certain point'.[85] At the same time, the plays do not express their utopian visions in the form of representing alternative worlds. Unlike the utopian plays of Aristophanes, Cavendish, Shaw, and Brenton, these works do not dramatize a utopian society, as such. Their dialogic strategies intervene in the present, offering prescient interruptions of

---

[84] Simpson, *As We Have Always Done*, 9.
[85] Kodwo, in Geert Lovink, 'A Speculative Dialogue with Kodwo Eshun', *Telepolis*, 10 July 2000, https://www.heise.de/tp/features/Everything-was-to-be-done-All-the-adventures-are-still-there-3447386.html

the known world. Their dramaturgies are determinations out of our hemmed in structures of knowing. They insist on the value of thinking society otherwise. The dialogics of these works retain hope as a political principle, and – *contre* Edelman's queer antifuturism – a commitment to the future as radically unknowable.

Out of this Woods collective writes:

> it is not so much 'no future' as *no to the future* as the continuation of a present that is impossible and undesirable. No to a politics that begins in the future rather than with an analysis of present tendencies. We must undo and remake the world. *In doing this we might return the future to us as a space of collective possibility.*[86]

Utopian drama in the twenty-first century retains the future as an essential category for political theatre but insists on the importance of its essential difference – the future marked as the scene of dismantlement of the systemic status quo – as radically open and unknowable. There are utopian moments of possibility in a broad range of contemporary theatre, and particularly in dystopian and post-apocalyptic plays focused on the climate emergency. However, utopian plays – plays that engage explicitly with utopianism, sustain a utopian impulse, figure the future as radically open, centralize hope (against hope) as an organizing principle – are mostly taking the form of the dialogic mode of the conversation. All three plays discussed in this chapter locate utopian politics in the here and now of a contemporary dialogic exchange, but equally they retain the power of the holistic utopian vision with the concomitant political effects generated by an encounter with systemic otherness.

---

[86] Out of the Woods Collective, *Hope Against Hope*, 146.

Epilogue

A key concern of this book is to consider the implications of taking utopian drama seriously. That there are few fully utopian plays in existence has made possible the close examination of much of what is available in English (the only material considered in translation is Greek Comedy). Examining utopian plays across time has made visible historical continuities and discontinuities of utopian tropes and conventions, variations in uses of genre, and differing political interests and interventions. The small number of utopian plays across a vast expanse of time, the distinctiveness of each example, and the plays' specific entanglements in their respective sociopolitical historical contexts makes drawing conclusions generalizable to all the works challenging. Even so, examining these plays together has brought into view fascinating connections in the ways playwrights have utilized the concept of utopia, our understandings of the later plays gaining from the mobilization of the utopian forms and politics registered in the early work.

Dan Rebellato claims 'utopia cannot be shown. That one can imagine the purely Other, the Beyond, the Noumenal, is a fantasy only held by a few Deleuzian postmodernists.'[1] If this is the case, it must apply to all forms of utopian art, and yet it has not stopped thousands of prose narratives from offering accounts of utopian societies. The attempt to represent, articulate, dramatize, or perform utopia might always fail (at least according to Rebellato's conception of utopia as other) but there is, at the same time, much to gain from the effort. Darren Webb values the holistic utopia's 'newly discovered structure of feeling, experienced as a form of recognition'.[2] Showing what utopia could look like encourages imaginative exchanges with alternative futures, and expands the parameters of what is permissible to

---

[1] Dan Rebellato, '"And I Will Reach Out My Hand with a Kind of Infinite Slowness and Say the Perfect Thing": The Utopian Theatre of Suspect Culture', *Contemporary Theatre Review* 13.1 (2003): 61–80, 76. This is in the context of Rebellato's discussion of Scottish experimental theatre company Suspect Culture. He continues, '[i]t is the *possibility* of utopia that is affirmed, more than any specific plan of how such a society would function.' (Ibid.).

[2] Darren Webb, 'Critical Pedagogy, Utopia and Political (Dis)Engagement, *Power and Education* 5 (3): 280–90, 286.

contemplate. Its failure too can be generative. Fredric Jameson identifies utopia as negative, its function lying 'not in helping us to imagine a better future but rather in demonstrating our utter incapacity to imagine such a future – our imprisonment in a non-utopian present without historicity or futurity'.[3] Utopian plays have always recognized the impediments to crafting new social forms from existing apparatus, and in this recognition, there is value.

An additional point of interest in the book is the discovery that utopian plays from a range of historical periods emerge in comic forms. Comedy and satire provide supple, anarchic languages well suited to articulating alternative worlds. Unlike the more earnest registers of utopian prose fiction, utopian drama is less concerned with persuading the reader/spectator of the plausibility of the utopia. Instead, it exploits a particular mode of attention produced through the genre expectations of comedy. The world imagined is not a real utopian society. This is comedy. This is playful, satirical, ridiculous even. Yet, serious ideas and political alternatives form equal parts of the mix. The theatrical experience is at once frivolously entertaining, and entertaining *of* subversive ideas and utopian alternatives to the prevailing system of the playwright. Comedy is a capricious form whose mutability unleashes alternative thinking, flights of fantasy, subversions, and rebellions, at the same time as undermining the validity of these propositions.

We also see in much utopian drama a merging of the city and body utopias, categorizations of utopian worlds usually appearing separately in prose narrative. The city utopia (underpinned by human reason, effort, and progress) and the body utopia (an ahistorical scene of bodily satiation) combine in utopian dramas to produce worlds where human effort, social order, sensual pleasure, and temporal plasticity form part of the same articulation. Human reason and agency undergird the mechanisms by which the better society is created, but bodily appetites, revelry, whimsy, and fantasy form the primary means through which the utopia is experienced. Utopian drama's blend of the city and body utopia equally means fantasy, the supernatural, and fictions of the past as well as the future are stitched into a utopian pattern simultaneously inclusive of rational planning or technological advancements. Hence, Aristophanes mixes solid walls, new laws, and talking birds in *The Birds*. Lady Happy's feminist community in *The Convent of Pleasure* depends on rational planning but is striking for a utopian culture expressed through sensual appreciation of fine silks, perfumes, good food, dancing, and erotic queer encounters. Bernard Shaw's *Back to Methuselah* begins in Biblical time and culminates many thousands of years into

---

[3] Fredric Jameson, 'The Politics of Utopia', *New Left Review* 25 (2004): 35–54, 46.

the future, interweaving eccentric ideas about extreme (and willed) longevity with rational political theory. Brenton's *Greenland* conjoins so-called primitive life (oilskins and walking as the only means of travel), highly developed communication skills (telepathy), and frivolous use of advanced technology (hologram nail varnish). This melding of plausible political theory and scientific innovation with the fantastical is sustained in contemporary utopian plays: Cesi Davidson's 'Voice Lessons' interweaves brutal histories of enslavement and dispossession with superhuman celestial powers. Mojisola Adebayo's *STARS* combines space travel, afrofuturist histories, sexual pleasure in old age, and the hedonism of a nightclub. In fusing sf, fantasy, rational planning, sensual satisfaction, political critique, and carnivalesque revelry, utopian drama exploits its origins as a form and practice in public ritual and festivity – at once entertaining and political.

Utopian plays are crafted from drama's distinctive method of using bodily performance and dialogue. In place of offering descriptions of a utopian world or complicated rhetorical framing (both of which utopian prose narratives deploy as an attempt to make the utopia seem plausible), utopian plays work *with* the limitations and comic implications of the human body in performance and express knowingness of the difficulty of signifying an alternative world from the aesthetic tools of this one. The utopian worlds are either proximate to the non-utopian contexts of the playwright (Aristophanes and Cavendish), contain no serious attempt to signify their other worldliness (Bernard Shaw and Davidson), emphasize the ordinariness of life in utopia (Brenton), or are glimpsed in intersubjective encounters structured through the dialogics of conversation (MacDonald, Davidson, and Adebayo). It is striking that a central tenet of drama – actors on stage engaged in dialogue – forms the primary means for articulating utopia in contemporary plays. Borrowing from postdramatic theatre, these recent plays exploit the conventions of drama that most lend themselves to crafting a dramatic encounter with utopia. Attempts to show a utopian society are replaced with a form of dialogics that refigure subjectivity and connectedness as part of a collaborative effort to prize the present open for utopian futures. Utopia is interpellated differently in these conversations. No longer separately apart spatially or temporally, utopia becomes multiply positioned – located both within the here and now of the present (which it critiques and resists) and as part of a radically different future.

That utopian drama is conscious of its own limitations likens it to the critical utopia, as developed by Tom Moylan. Comedic forms, self-referentiality, provisionality, mixed genres, the foregrounding of character and action at the expense of description and setting are common to both utopian drama and the critical utopia. Yet, Moylan is rightly wary of misapplying the label of the critical utopia – a type of literary utopia characterized by formal and thematic experimentation but equally grounded in 1960s feminist and socialist radicalism. He warns that 'one-dimensional applications could (as in the "cleansing" of the radical politics and aesthetics of Bertolt Brecht [...]) simply aestheticize the critical utopia as a purely formal strategy and therefore deny or suppress the specific political motivation and intention of critical utopianism'.[4] Applying the term critical utopia to utopian plays would fail to recognize the separate generic contexts of prose narrative and drama. While experimental disruptions to realism and radical politics are co-performed in the prose narrative critical utopias of the 1970s, the generic trajectory of utopian drama – within comic forms – has meant the dramatic and theatrical structures of utopian plays have always included some of the formal features of the critical utopia, these comfortably accommodated within the mainstream generic expectations of comic drama.

How then to offer a concluding pithy definition of utopian drama when the politics and style of this genre of plays across such a considerable expanse of time are so diverse? Utopian drama's comic qualities involve a distinctive coarticulation of sensuality, fantasy, human contrivance, and scientific rationalism – actions and affects usually present in separate forms. Hesiod's *Theogony* positions Eros as pre-existing the other gods, a location that privileges passion, libidinal desires, and erotic energies as foundational. Explicit mention is made of this in one of the parabases in Aristophanes' *The Birds*: 'the universe contained no gods, till Eros mingled all'.[5] Libidinal vitality constitutes a key economy across the genre of utopian drama, including in recent plays. The final work discussed in this book – Adebayo's *STARS* – stages an old woman's search for her orgasm. Notably, the bodily as a key site of experiential encounter with the utopian is conspicuously absent in the city states of Plato, More, Bacon, Bellamy, and Wells. Bodily appetites – registered in varying degrees as excessive, threatening, or embarrassing – are contained and disciplined in city utopias. But in drama – a form communicated through bodies (voice, breath, smell, touch) – fleshly kinetics power the performance. Sensory pleasures, frivolity and foolishness, and vertiginous affects are not constrained, but rather celebrated in utopian drama.

I hope this book has shown the variety of fascinating ways in which utopian plays have exploited their comic forms, multiple sign systems, and affective potential to draw on the utopian imagination in contemplation of alternative worlds and ways of living. In the process of analysing this work, I

---

[4] Tom Moylan, *Demand the Impossible: Science Fiction and the Utopian Imagination*, ed. Raffaella Baccolini (Oxford: Peter Lang, 2014), xxiv.
[5] Aristophanes, *The Birds*, in trans. David Barrett and Alan H. Sommerstein, *The Birds and Other Plays*, London: Penguin, 190.

have tried to establish generic and thematic continuities and discontinuities across the diversity of the drama, and offer an analysis of the political interventions of these plays in the context of their own historical moments. The book has also considered the implications of privileging prose narrative utopias within the field of Utopian Studies, which has additionally involved the neglect of the influence of drama on utopian fiction as well as an underappreciation of the deep roots of utopian drama and its specific contributions to utopian aesthetics and utopian ideas more generally. I hope *Utopian Drama* enables new scholarship that can build on its findings, including expanding the geographical parameters – particularly to include studies that examine utopian plays from outside Europe and North America – and developing theories and concepts that further facilitate understanding of the specificities of utopian plays.

Drama has a particular set of qualities that enable it to craft encounters with utopian alternatives in distinctive ways. The resources helpful for a utopian act of imagination are, as Rob Hopkins observes, 'multisensory, encompassing smell, touch, sound, emotion and taste'.[6] Drama is both an embodied and dialogic experience, an experience befitting a performance of critical engagement with the prevailing system, as well as an opportunity to participate in a collective act of social dreaming. Ezra Brain, a trans theatre practitioner from New York writes, '[t]he world is broken – any child can tell you that. So, instead of simply churning out play after play that tells our audiences the world is broken, we should try to paint an image of the future. What could a future world look like? How do we get there? We should begin to think about creating visions of liberation, not just constant performances of oppression'.[7] They are right. We need utopian drama to help us do this.

---

[6] Rob Hopkins, *From What Is to What If: Unleashing the Power of Imagination to Create the Future We Want* (London: Chelsea Green Publishing, 2019), 11.
[7] Ezra Brain, 'Towards a Marxist Theatre', *HowlRound Theatre Commons*, 15 April 2021, http://howlround.com/towards-marxist-theatre

Bibliography

Adebayo, Mojisola. *STARS*. In *Mojisola Adebayo: Plays Two*, introduced by Lynette Goddard, 187–246. London: Oberon Books, 2019.
Adebayo, Mojisola. Interview. In *Theatre in Times of Crisis: 20 Scenes for the Stage in Troubled Times*, edited by Dom O'Hanlon, 1–5. London: Bloomsbury, 2020.
Adiseshiah, Siân. 'Utopian Space in Caryl Churchill's History Plays: *Light Shining in Buckinghamshire* and *Vinegar Tom*'. *Utopian Studies* 16.1 (Spring 2005): 3–26.
Adiseshiah, Siân. *Churchill's Socialism: Political Resistance in the Plays of Caryl Churchill*. Newcastle: Cambridge Scholars Publishing, 2009.
Adiseshiah, Siân. '"We Said We Wouldn't Look Back": Utopia and the Backward Glance in Dorothy Reynolds and Julian Slade's *Salad Days*'. *Studies in Musical Theatre* 5.2 (2011): 149–61.
Adiseshiah, Siân. '"I just die for some authority!" Barriers to Utopia in Howard Brenton's *Greenland*'. *Comparative Drama* 46.1 (Spring 2012): 41–55.
Adiseshiah, Siân. '"The Times" of Caryl Churchill'. In *The Theatre of Caryl Churchill*, edited by R. Darren Gobert, 214–24. London: Bloomsbury, 2014.
Adiseshiah, Siân. 'Spectatorship and the New (Critical) Sincerity: The Case of Forced Entertainment's *Tomorrow's Parties*'. *Contemporary Drama in English* 4.1 (May 2016): 180–95.
Adiseshiah, Siân. 'The Utopian Potential of Aging and Longevity in Bernard Shaw's *Back to Methuselah*'. *Age, Culture, Humanities: An Interdisciplinary Journal* 4 (May 2019): https://ageculturehumanities.org/WP/the-utopian-potential-of-ageing-and-longevity-in-bernard-shaws-back-to-methuselah-1921/
Adorno, Theodor W. 'The Essay as Form'. *New German Critique* 32 (Spring–Summer, 1984): 151–71.
Agamben, Georgio. 'What is the Contemporary?'. In *What is an Apparatus? And Other Essays*, translated by David Kishik and Stefan Pedatella, 39–54. Redwood City, CA: Stanford University Press, 2009.
Alderman, Naomi. *The Power*. New York: Viking, 2016.
Ambler, Wayne. 'Tyranny in Aristophanes's *Birds*'. *The Review of Politics* 74 (2012): 185–206.
Ambler, Wayne. 'On the Anabasis of Trygaeus: An Introduction to Aristophanes' *Peace*'. In *The Political Theory of Aristophanes: Explorations in Poetic Wisdom*, edited by Jeremy J. Mhire and Bryan-Paul Frost, 137–159. New York: State University of New York Press, 2014.
Anderson, Tammy L., and Philip R. Kavanaugh. 'A "Rave" Review: Conceptual Interests and Analytical Shifts in Research on Rave Culture'. *Sociology Compass* 1/2 (2007): 499–519.

Appelbaum, Robert. *Literature and Utopian Politics in Seventeenth-century England*. Cambridge: Cambridge University Press, 2002.

Aristophanes, *The Birds of Aristophanes*. Translated by H. R. Cary. London: Taylor and Hessey, 1824.

Aristophanes, *The Birds of Aristophanes*. Translated by B. H. Kennedy. London: Macmillan and Co., 1874.

Aristophanes, *The Birds*. In *The Birds and Other Plays*. Translated by David Barrett and Alan H. Sommerstein, 153–214. London: Penguin, 2003.

Aristophanes, *The Assemblywomen*. In *The Birds and Other Plays*. Translated by David Barrett and Alan H. Sommerstein, 221–64. London: Penguin, 2003.

Arnheim, Rudolf. 'On the Late Style of Life and Art'. *Michigan Quarterly Review* 17.2 (1978): 149–56.

Arrowsmith, William. 'Aristophanes' *Birds*: The Fantasy Politics of Eros'. *Arion: A Journal of Humanities and the Classics* 1.1 (1973): 119–67.

Asimov, Isaac. *I, Robot*. New York: Gnome Press, 1950.

Astell, Mary. *A Serious Proposal to the Ladies*. 1684. Edited by Sharon L. Jansen. Steilacoom, WA: Saltar's Point Press, 2014.

Augé, Marc. *The Future*, translated by John Howe. London: Verso, 2015.

Baccolini, Raffaella. '"Hope isn't stupid": The Appropriation of Dystopia', *mediAzioni* 27 (2020): http://www.mediazioni.sitlec.unibo.it/index.php/no-27-2020/120-dossier-the-domestication-of-utopia/402-hope-isnt-stupid-the-appropriation-of-dystopia.html

Bacon, Francis. *New Atlantis*. 1627. Edited by G. C. Moore-Smith. Cambridge: Cambridge University Press, 2014.

Bacon, Francis. *The New Atlantis*. Seattle, WA: Amazon Publishing, 2017.

Baggesen, Søren. 'Utopian and Dystopian Pessimism: Le Guin's *The Word for World is Forest* and Tiptree's "We Who Stole the Dream"'. *Science Fiction Studies* 14 (1987): 34–43.

Baker-Putt, Alyce R. 'Defining the Female Self Through Female Communities: Margaret Cavendish's *The Female Academy, The Convent of Pleasure*, and *Bell in Campo*'. *Shakespeare and Renaissance Association of West Virginia* 29 (2006): 37–46.

Bakhtin, M. M. *Rabelais and His World*. 1965. Translated by Hélène Iswolsky. Cambridge, MA: MIT Press, 1968.

Bakhtin, Mikhail. 'Epic and Novel: Toward a Methodology for the Study of the Novel'. In *Modern Genre Theory*, edited by David Duff, 68–81. Essex: Longman, 2000.

Baldwin, James. 'Of the Sorrow Songs: The Cross of Redemption'. 1979. In *The Picador Book of Blues and Jazz*, edited by James Campbell, 324–31. London: Picador, 1996.

Banks, Iain M. *Excession*. London: Orbit, 1996.

Barrett, David. 'Introductory Note to *The Birds*'. In Aristophanes. *The Birds and Other Plays*, translated by David Barrett and Alan H. Sommerstein, 149–51. London: Penguin, 2003.

Barrett, David. 'Introductory Note to *The Assemblywomen*'. In Aristophanes. *The Birds and Other Plays*, translated by David Barrett and Alan H. Sommerstein, 217–20. London: Penguin, 2003.

Bartkowski, Frances. *Feminist Utopias*. Lincoln, NE and London: University of Nebraska Press, 1989.

Bastin-Hammou, Malika. 'Aristophanes' *Peace* on the Twentieth-Century French Stage: From Political Statement to Artistic Failure'. In *Aristophanes in Performance 421BC-AD2007: Peace, Birds and Frogs*, edited by Edith Hall and Amanda Wrigley, 247–54. London: MHRA and Maney Publishing, 2007.

Behn, Aphra, 'The Golden Age'. 1684. In *The Works of Aphra Behn*, edited by Montague Summers, 6 vols, 138–44. New York: Phaeton, 1967.

Bellamy, Edward. *Looking Backward 2000–1887*. 1888. Oxford: Oxford University Press, 2007.

Biles, Zachary P. 'The Rivals of Aristophanes and Menander'. In *The Cambridge Companion to Greek Comedy*, edited by Martin Revermann, 43–59. Cambridge: Cambridge University Press, 2014.

Bishop, G. W. *Barry Jackson and the London Theatre*. London: Arthur Barker, 1933.

Blaikie, Andrew. *Ageing and Popular Culture*. Cambridge: Cambridge University Press, 1999.

Blasing, Mutlu Konuk. *Lyric Poetry: The Pain and Pleasure of Words*. Princeton, NJ: Princeton University Press, 2006.

Boal, Augusto. *Theatre of the Oppressed*. 1974. London: Pluto, 2019.

Bogart, Anne. 'Utopia Forum'. *Theater* 26.1–2 (1995): 182–9.

Bonin, Erin Lang. 'Margaret Cavendish's Dramatic Utopias and the Politics of Gender'. *Studies in English Literature 1500–1900* 40.2 (2000): 339–54.

Bonnette, Amy L. 'Aristophanes' Feminine Comedies and Socratic Political Science'. In *The Political Theory of Aristophanes*, edited by Jeremy J. Mhire and Bryan-Paul Frost, 303–27. New York: State University of New York Press, 2014.

Boon, Richard. 'Retreating to the Future: Brenton in the Eighties'. *Modern Drama* 33.1 (1990): 30–41.

Boon, Richard. *Brenton: The Playwright*. London: Methuen Drama, 1991.

Boyle, Deborah. 'Margaret Cavendish on Gender, Nature, and Freedom'. *Hypatia* 28.3 (Summer 2013): 516–32.

Branham, R. Bracht. Ed. *Bakhtin and the Classics*. Evanston, IL: Northwestern University Press, 2002.

Brant, Clare and Diane Purkiss. 'Introduction: Minding the Story'. In *Women, Texts and Histories 1575–1760*, ed. Clare Brant and Diane Purkiss, 8. London and New York: Routledge, 1992.

Brenton, Howard. *Sore Throats*. 1979. In *Howard Brenton Plays 1*, 337–90. London: Methuen, 1986.

Brenton, Howard. 'The Red Theatre under the Bed'. *New Theatre Quarterly* 3 (1987): 195–206.

Brenton, Howard. *Bloody Poetry*. London: Methuen Drama, 1988.

Brenton, Howard. *Greenland*. London: Methuen Drama, 1988.
Brenton, Howard. 'On Writing the Utopian Plays'. In *Greenland*, 3. London: Methuen, 1988.
Brenton, Howard. 'Brenton's Erehwon'. Interview with Robert Gore-Langton. *Plays and Players* (April 1988): 10–11.
Brenton, Howard. *Hot Irons: Diaries, Essays, Journalism*. London: Nick Hern, 1995.
Brenton, Howard. 'Interview'. *Making Plays: Interviews with Contemporary British Dramatists and Directors*, edited by Duncan Wu. Basingstoke: Palgrave, 2000.
Brenton, Howard. 'Preface'. *Howard Brenton Plays 2*, viii–xvi. London: Methuen, 2013.
Brenton, Howard. Skype interview with author, 15 June 2020.
Brustein, Robert. *The Theatre of Revolt: Studies in Modern Drama from Ibsen to Genet*. Chicago, IL: Ivan R. Dee, 1991.
Burdekin, Katharine. *Swastika Night*. 1937. New York: The Feminist Press, 1985.
Burke, Kenneth. *A Grammar of Motives and A Rhetoric of Motives*. Cleveland, OH: Meridian Books/World, 1962.
Burns, Lori. 'The Concept Album as Visual-Sonic-Textual Spectacle: The Transmedial Storyworld of Coldplay's Mylo Xyloto'. *IASPM Journal* 6: 2 (2016): 91–116.
Burwell, Jennifer. *Notes on Nowhere: Feminism, Utopian Logic, and Social Transformation*. London: University of Minnesota Press, 1997.
Busby, Selina. *Applied Theatre: A Pedagogy of Utopia*. London: Bloomsbury, 2001.
Campanella, Tommaso. *City of the Sun*. 1602. Translated by Thomas W. Halliday. Newton Stewart: Anodos Books, 2017.
Carey, John. Ed. *The Faber Book of Utopias*. London: Faber, 1999.
Cary, Mary. *A New and More exact Mappe of New Jerusalems Glory when Jesus Christ and his Saints with him shall Reign on Earth a Thousand Years, and Possess all Kingdoms*. London, 1651.
Cavendish, Margaret. 'A True Relation of my Birth, Breeding, and Life'. In *Natures Pictures Drawn by Fancies Pencil to the Life. Written by the thrice Noble, Illustrious, and Excellent Princess, the Lady Marchioness of Newcastle*, 368–91. London, 1656.
Cavendish, Margaret. 'To the Readers'. Front Matter to *Playes*. 1662. In *The Convent of Pleasure and Other Plays*, edited by Anne Shaver, 255–56. Baltimore and London: The Johns Hopkins University Press, 1999.
Cavendish, Margaret. *The Female Academy*. 1662. Edited by Sharon L. Jansen, 107–54. Steilacoom, WA: Saltar's Point Press, 2017.
Cavendish, Margaret. *Bell in Campo*. 1662. In *The Convent of Pleasure and Other Plays*, edited by Anne Shaver, 107–69. London: The Johns Hopkins University Press.
Cavendish, Margaret. *The Blazing World and Other Writings*. 1666. Edited by Kate Lilley. London: Penguin, 1994.
Cavendish, Margaret. *The Convent of Pleasure*. 1668. Edited by Sharon L. Jansen. Steilacoom, WA: Saltar's Point Press, 2016.

Cavendish, Margaret. 'Author's Epistle Preceding *Plays, Never Before Printed*, 1668'. *The Convent of Pleasure and Other plays*, edited by Anne Shaver, 273. Baltimore, MD: The Johns Hopkins University Press, 1999.

Ceccarelli, Paola. 'Life Among the Savages and Escape from the City'. In *The Rivals of Aristophanes: Studies in Athenian Old Comedy*, edited by David Harvey and John Wilkins, 453–71. Duckworth: The Classical Press of Wales, 2000.

Cervantes, Miguel de. *Galatea*. 1585. Newark, NJ: Palala Press, 2015.

Chalmers, Hero. 'Dismantling the Myth of "Mad Madge": The Cultural Context of Margaret Cavendish's Authorial Self-Presentation'. *Women's Writing* 4.3 (1997): 323–40.

Chalmers, Hero. 'The Politics of Feminine Retreat in Margaret Cavendish's *The Female Academy* and *The Convent of Pleasure*'. *Women's Writing* 6.1 (1999): 81–94.

Chappelow, Alan. *Shaw – 'The Chucker-Out': A Biographical Exposition and Critique*. New York: AMS Press, 1971.

Chase, Karen. *The Victorians and Old Age*. Oxford: Oxford University Press, 2009.

Claeys, Gregory. Ed. *The Cambridge Companion to Utopian Literature*. Cambridge: Cambridge University Press, 2010.

Claeys, Gregory. 'The Origins of Dystopia: Wells, Huxley and Orwell'. In *The Cambridge Companion to Utopian Literature*, edited by Gregory Claeys, 107–31. Cambridge: Cambridge University Press, 2010.

Clarke, Arthur C. *2001 A Space Odyssey*. London: Hutchinson, 1968.

Clifton, Glenn. 'An Imperfect Butlerite: Aging and Embodiment in *Back to Methuselah*'. *Shaw: The Annual of Bernard Shaw Studies* 34 (2014): 108–26.

Cole, Thomas R. 'Introduction'. In *What Does it Mean to Grow Old? Reflections from the Humanities*, edited by Thomas R. Cole and Sally A. Gadow, 3–7. Durham, NC: Duke University Press, 1986.

Cole, Thomas R. 'The "Enlightened" View of Aging: Victorian Morality in a New Key'. In *What Does it Mean to Grow Old? Reflections from the Humanities*, edited by Thomas R. Cole and Sally A. Gadow, 117–30. Durham, NC: Duke University Press, 1986.

Conrad, Christoph. 'Old Age in the Modern and Postmodern Western World'. In *Handbook of the Humanities and Aging*, edited by Thomas R. Cole, David D. Van Tassel and Robert Kastenbaum, 62–95. New York: Springer Publishing Company, 1992.

Cooper, Sam. '"Enemies of Utopia for the Sake of its Realisation": Futurism, Surrealism, Situationism and the Problem of Utopia'. In *Utopia: The Avant-Garde, Modernism and (Im)possible Life*, edited by David Ayers, Benedikt Hjartarson, Tomi Huttunem, and Harri Velvo, 17–32. Berlin: De Gruyter, 2015.

Corbett, John. 'Anthony Braxton's Bildungsmusik: Thoughts on Composition 171'. In *Mixtery: A Festschrift for Antony Braxton*, edited by Graham Lock, 185–6. Exeter: Stride, 1995.

Crates, *Wild Beasts*. Fragment 16. In *Fragments of Old Comedy, Volume 1, Alcaeus to Diocles*, edited and translated by Ian C. Storey, 341–54. Cambridge, MA: Harvard University Press, 2011.

Crawford, Julie. 'Convents and Pleasures: Margaret Cavendish and the Drama of Property'. *Renaissance Drama* 32 (2003): 177–23.

Cressy, David. 'Early Modern Space Travel and the English Man in the Moon'. *American Historical Review* 111.4 (October 2006): 961–82.

Davidson, Cesi. 'Voice Lessons'. In *Articulation: Short Plays to Nourish the Mind & Soul*, 103–17. Seattle, WA: Aqueduct Press, 2019.

Davidson, Cesi. Introduction. *Articulation: Short Plays to Nourish the Mind & Soul*, 1–2. Seattle, WA: Aqueduct Press, 2019.

Davis, Laurence. Ed. 'The Domestication of Utopia'. Special Issue. *Mediazoni* 27 (2020): http://www.mediazioni.sitlec.unibo.it/index.php/no-27-2020/120-dossier-the-domestication-of-utopia/401-introduction-special-issue-on-the-domestication-of-utopia.html

Day, Jessica. 'Sexual Pleasure and Utopian Desire in Twenty-First Century Fictional Forms and Cultural Practice'. PhD Thesis. University of Lincoln, 2019.

de Ste Croix, G. E. M. *The Origins of the Peloponnesian War*. Ithaca, NY: Cornell University Press, 1972.

Debord, Guy. *The Society of the Spectacle*. 1969. Translated by Ken Knabb. London: Rebel Press, 1983.

Di Simoni, Laura. 'Staging the Dark Times: Contemporary Dystopian Theatre in the UK 2000–2019'. PhD Thesis. University of Nottingham, 2021.

Dick, Philip K. *Do Androids Dream of Electric Sheep?* New York: Doubleday, 1968.

D'Monté, Rebecca. 'Mirroring Female Power: Separatist Spaces in the Plays of Margaret Cavendish, Duchess of Newcastle'. In *Female Communities, 1600–1800: Literary Visions and Cultural Realities*, edited by Rebecca D'Monté and Nicole Pohl, 93–110. Basingstoke: Macmillan, 2001.

Dobrov, Gregory W. 'Introduction'. In *The City as Comedy: Society and Representation in Athenian Drama*, edited by Gregory W. Dobrov, ix–xix. Chapel Hill, NC: University of North Carolina Press, 1997.

Dobrov, Gregory W. 'Language, Fiction, and Utopia'. In *The City as Comedy: Society and Representation in Athenian Drama*, edited by Gregory W. Dobrov, 95–132. Chapel Hill, NC: University of North Carolina Press, 1997.

Dobrov, Gregory W. Ed. *The City as Comedy: Society and Representation in Athenian Drama*. Chapel Hill, NC: University of North Carolina Press, 1997.

Dolan, Jill. *Utopia in Performance: Finding Hope at the Theater*. Ann Arbor, MI: University of Michigan Press, 2005.

Donawerth, Jane L. and Carol A. Kolmerten. 'Introduction'. In *Utopian and Science Fiction by Women: Worlds of Difference*, edited by Jane L. Donawerth and Carol A. Kolmerten, 1–14. Liverpool: Liverpool University Press, 1994.

Donoghue, Emma. *Passions Between Women: British Lesbian Culture 1668–1801*. New York: Harper, 1995.

Dutton, Danielle. *Margaret the First*. New York: Catapult, 2016.
Ebbott, Mary. 'Tell Me How it Hurts: An Intersection of Poetry and Pain in the *Iliad*'. *New England Review* 37.2 (2016): 31–47.
Edelman, Lee. *No Future: Queer Theory and the Death Drive*. Durham, NC: Duke University Press, 2004.
Edgar, David. *The Second Time as Farce*. London: Lawrence and Wishart, 1988.
Edmondson, Ricca. *Ageing, Insight and Wisdom: Meaning and Practice Across the Lifecourse*. Bristol: Policy Press, 2015.
Edwards, Anthony. 'Historicizing the Popular Grotesque: Bakhtin's *Rabelais and His World* and Attic Old Comedy'. In *Bakhtin and the Classics*, edited by R. Bracht Branham, 27–55. Evanston, IL: Northwestern University Press, 2002.
Edwards, Caroline. *Utopia and the Contemporary British Novel*. Cambridge: Cambridge University Press, 2019.
Ehn, Erik. 'Translations and Fragments From the New Panic Compound in Damascus, Kansas'. *Theater* 26.1–2 (1995): 126–38.
Elliott, Robert C. *The Shape of Utopia: Studies in a Literary Genre*. Chicago and London: University of Chicago Press, 1970.
Eshun, Kodwo. *More Brilliant than the Sun: Adventures in Sonic Fiction*. London: Quartet Books, 1998.
Etchells, Tim. 'You Did Not Know Who You Were'. In Claire MacDonald, 3–6. *Utopia: Three Plays for a Postdramatic Theatre*. Bristol: Intellect, 2015.
Evans Arthur B. Ed. *Vintage Visions: Essays on Early Science Fictions*. Middletown, CT: Wesleyan University Press, 2014.
Evans, Rhiannon. *Utopia Antiqua: Readings of the Golden Age and the Decline at Rome*. London: Routledge, 2008.
Evans, T. F. 'The Later Shaw'. In *The Cambridge Companion to George Bernard Shaw*, edited by Christopher Innes, 240–258. Cambridge: Cambridge University Press, 1998.
Eynat-Confino, Irene. *On the Uses of the Fantastic in Modern Theatre: Cocteau, Oedipus, and the Monster*. New York: Palgrave Macmillan, 2008.
Farley-Hills, David. 'Jonson and the Neo-classical Rules in *Sejanus* and *Volpone*'. *Review of English Studies* 46 (1995): 53–73.
Faver, Cheryl. 'Refracted, Distracted, and Hopeful'. *Theater* 26.1–2 (1995): 139–55.
Ferguson, John. *Utopias of the Classical World*. London: Thames and Hudson, 1975.
Foley, Helene P. 'The "Female Intruder" Reconsidered: Women in Aristophanes' *Lysistrata* and *Ecclesiazusae*'. *Classical Philology* 77.1 (1982): 1–21.
Forrest, Katherine V. *Daughters of an Emerald Dusk*. Tallahassee, FL: Bella Books, 2005.
Foucault, Michel. 'Of Other Spaces.' *Diacritics* 16 (Spring 1986): 22–27.
Fourier, Charles. *The Theory of the Four Movements*, edited by Gareth Stedman Jones and Ian Patterson. Cambridge: Cambridge University Press, 1996.

Franko, Carol. 'Dialogic Narration and Ambivalent Utopian Hope in Lessing's *Shikasta* and Le Guin's *Always Coming Home*'. *Journal of the Fantastic in the Arts* 2.3 (7) (1990): 23–33.

Freytag, Gustav. *Freytag's Technique of the Drama: An Exposition of Dramatic Composition and Art*. Los Angeles, CA: Hardpress Publishing, 2012.

Friedan, Betty. *The Fountain of Age*. London: Jonathan Cape, 1993.

Frow, John. *Genre*. London: Routledge, 2015.

Frye, Northrop. *Anatomy of Criticism: Four Essays*. Princeton, NJ: Princeton University Press, 1959.

Gadow, Sally A. 'Frailty and Strength: The Dialectic of Aging'. In *What Does it Mean to Grow Old? Reflections from the Humanities*, edited by Thomas R. Cole and Sally A. Gadow, 237–43. Durham, NC: Duke University Press, 1986.

Gahan, Peter. 'The Achievement of Shaw's Later Plays, 1920–1939'. *Shaw: The Annual of Bernard Shaw Studies* 23 (2003): 27–35.

Gearhart, Sally Miller. *The Wanderground*. Watertown, MA: Persephone Press, 1978.

Geduld, H. M. '*Back to Methuselah* and The Birmingham Repertory Company'. *Modern Drama* 2.2 (1959): 115–29.

G'Fellers, Jeanne. *No Sister of Mine*. Tallahassee, FL: Bella Books, 2005.

Gibson, William. *Neuromancer*. New York: Ace, 1985.

Giesecke, Annette Lucia. 'Homer's Eutopolis: Epic Journeys and the Search for an Ideal Society'. *Utopian Studies* 14.2 (2003): 23–40.

Gilman, Charlotte Perkins. *Herland*. 1915. In *Herland and The Yellow Wallpaper*, introduced by Lindy West, London: Vintage Classics, 2015.

Goddard, Lynette. 'Introduction'. In *Mojisola Adebayo: Plays Two*, 13–18. London: Oberon Books, 2019.

Gore-Langton, Robert. 'Brenton's Erehwon'. *Plays & Players* (April 1988): 10–11.

Goulding, Christina and Avi Shankar. 'Age is Just a Number: Rave Culture and the Cognitively Young "Thirty Something"'. *European Journal of Marketing* 38 (2004): 641–58.

Gray, John. *Black Mass: Apocalypse, Religion and the Death of Utopia*. London: Allen Lane, 2007.

Gray, Susan and Christos Callow Jr. 'Past and Future of Science Fiction Theatre'. *Foundation* 117 (Spring 2014): 60–9.

Gregoriou, Zelia. 'Pedagogy and Passages: The Performativity of Margaret Cavendish's Utopian Fiction'. *Journal of Philosophy of Education* 47.3 (2013): 457–75.

Gutmann, David. *Reclaimed Powers*. New York: Basic Books, 1987.

Hale, Piers J. 'Of Mice and Men: Evolution and the Socialist Utopia. William Morris, H. G. Wells, and George Bernard Shaw'. *Journal of the History of Biology* 43.1 (2010): 17–66.

Hall, Edith. 'Comedy and Athenian Festival Culture'. In *The Cambridge Companion to Greek Comedy*, edited by Martin Revermann, 306–21. Cambridge: Cambridge University Press, 2014.

Hall, Sarah. *The Carhullan Army*. London: Faber, 2007.

Halliwell, Stephen. 'Laughter'. In *The Cambridge Companion to Greek Comedy*, edited by Martin Revermann, 189–205. Cambridge: Cambridge University Press, 2014.

Haraway, Donna. *A Cyborg Manifesto: Science, Technology, and Socialist-Feminism in the Late Twentieth Century*. Minneapolis, MN: University of Minnesota Press, 2016.

Hartung, Heike. 'Longevity Narratives: Darwinism and Beyond'. *Journal of Aging Studies* 47 (2018): 84–7.

Harvey, David. *Spaces of Hope*. Edinburgh: Edinburgh University Press, 2000.

Harvey, David and John Wilkins. *The Rivals of Aristophanes: Studies in Athenian Old Comedy*. Duckworth: The Classical Press of Wales, 2000.

Heddon, Deirdre. 'Letter to Claire MacDonald 30 September 2013'. In *Utopia: Three Plays for a Postdramatic Theatre*, Claire MacDonald, 47–9. Bristol: Intellect, 2015.

Henderson, Jeffrey. *Aristophanes: Essays in Interpretation*. Cambridge: Cambridge University Press, 1980.

Henderson, Jeffrey. '*Lysistrate*: The Play and its Themes'. In *Aristophanes: Essays in Interpretation*, edited by Jeffrey Henderson, 153–218. Cambridge: Cambridge University Press, 1980.

Henderson, Jeffrey. 'Mass versus Elite and the Comic Heroism of Peisetairos'. In *The City as Comedy: Society and Representation in Athenian Drama*, edited by Gregory W. Dobrov, 135–48. London: University of North Carolina Press, 1997.

Hesiod, *Works and Days*. In *Theogony* and *Works and Days*, translated by M. L. West, 35–61. Oxford: Oxford University Press, 1988.

Hexter, J. H. *More's Utopia: The Biography of an Idea*. Princeton, NJ: Princeton University Press, 1952.

Hill, Christopher. *The World Turned Upside Down: Radical Ideas During the English Revolution*. 1972. London: Penguin, 1991.

Hobby, Elaine. *Virtue of Necessity: English Women's Writing 1649–88*. London: Virago, 1988.

Holmesland, Oddvar. *Utopian Negotiation: Aphra Behn and Margaret Cavendish*. New York: Syracuse University Press, 2003.

Holroyd, Michael. *Bernard Shaw*. London: Vintage, 1998.

Homer, *The Odyssey*. Translated by D. C. H. Rieu. London: Penguin, 2003.

Hopkins, Rob. *From What Is to What If: Unleashing the Power of Imagination to Create the Future We Want*. London: Chelsea Green Publishing, 2019.

Horwood, Joel. *This Changes Everything*. London: Nick Hern, 2015.

Hubbard, Thomas K. 'Utopianism and the Sophistic City in Aristophanes'. In *The City as Comedy: Society and Representation in Athenian Drama*, edited by Gregory W. Dobrov, 23–50. London: University of North Carolina Press, 1997.

Hummert, Paul A. *Bernard Shaw's Marxian Romance*. Lincoln, NE: University of Nebraska Press, 1973.

Hurwit, Jeffrey M. *The Art and Culture of Early Greece 1100–480 B.C.* Ithaca, NY: Cornell University Press, 1985.

Hustvedt, Siri. *The Blazing World*. New York: Simon & Schuster, 2014.
Hutson, Scott. 'The Rave: Spiritual Healing in Modern Western Subcultures'. *Anthropological Quarterly* 73.1 (2000): 35–49.
Hutton, Sarah. 'Science and Satire: The Lucianic Voice of Margaret Cavendish's *Description of a New World Called the Blazing World*'. In *Authorial Conquests: Essays on Genre in the Writings of Margaret Cavendish*, edited by Line Cottegnies and Nancy Weitz, 161–78. London: Associated University Presses, 2003.
Huxley, Aldous. *Brave New World*. 1932. London: Vintage, 2007.
Innes, Christopher. 'Utopian Apocalypses: Shaw, War, and H. G. Wells'. *The Annual of Bernard Shaw Studies* 23 (2003): 37–46.
Jackson, Michael. 'Designed by Theorists: Aristotle on Utopia'. *Utopian Studies* 12.2 (2001): 1–12.
Jameson, Fredric. 'Longevity as Class Struggle'. In *Immortal Engines: Life Extension Immortality in Science Fiction and Fantasy*, edited by George Slusser, Gary Westfahl, and Eric S. Rabkin, 4–42. Athens, GA: University of Georgia Press, 1996.
Jameson, Fredric. 'The Politics of Utopia'. *New Left Review* 25 (2004): 35–54.
Jameson, Fredric. *Archaeologies of the Future: The Desire Called Utopia and Other Science Fictions*. London: Verso, 2005.
Jameson, Fredric. 'An American Utopia'. In *An American Utopia: Dual Power and the Universal Army*, edited by Slavoj Žižek, 1–96. London: Verso Books, 2016.
Jankowski, Theodora A. *Pure Resistance: Queer Virginity in Early Modern English Drama*. Philadelphia, PA: University of Pennsylvania Press, 2000.
Johns, Alessa. 'Mary Astell's "Excited Needles": Theorizing Feminist Utopia in Seventeenth-Century England'. *Utopian Studies* 7.1 (1996): 60–74.
Kellett, Katherine R. '*Performance, Performativity, and Identity in Margaret Cavendish's The Convent of Pleasure Studies*'. *SEL Studies in English Literature 1500–1900* 48.2 (Spring 2008): 419–42.
Kendall, Walter. *The Revolutionary Movement in Britain in 1900–21: The Origins of British Communism*. London: Weidenfeld and Nicolson, 1969.
Khanna, Lee Cullen. 'Utopian Exchanges: Negotiating Difference in Utopia'. In *Gender and Utopia in the Eighteenth Century: Essays in English and French Utopian Writing*, edited by Brenda Tooley and Nicole Pohl, 17–37. London: Routledge, 2007.
King, Kimball. 'Howard Brenton's Utopia Plays'. In *Howard Brenton: A Casebook*, edited by Ann Wilson, 117–25. New York and London: Garland, 1992.
Klaić, Dragan. *The Plot of the Future: Utopia and Dystopia in Modern Drama*. Ann Arbor, MI: University of Michigan Press, 1991.
Klaić, Dragan. 'Utopia Sustained'. *Theater*, 26.1–2 (1995): 60–9.
Knight, Diana. *Barthes and Utopia: Space, Travel, Writing*. Oxford: Clarendon Press, 1997.
Konstan, David. 'The Greek Polis and Its Negations: Versions of Utopia in Aristophanes' *Birds*'. In *The City as Comedy: Society and Representation in Athenian Drama*, edited by Gregory W. Dobrov, 3–22. Chapel Hill, NC: University of North Carolina Press, 1997.

Konstan, David. 'Defining the Genre'. In *The Cambridge Companion to Greek Comedy*, edited by Martin Revermann, 27–42. Cambridge: Cambridge University Press, 2014.
Korstevdt, Benjamin. *Listening for Utopia in Ernst Bloch's Musical Philosophy*. Cambridge: Cambridge University Press, 2010.
Kumar, Krishan. *Utopianism*. Milton Keynes: Open University Press, 1991.
Langner, Lawrence. *The Magic Curtain*. London: Harrap, 1952.
Lape, Susan and Alfonso Moreno. 'Comedy and the Social Historian'. In *The Cambridge Companion to Greek Comedy*, edited by Martin Revermann, 336–69. Cambridge: Cambridge University Press, 2014.
Laudien, Heidi. 'Aphra Behn: Pastoral Poet'. *Women's Writing* 12.1 (2005): 43–58.
Le Guin, Ursula. *The Left Hand of Darkness*. 1969. London: Penguin, 2016.
Le Guin, Ursula. *The Word for World is Forest*. 1972. New York: Berkley Books, 1976.
Le Guin, Ursula. *The Dispossessed: An Ambiguous Utopia*. New York: Harper and Row, 1974.
Lenker, Lagretta Tallent. 'Why? Versus Why Not?: Potentialities of Aging in Shaw's *Back to Methuselah*. In *Aging and Identity: A Humanities Perspective*, edited by Sarah Munson Deats and Lagretta Tallent Lenker, 47–60. Westport, CT and London: Praeger, 1999.
Levitas, Ruth. 'Preface to the Student Edition'. In *The Concept of Utopia*, ix–xv. Oxford: Peter Lang, 2011.
Lilley, Kate. 'Blazing Worlds: Seventeenth-Century Women's Utopian Writing'. In *Women, Texts and Histories 1575–1760*, edited by Clare Brant and Diane Purkiss, 102–33. London and New York: Routledge, 1992.
Lock, Graham. *Blutopia: Visions of the Future and Revisions of the Past in the Work of Sun Ra, Duke Ellington, and Anthony Braxton*. Durham, NC: Duke University Press 2000.
London, Jack. *The Iron Heel*. 1908. Orinda, CA: SeaWolf Press, 2017.
MacDonald, Claire. 'Written Worlds'. In *Utopia: Three Plays for a Postdramatic Theatre*, xiii–xxx. Bristol: Intellect, 2015.
MacDonald, Claire. *An Imitation of Life*. In *Utopia: Three Plays for a Postdramatic Theatre*, 7–23. Bristol: Intellect, 2015.
MacDonald, Claire. *Storm from Paradise*. In *Utopia: Three Plays for a Postdramatic Theatre*, 25–42. Bristol: Intellect, 2015.
MacDonald, Claire. *Correspondence*. In *Utopia: Three Plays for a Postdramatic Theatre*. 51–68. Bristol: Intellect, 2015.
Mander, Raymond and Joe Mitchenson. *Theatrical Companion to Shaw: A Pictorial Record of the First Performances of the Plays of George Bernard Shaw*. London: Rockliffe, 1954.
Manuel, Frank E. and Fritzie P. Manuel. *Utopian Thought in The Western World*. Oxford: Blackwell, 1979.
Marlow, Christopher. '"Worse in Singularity"?: Kant, Derrida, and Aesthetics in Margaret Cavendish's *The Blazing World*'. *Restoration* 41.1 (Spring 2017): 59–80.

Marshall, C. W. 'Dramatic Technique and Athenian Comedy'. In *The Cambridge Companion to Greek Comedy*, edited by Martin Revermann, 131–46. Cambridge: Cambridge University Press, 2014.

Marx, Karl. 'Critique of the Gotha Programme'. 1891. In *The Portable Karl Marx*, edited by Eugene Kamenka, 533–55. London: Penguin, 1983.

Mascetti, Yaakov A. 'A "World of Nothing, but Pure Wit": Margaret Cavendish and the Gendering of the Imaginary'. *Journal of Literature and the History of Ideas* 6.1 (January 2008): 1–31.

May, William F. 'The Virtues and Vices of the Elderly'. In *What Does it Mean to Grow Old? Reflections from the Humanities*, edited by Thomas R. Cole and Sally A. Gadow, 43–61. Durham, NC: Duke University Press, 1986.

McGrath, John. *The Bone Won't Break*. London: Methuen, 1990.

Meiggs, R. *The Athenian Empire*. Oxford: Oxford University Press, 1972.

Mellor, Anne K. 'On Feminist Utopias'. *Women's Studies* 9 (1982): 241–62.

Melucci, Alberto. *Challenging Codes: Collective Action in the Information Age*. Cambridge: Cambridge University Press, 1996.

Metagenes, *Thurio-Persians* Fragment 6. In *Fragments of Old Comedy II: Diopeithes to Pherecrates*, edited by Ian C. Storey, 359–61. Cambridge, MA: Harvard University Press, 2011.

Miéville, China. 'Afterword: Cognition as Ideology: A Dialectic of SF Theory'. In *Marxism and Science Fiction*, edited by Mark Bould and China Miéville, 231–48. London: Pluto Press, 2009.

Miller, Arthur. *The Creation of the World and Other Business*. New York: Viking, 1973.

Minois, George. *History of Old Age: From Antiquity to the Renaissance*. Oxford: Polity Press, 1989.

Moodie, Erin K. 'Aristophanes, The *Assemblywomen* and the Audience: The Politics of Rapport'. *The Classical Journal* 107.3 (2012): 257–81.

Moody, Harry R. 'The Meaning of Life and the Meaning of Old Age'. In *What Does it Mean to Grow Old? Reflections from the Humanities*, edited by Thomas R. Cole and Sally A. Gadow, 9–40. Durham, NC: Duke University Press, 1986.

Moody, Harry R. 'From Successful Aging to Conscious Aging'. In *Successful Aging Through The Life Span: Intergenerational Issues in Health*, edited by M. Wykle, P. Whitehouse, and D. Morris, 55–68. New York: Springer, 2004.

More, Thomas. *Utopia*. 1516. Translated and edited by Paul Turner. London: Penguin, 2003.

Morgan, Margery. *The Shavian Playground*. London: Methuen, 1972.

Morris, William. *News from Nowhere*. 1890. Edited by Clive Wilmer. London: Penguin, 1993.

Mosher, Joyce Devlin. 'Female Spectacle as Liberation in Margaret Cavendish's Plays'. *Early Modern Literary Studies* 11.1 (May 2007): 1–28.

Moulton, Carroll. *Aristophanic Poetry*. Göttingen: Vandenhoeck und Ruprecht, 1981.

Moylan, Tom. *Demand the Impossible: Science Fiction and the Utopian Imagination*, edited by Raffaella Baccolini. Rev. edn. Oxford: Peter Lang, 2014.
Muldoon, Roland. 'Interview'. In *Fringe First: Pioneers of Fringe Theatre on Record*, edited by Roland Reese, 68–76. London: Oberon Books, 1992.
Mumford, Lewis. *The Story of Utopias*. Gloucester, MA: Peter Smith, 1959.
Muñoz, José Esteban. *Cruising Utopia: The Then and There of Queer Futurity*. Rev. edn. New York and London: New York University Press, 2019.
Munk, Erika and Tom Sellar, 'Up Front: An Invitation to Utopia'. *Theater* 26.1–2 (1995): 5–6.
Munk, Erika. 'Exiled From Nowhere'. *Theater* 26.1–2 (1995): 101–12.
Nelson, Stephanie. 'Aristophanes and the Polis'. In *The Political Theory of Aristophanes: Explorations in Poetic Wisdom*, edited by Jeremy J. Mhire and Bryan-Paul Frost, 109–36. New York: State University of New York Press, 2014.
Nichols, Peter. 'The Comedy of the Just City: Aristophanes' *Assemblywomen* and Plato's *Republic*'. In *The Political Theory of Aristophanes: Explorations in Poetic Wisdom,* edited by Jeremy J. Mhire and Bryan-Paul Frost, 259–74. New York: State University of New York Press, 2014.
Olbricht, Erika Mae. 'Using Sex: Margaret Cavendish's "The Lady Contemplation" and the Authorial Fantasy of Class Permanence'. *Pacific Coast Philology* 38 (2003): 77–98.
Orwell, George. *1984*. 1949. London: Penguin, 2019.
Osborne, Deirdre. 'Skin Deep, a Self-Revealing Act: Monologue, Monodrama, and Mixedness in the Work of SuAndi and Mojisola Adebayo'. *Journal of Contemporary Drama in English* 2013–1(1): 54–69.
Out of the Woods Collective. *Hope Against Hope: Writers on Ecological Crisis*. New York: Commons Notions, 2020.
Paloma, Dolores. 'Margaret Cavendish: Defining the Female Self'. *Women's Studies* 7 (1980): 55–66.
Parrinder, Patrick. 'Utopia and Romance'. In *The Cambridge Companion to Utopian Literature*, edited by Gregory Claeys, 154–73. Cambridge: Cambridge University Press, 2010.
Pasupathi, Vimala C. 'New Model Armies: Re-contextualizing The Camp in Margaret Cavendish's *Bell in Campo*'. *ELH* 78.3 (Fall 2011): 657–85.
Patrick, J. Max. 'Introduction'. In 'Utopias and Dystopias, 1500–1750'. Section IX compiled by R. W. Gibson, 293–300. *St. Thomas More: A Preliminary Bibliography of His Works and of Moreana to the Year 1750*, compiled by R. W. Gibson and J. Max Patrick. New Haven, CT: Yale University Press, 1961.
Payne, Linda R. 'Dramatic Dreamscape: Women's Dreams and Utopian Vision in the Works of Margaret Cavendish, Duchess of Newcastle'. In *Curtain Calls: British and American Women and the Theater, 1660–1820*, edited by Mary Anne Schofield and Cecilia Macheski, 18–33. Athens, OH: Ohio University Press, 1991.

Peace, David. 'David Peace: Why I'm Letting Red Ladder Stage *The Damned United*'. Interview by Chris Wiegand, *Guardian* http://www.theguardian.com/stage/2014/oct/22/david-peace-red-ladder-stage-the-damned-united-brian-clough-theatre 22 October 2014.

Peacock, D. Keith. *Thatcher's Theatre*. London: Greenwood, 1999.

Pepys, Samuel. *The Diary of Samuel Pepys*. 1825. Edited by Robert Latham and William Matthews, 11 vols. London: G. Bell and Sons, 1976.

Perry, Ruth. 'Mary Astell's Response to the Enlightenment'. In *Women and the Enlightenment*, edited by Margaret Hunt, Margaret Jacob, Phyllis Mack, and Ruth Perry, 13–40. New York: Haworth Press, 1984.

Pharand, Michel W. *Bernard Shaw and the French*. Gainesville, FL: University Press of Florida, 2000.

Philmus, Robert M. 'The Language of Utopia'. *Studies in the Literary Imagination* 6 (1973): 61–78.

Piercy, Marge. *Woman on the Edge of Time*. New York: Alfred A. Knopf, 1976.

Plato. *The Republic*. Translated by Desmond Lee. London: Penguin, 1987.

Pohl, Nicole. 'Utopianism after More: The Renaissance and Enlightenment'. In *The Cambridge Companion to Utopian Literature*, edited by Gregory Claeys, 51–78. Cambridge: Cambridge University Press, 2010.

Popper, Karl. *The Open Society and Its Enemies*. Rev. edn. Princeton, NJ: Princeton University Press, 1950.

Popper, Karl. 'Utopia and Violence'. *World Affairs* 149.1 (Summer 1986): 3–9.

Pozzi, Dora C. 'The Pastoral Ideal in *The Birds* of Aristophanes'. *The Classical Journal* 81.2 (1986): 119–29.

Purkiss, Diane. *The English Civil War: A People's History*. London: Perennial, 2007.

Rabelais, François. *Gargantua and Pantagruel*. 1534. Translated and edited by M. E. Screech. London: Penguin, 2006.

Raber, Karen L. 'Warrior Women in the Plays of Cavendish and Killigrew'. *Studies in English Literature, 1500–1900* 40.3 (2000): 413–33.

Rayner, Alice. 'The Audience: Subjectivity, Community and the Ethics of Listening', *Journal of Dramatic Theory and Criticism* 7.2 (Spring 1993): 3–23.

Rebellato, Dan. '"And I Will Reach Out My Hand With A Kind of Infinite Slowness And Say The Perfect Thing": The Utopian Theatre of Suspect Culture'. *Contemporary Theatre Review* 13.1 (2003): 61–81.

Redfield, James. 'Drama and Community: Aristophanes and Some of His Rivals'. In *Nothing to do with Dionysos? Athenian Drama in its Social Context*, edited by John J. Winkler and Froma I. Zeitlin, 314–35. Princeton, NJ: Princeton University Press, 1990.

Rees, Emma L. *Margaret Cavendish: Gender, Genre, Exile*. Manchester: Manchester University Press, 2003.

Reid, Trish. 'The Dystopian Near-future in Contemporary British Drama'. *Journal of Contemporary Drama in English* 7.1 (2019): 72–88.

Reinelt, Janelle. 'Selected Affinities: Bertolt Brecht and Howard Brenton'. In *Howard Brenton: A Casebook*, edited by Ann Wilson, 39–58. New York and London: Garland, 1992.

Revermann, Martin. Ed. *The Cambridge Companion to Greek Comedy*. Cambridge: Cambridge University Press, 2014.
Revermann, Martin. 'Divinity and religious practice'. In *The Cambridge Companion to Greek Comedy*, edited by Martin Revermann, 275–287. Cambridge: Cambridge University Press, 2014.
Reynolds, Simon. *Generation Ecstasy: Into the World of Techno and Rave Culture*. New York: Routledge, 1999.
Rieu, E. V. Introduction. Homer, *The Odyssey*, xi–xlv. London: Penguin, 2003.
Riley, Sarah C. E., Christine Griffin, and Yvette Morey, 'The Case for "Everyday Politics": Evaluating Neo-tribal Theory as a Way to Understand Alternative Forms of Political Participation, Using Electronic Dance Music Culture as an Example'. *Sociology* 44.2 (2010): 345–63.
Romer, F. E. 'Good Intentions and the ὁδὸς ἡ ἐς κόρακας'. In *The City as Comedy: Society and Representation in Athenian Drama*, edited by Gregory W. Dobrov, 51–74. London: University of North Carolina Press, 1997.
Roselli, David Kawalko. 'Social Class'. In *The Cambridge Companion to Greek Comedy*, edited by Martin Revermann, 241–58. Cambridge: Cambridge University Press, 2014.
Rosen, Ralph M. 'Lucian's Aristophanes: On Understanding Old Comedy in the Roman Imperial Period'. In *Athenian Comedy in the Roman Empire*, edited by C. W. Marshall and Tom Hawkins, 141–287. London: Bloomsbury, 2016.
Rothwell, Kenneth S. *Politics and Persuasion in Aristophanes' Ecclesiazusae*. Leiden and New York: E. J. Brill, 1990.
Rousseau, Jean-Jacques. *The Social Contract*. 1762. London: Penguin, 1968.
Rowbotham, Sheila. 'Hopes, Dreams and Dirty Nappies'. *Marxism Today* (December 1984): 8–12.
Ruffell, Ian. 'The World Turned Upside Down: Utopia and Utopianism in The Fragments Of Old Comedy'. In *The Rivals of Aristophanes: Studies in Athenian Old Comedy*, edited by David Harvey and John Wilkins, 473–506. Duckworth: The Classical Press of Wales, 2000.
Ruffell, Ian. 'Utopianism'. In *The Cambridge Companion to Greek Comedy*, edited by Martin Revermann, 206–21. Cambridge: Cambridge University Press, 2014.
Runcie, Charlotte. 'Is this the first ever sci-fi novel?' *The Telegraph* 7 November 2013 http://www.telegraph.co.uk/culture/books/10432784/Is-this-the-first-ever-sci-fi-novel.html
Russ, Joanna. *The Female Man*. New York: Bantum Books, 1975.
Sargent, Lyman Tower. 'Women in Utopia'. *Comparative Literature Studies* 10.4 (1973): 302–16.
Sargent, Lyman Tower. 'The Three Faces of Utopianism Revisited'. *Utopian Studies* 5 (1994): 1–37.
Sargent, Lyman Tower. 'What is a Utopia?' *Morus: Utopia e Renascimento*: 2 (2005): 153–60.
Sargent, Lyman Tower. *Utopianism: A Very Short Introduction*. Oxford: Oxford University Press, 2010.

Sargent, Lyman Tower. 'Utopian Literature in English: An Annotated Bibliography From 1516 to the Present'. http://openpublishing.psu.edu/utopia/

Sargisson, Lucy. *Contemporary Feminist Utopianism*. London: Routledge, 1996.

Schmidt, Paul. 'Observations on Ideal Stage Languages'. *Theater* 26.1–2 (1995): 162–4.

Schonfield, Victor. Ed. *Sun Ra: Intergalactic Research Arkestra*. Concert program (London: Music Now, 1970).

Scott, Sarah. *Millenium Hall*. 1762. Edited by Gary Kelly. Peterborough, Ont.: Broadview Press. 1995.

Segal, Lynne. *Radical Happiness: Moments of Collective Joy*. London: Verso, 2017.

Sellar, Tom. 'A Philosophy Which Knows Its Stage'. *Theater* 26.1–2 (1995): 83–8.

Shakespeare, William. *The Tempest*. 1611. Edited by Alden T. Vaughan and Virginia Mason Vaughan. London: Arden, 2011.

Shaw, George Bernard. 'Preface on Days of Judgment'. In *The Simpleton of the Unexpected Isles*, 1–18. In *The Simpleton, The Six, and the Millionaires: Three Plays*. London: Constable, 1936.

Shaw, George Bernard. *The Simpleton of the Unexpected Isles*. In *The Simpleton, The Six, and the Millionaires: Three Plays*, 19–81. London: Constable, 1936.

Shaw, George Bernard. Preface. In *Farfetched Fables*. 1950. In *The Bodley Head Bernard Shaw: Collected Plays with Their Prefaces*, edited by Dan H. Laurence, 1–18. London: Max Reinhardt The Bodley Head, 1974.

Shaw, George Bernard. *Farfetched Fables*. In *The Bodley Head Bernard Shaw, Collected Plays with their Prefaces*, edited by Dan H. Laurence, 430–66. London: Max Reinhardt The Bodley Head, 1974.

Shaw, George Bernard. *Back to Methuselah*. 1921. London: Penguin, 1987.

Shaw, George Bernard. *Buoyant Billions*. 1948. In *Bernard Shaw: Last Plays*, edited by Dan Laurence. London: Penguin, 1994.

Shelley, Mary. *Frankenstein*. 1818. Edited by Maurice Hindle. London: Penguin, 2003.

Short, Mick. *Exploring the Language of Poems, Plays and Prose*. London and New York: Longman, 1996.

Sidwell, Keith. 'Fourth-century Comedy Before Menander'. In *The Cambridge Companion to Greek Comedy*, edited by Martin Revermann, 60–78. Cambridge: Cambridge University Press, 2014.

Sierra, Horacio. 'Convents as Feminist Utopias: Margaret Cavendish's *The Convent of Pleasure* and the Potential of Closeted Dramas and Communities'. *Women's Studies* 38 (2009): 647–69.

Silver, Arnold. *Bernard Shaw: The Darker Side*. Redwood City, CA: Stanford University Press, 1982.

Simpson, Leanne Betasamosake. *As We Have Always Done: Indigenous Freedom Through Radical Resistance*. Minneapolis and London: University of Minnesota Press, 2017.

Situationist International. 'Détournement as Negation and Prelude'. *Internationale Sittuationist* #3. 1959. In *The Situationist International Anthology: Revised and Expanded Edition*, edited and translated by Ken Knapp, 67–68. Berkeley, CA: Bureau of Public Secrets, 2006.

Situationist International. '"Situationists": International Manifesto'. 1960. In *Programs and Manifestoes on 20th Century Architecture*, edited by Ulrich Conrads, 172–4. Cambridge, MA: MIT Press, 1990.

Sklar, Zachary. 'Foreword'. In Cesi Davidson. *Articulation: Short Plays to Nourish the Mind & Soul*, iii–v. Seattle, WA: Aqueduct Press, 2019.

Slater, Niall W. 'Performing the City in *Birds*'. In *The City as Comedy: Society and Representation in Athenian Drama*, edited by Gregory W. Dobrov, 75–94. Chapel Hill, NC: University of North Carolina Press, 1997.

Smith, Anna Deavere. 'A System of Lights'. *Theater* 26-1 and 2 (1995): 50–2.

Smith, Nicholas D. 'Political Activity and Ideal Economics: Two Related Utopian Themes in Aristophanic Comedy'. *Utopian Studies* 3 (1992): 84–94.

Sommerstein, Alan. 'The Politics of Greek Comedy'. In *The Cambridge Companion to Greek Comedy*, edited by Martin Revermann, 291–305. Cambridge: Cambridge University Press, 2014.

Soper, Kate. *Post-Growth Living: For an Alternative Hedonism*. London: Verso, 2020.

Sparks, Julie. 'The Evolution of Human Virtue: Precedents for Shaw's "World Betterer" in the Utopias of Bellamy, Morris, and Bulwer-Lytton'. In *Shaw and Other Matters*, edited by Susan Rusinko, 63–82. Selinsgrove, PA: Susquehanna University Press, 1998.

Spivey, Nivel. *Enduring Creation: Art, Pain, and Fortitude*. Oakland, CA: University of California Press, 2001.

Stauffer, Devin. 'Leo Strauss's UnSocratic Aristophanes?'. In *The Political Theory of Aristophanes: Explorations in Poetic Wisdom*, edited by Jeremy J. Mhire and Bryan-Paul Frost, 331–51. New York: State University of New York Press, 2014.

Steintrager, James. 'Plato and More's *Utopia*'. *Social Research* 36.3 (1969): 357–72.

Stone Stanton, Kamille. '"An Amazonian Heroickess": The Military Leadership of Queen Henrietta Maria in Margaret Cavendish's *Bell in Campo* (1662)'. *Early Theatre* 10.2 (2007): 71–86.

Storey, Ian C. Ed. and trans. *Fragments of Old Comedy I: Alcaeus to Diocles*. Cambridge, MA: Harvard University Press, 2011.

Storey, Ian C. Ed. and trans. *Fragments of Old Comedy II: Diopeithes to Pherecrates*. Cambridge, MA: Harvard University Press, 2011.

Storey, Ian C. Ed. and trans. *Fragments of Old Comedy III: Philonicus to Xenophon*. Cambridge, MA: Harvard University Press, 2011.

Stott, Andrew. *Comedy*. London: Routledge, 2004.

Sullivan, John. 'Utopia Forum'. *Theater* 26.1–2 (1995): 182–89.

Sun Ra and his Intergalactic Infinity Arkestra. *Space is the Place*. Beverly Hills, CA: Blue Thumb Records, 1973.

Suvin, Darko. *Metamorphosis of Science Fiction: On the Poetics and History of a Literary Genre*. New Haven and London: Yale University Press, 1979.

Switzky, Lawrence. 'Shaw Among the Modernists'. *Shaw: The Annual of Bernard Shaw Studies* 1.31 (2011): 133–48.

Takashi, Melanie and Tim Olaveson. 'Music, Dance and Raving Bodies: Raving as Spirituality in the Central Canadian Rave Scene'. *Journal of Ritual Studies* 17.2 (2003): 72–96.

Tasso, Torquato. *Aminta*. 1573. Edited by Irene Marchegiani Jones and Charles Jernigan. New York: Italica Press, 2008.

Thesleff, Holger. 'Platonic Chronology'. *Phronesis* 34.1 (1989): 1–26.

Thornton, Sarah. *Club Cultures: Music, Media, and Subcultural Capital*. London: Wesleyan University Press, 1996.

Titmuss, Richard M. and Kay Titmuss. *Parents Revolt: A Study of the Declining Birth-Rate in Acquisitive Societies*. London: Secker and Warburg, 1942.

Tompkins, Joanne. *Theatre's Heterotopias: Performance and the Cultural Politics of Space*. Basingstoke: Palgrave, 2014.

Tönnies, Merle. 'The Immobility of Power in British Political Theatre after 2000: Absurdist Dystopias'. *Journal of Contemporary Drama in English* 5.1 (2017): 156–72.

Troxel, Patricia. 'Haunting Ourselves: History and Utopia in Howard Brenton's *Bloody Poetry* and *Greenland*'. In *Text and Representation*, edited by Karelisa Hartigan, 97–103. New York and London: University of America Press, 1990.

Turner, Cathy. *Dramaturgy and Architecture: Theatre, Utopia and the Built Environment*. Basingstoke: Palgrave, 2015.

Turner, Paul. 'Introduction'. In Thomas More. *Utopia*, xi–xxviii. London: Penguin, 2003.

Ubersfeld, Anne. *Reading Theatre*. Toronto, Ont.: University of Toronto Press, 1999.

Ussher, R. G. *Aristophanes: Ecclesiazusae*. Oxford: Oxford University Press, 1986.

Vieira, Fátima. 'The Concept of Utopia'. In *The Cambridge Companion to Utopian Literature*, edited by Gregory Claeys, 3–27. Cambridge: Cambridge University Press, 2010.

Voigts, Eckart and Merle Tönnies. 'Posthuman Dystopia: Animal Surrealism and Permanent Crisis in Contemporary British Theatre'. *Journal of Contemporary Drama in English* 8.2 (2020): 295–312.

Waidner, Isabel. 'Liberating the Canon: Intersectionality and Innovation in Literature'. In *Liberating the Canon: An Anthology of Innovative Literature*, edited by Isabel Waidner, 7–20. Manchester: Dostoyevsky Wannabe Publishing, 2018.

Warburton, Rachel. '"[A] Woman hath no … Reason to desire Children for her Own Sake": Margaret Cavendish Reads Lee Edelman'. *Lit: Literature Interpretation Theory* 27.3 (2016): 234–51.

Webb, Darren. 'Critical Pedagogy, Utopia and Political (Dis)Engagement'. *Power and Education* 5.3 (2013): 280–90.

Wells, H. G., *The Time Machine*, 1895. Edited by Patrick Parrinder. London: Penguin, 2005.

Wells, H. G. *A Modern Utopia*, 1905. Edited by Gregory Claeys. London: Penguin, 2005.
West, M. L. Introduction. Hesiod, *Theogony* and *Works and Days*, vii–xxi. Oxford: Oxford University Press, 1988.
Wherly, Eric S. *Shaw for the Million*. London: Gulliver Books, n.d.
Wilkins, John. 'Edible Choruses'. In *The Rivals of Aristophanes: Studies in Athenian Old Comedy*, edited by David Harvey and John Wilkins, 341–54. Duckworth: The Classical Press of Wales, 2000.
Willi, Andreas. 'The Language(s) of Comedy'. In *The Cambridge Companion to Greek Comedy*, edited by Martin Revermann, 168–83. Cambridge: Cambridge University Press, 2014.
Williams, Gweno. '"Why May Not a Lady Write a Good Play?" Plays by Early Modern Women Reassessed as Performance Texts'. In *Readings in Renaissance Women's Drama: Criticism, History, and Performance 1594–1998*, edited by S. P. Cerasano and Marian Wynne-Davis, 95–107. London: Routledge, 1998.
Wilson, Nigel. 'The Transmission of Comic Texts'. In *The Cambridge Companion to Greek Comedy*, edited by Martin Revermann, 424–32. Cambridge: Cambridge University Press, 2014.
Winkler, John J. and Froma I. Zeitlin. *Nothing to do with Dionysos? Athenian Drama in its Social Context*. Princeton, NJ: Princeton University Press, 1990.
Winstanley, Gerrard. *The Law of Freedom.*1952. In *Winstanley: The Law of Freedom and Other Writings*, edited by Christopher Hill. London: Penguin, 1973.
Wiseman, Susan. 'Gender and Status in Dramatic Discourse: Margaret Cavendish, Duchess of Newcastle'. In *Women, Writing, History 1640–1740*, edited by Isobel Grundy and Susan Wiseman, 159–87. London: Batsford, 1992.
Wittig, Monique, *Les Guérillères*. 1969. Translated by David Le Vay. London: Picador, 1972.
Wohl, Victoria. 'Comedy and Athenian Law'. In *The Cambridge Companion to Greek Comedy*, edited by Martin Revermann, 322–35. Cambridge: Cambridge University Press, 2014.
Woolf, Virginia. *A Room of One's Own*. 1929. New York: Harvest Books, 1989.
Wood, Tanya Caroline. 'Brave New Worlds? The Gender Politics of Margaret Cavendish's Primary and Secondary Realms'. PhD thesis. Toronto, Ont.: University of Toronto, 2001.
Wu, Duncan. Ed. *Making Plays: Interviews with Contemporary British Dramatists and their Directors*. Basingstoke: Palgrave Macmillan, 2000.
Yde, Matthew. *Bernard Shaw and Totalitarianism: Longing for Utopia*. London: Palgrave, 2013.
Zamalin, Alex. *Black Utopia: The History of an Idea from Black Nationalism to Afrofuturism*. New York: Columbia University Press, 2019.
Zamyatin, Yevgeny, *We*. 1921. Translated by Clarence Brown. London: Penguin, 1993.

Zeitlin, Froma I. 'Playing the Other: Theater, Theatricality, and the Feminine in Greek Drama'. In *Nothing to do with Dionysos? Athenian Drama in its Social Context*, edited by John J. Winkler and Froma I. Zeitlin, 63–96. Princeton, NJ: Princeton University Press, 1990.

Zumbrunnen, John. 'Fantasy, Irony, and Economic Justice in Aristophanes' *Assemblywomen* and *Wealth*'. *The American Political Science Review* 100.3 (August 2006): 319–33.

Newspaper reviews and articles

Brain, Ezra. 'Towards a Marxist Theatre'. *HowlRound Theatre Commons*. http://howlround.com/towards-marxist-theatre 15 April 2021.

Bulloch, J. M. 'Memories of Methuselah'. *Graphic*, 1 March 1924.

Coldstream, John. Review of *Sore Throats*. *Daily Telegraph*, 27 April 1988. In Reviews of *Sore Throats*. In *London Theatre Record* 22 April – 5 May 1988, 533–6.

Coveney, Michael. Review of *Sore Throats*, *Financial Times* 26 April 1988. In Reviews of *Sore Throats*. In *London Theatre Record* 22 April – 5 May 1988, 533–6.

Devlin, Hannah. 'Ageing Process May be Reversible, Scientists Claim', *the Guardian* 15 December 2016, https://www.theguardian.com/science/2016/dec/15/ageing-process-may-be-reversible-scientists-claim

Dukes, Ashley. 'The Stage of the Day'. *Illustrated Sporting and Dramatic News*, 1 March 1924.

Finch, David. 'Live Long and Prosper? Demographic Trends and their Implications for Living Standards', 16 January 2017, http://www.resolutionfoundation.org/publications/live-long-and-prosper-demographic-trends-and-their-implications-for-living-standards/

Freebody, Debenham K. 'Back to Methuselah: A Sombre Week of Shaw'. *The Era* 27 February 1924.

Hiley, Jim. Review of *Sore Throats*, *Listener*, 5 May 1988. In Reviews of *Sore Throats*, in *London Theatre Record* 22 April – 5 May 1988, 5 33–6.

Hulbert, Dan. 'Back-To-Back *Methuselah*'. *American Theatre* (October 2000).

Jobson, Baz. 'Bearcubs – 3am – Cadence Sampler', http://www.covertmag.com/2012/06/bearcubs-3am-cadence-sampler/ 4 June 2012.

Lovink, Geert. 'A Speculative Dialogue with Kodwo Eshun', *Telepolis*, 10 July 2000, https://www.heise.de/tp/features/Everything-was-to-be-done-All-the-adventures-are-still-there-3447386.html

Moore, Marcus J. Review of Floating Points, 'Peroration Six'. *Pitchfork News* 5 November 2015 https://pitchfork.com/reviews/tracks/17800-floating-points-peroration-six/

Muggs, Joe. 'Return to the chill-out room: when did ambient music last have it so good?'. *Fact* 9 October 2014, https://www.factmag.com/2014/10/09/ambient-2014-round-up-joe-muggs/

Prasad, Aarathi. 'How artificial wombs will change our ideas of gender, family and equality'. *The Guardian* 1 May 2017, https://www.theguardian.com/commentisfree/2017/may/01/artificial-womb-gender-family-equality-lamb

Ravens, Chal. Review of Lorenzo Senni, 'Sacco Matto'. *Pitchfork News* 29 April 2020, https://pitchfork.com/reviews/albums/lorenzo-senni-scacco-matto/

Sherburne, Philip. Review of Seven Davis Jr. 'Universes'. *Pitchfork News* 16 July 2015, https://pitchfork.com/reviews/albums/20756-universes/

St Félix, Doreen. 'The Otherworldly Concept Albums of Janelle Monáe'. *The New Yorker* 1 March 2018 https://www.newyorker.com/culture/culture-desk/the-otherworldly-concept-albums-of-janelle-monae

Weintraub, Stanley 'GBS and the Despots'. *The Times Literary Supplement* 22 August 2011, http://www.the-tls.co.uk/articles/public/george-bernard-shaw-and-the-despots/

Wilson, Greg. 'Electro-Funk – What did it all mean? Dance Culture's Missing Link'. *ElectroFunk Roots* November 2003, https://www.electrofunkroots.co.uk/articles/what.html

Authorless newspaper reviews

Diss Express, 29 February 1924.
Aberdeen Press and Journal, 14 April 1924.
Gloucester Journal, 15 September 1923.
Nottingham Journal, 20 March 1928.
Sheffield Daily Telegraph, 6 March 1928.
Sheffield Daily Telegraph, 6 December 1924.

Websites

Adebayo, Mojisola. Staff profile (performance page). Queen Mary University of London. https://www.qmul.ac.uk/sed/staff/adebayom.html

Adebayo, Mojisola. Staff profile (public engagement page). Queen Mary University of London, https://www.qmul.ac.uk/sed/staff/adebayom.html

Adebayo, Mojisola. Staff profile (research page). Queen Mary University of London, https://www.qmul.ac.uk/sed/staff/adebayom.html

Complete Works of Margaret Cavendish project website: http://digitalcavendish.org/complete-works/

Idle Women website, https://idlewomen.org/about/

Smith, Andy. 'Plays for the People'. https://www.andysmiththeatre.com/plays-for-the-people

Index

absurdist 50, 60, 61
actors 29, 38, 95, 187
Adebayo, Debo (DJ DeboA) 174, 179
Adebayo, Mojisola, *Plays Two* 174
Adebayo, Mojisola, *STARS* 25, 161, 173–84, 187, 188
  Afrofuturism 176–8
  dialogics 175–6, 181–2
  innovation 174
  music 177–81
Adorno, Theodor S. 166
affect 4, 5, 7, 25, 29, 30, 79, 81, 121, 139, 160, 179, 181, 188
African diaspora 170, 172
Afrofuturism 176–8, 187
afterlife 14, 33, 35–6
Agamben, Giorgio 117
ageing 101, 105–8, 113–20, 126–8
agency, human 9, 25, 40, 46–7, 51, 104, 124–6
Alderman, Naomi *The Power* 94
Aldiss, Brian 19
altruism 60, 171
Amazonian women 67, 81, 94
Ambler, Wayne 50, 62
anachrony 117
anarchistic utopias 37, 67–8, 79
Ancients (in Shaw's *Back to Methuselah*) 114–20
Anderson, Tammy L. 180
animals, in drama 24–5, 45
anti-authoritarianism 42
anti-capitalist 13
anti-realist 43, 54
anti-Semitism 103
anti-utopianism 4–5, 44, 60–2, 102
Appelbaum, Robert 69, 80–1
appetites 33, 45, 46, 57, 88, 186, 188
Archippus, *Fishes* 45

archistic/anarchistic traditions 37, 67–8, 79
Aristophanes 33–4, 38, 77, 88, 96
  Acharnians 40
  The Assemblywomen 22, 34, 40, 44, 55–62, 86
  The Birds 22, 25, 40, 47–55, 57, 87, 123, 186, 188
  class identity 72
  Knights 41
  Lysistrata 40
  political views 41–2, 43
  Wealth 44
Aristotle 19–20, 21, 28
  Politics 9, 37
Arnheim, Rudolf 116
Arrowsmith, William 48
ascetic 9, 24, 88
Asquith, Herbert Henry 109
Astell, Mary, *A Serious Proposal to the Ladies* 69
Astor, Nancy 104
Athens 47, 52, 55, 57
Atlanta Theatre 113
Atwood, Margaret 19
audience 1, 26, 29, 30, 39, 56, 57, 59, 62, 157, 180
Augé, Marc 3–4, 164, 169, 173
Augustine of Hippo (Saint Augustine), *City of God* 33
authors, female 65, 69, 71, 78, 85–6
automatist utopianism 37, 44–7, 135

Baccolini, Raffaella 160
Bacon, Francis 18, 24, 87, 188
  New Atlantis 27, 65, 67, 78, 106
Baggesen, Søren 168, 169
Baker-Putt, Alyce R. 84
Bakhtin, Mikhail 19, 41, 151, 154
Baldwin, James 173

Barrett, David 49, 55
Behn, Aphra
   'The Golden Age' (poem) 69
   The Emperor of the Moon 9, 66
Bellamy, Edward, *Looking Backward* 16, 18–19, 22, 52, 78, 87, 102
Bergson, Henri, *Creative Evolution* 104
Bermuda pamphlets, the 69–70
Bible, the 26, 113, 120, 127
Birmingham Repertory Theatre 111–13
'Black Lives Matter' campaign 160
Blackness 170–4, 176, 178
Blade Runner (film) 178–9
Bloch, Ernst 168–9, 179
Boal, Augusto 173
body, human 118–19, 188
body utopias 24–6, 67, 88, 125, 126, 186
Bogart, Anne 28
Boon, Richard 130
boundaries 61, 84–7
Boyle, Deborah 90–1
Brain, Ezra 189
Branham, R. Bracht 42
Brant, Clare 96
Brecht, Bertolt
   Mother Courage 121
   Verfremdungseffekt 11
Brenton, Howard
   Bloody Poetry 129–30, 143–8, 158
   Greenland 25, 27, 106, 129–30, 132–3, 136–8, 145, 148–58, 187
   and More's *Utopia* 137, 150
   and Morris' *News from Nowhere* 136–8
   ordinary life, portrayal of 152, 154, 157, 158
   The Romans in Britain 150
   Situationism 129, 130, 133–6, 138, 149, 152, 159
   socialism 156–7
   Sore Throats 129–30, 138–43, 145, 146, 152, 157
Brenton, Howard and David Hare, *Pravda* 132
Brooks, Pete 164
Brown, Paul 151
Brustein, Robert 114, 119, 125
Burdekin, Katharine, *Swastika Night* 19
Burke, Kenneth 162
Burton, Robert, *The Anatomy of Melancholy* 65
Burwell, Jennifer 145
Bush Theatre, London 165
Butler, Samuel, *Luck or Cunning?* 104

Cambridge Companion to Utopian Literature 81
Campanella, Tommaso 18, 65, 78
   City of the Sun 67, 106
capitalism 99, 102, 123, 143, 157; *see also* post-capitalism
Carey, John 71, 72–3
   Faber Book of Utopias 81
carnival 24, 41, 67, 151, 154, 187
Cary, Mary, *A New and More exact Mappe of New Jerusalems Glory when Jesus Christ and his Saint with him shall reign on earth a Thousand years, and possess all Kingdoms* 68–9
CAST (Cartoon Archetypical Slogan Theatre) 132
Cavendish, Margaret 22, 25, 65
   Bell in Campo 65–7, 92–6
   biography 70
   The Blazing World 70, 71, 73, 76, 79, 81
   comparison with male authors 67, 96
   The Convent of Pleasure 24, 65, 66, 76, 81, 83, 86–92, 186
   critical reception 71–2

The Female Academy 65, 66, 76,
  82–6
 feminism 77–80
 innovation 97–8
 and More's *Utopia* 83, 88, 90
 Playes 74
 Plays, Never before Printed, 1668
  75, 76
 royalist views 65, 72–3, 87, 93
 subversion of dramatic rules 75
Ceccarelli, Paola 44
Cervantes, Miguel
 Don Quixote de La Mancha 67–8
 Galatea 106
Chalmers, Hero 71, 73, 87
Chase, Karen 107
childbirth, dramatic representation of
  89–90
chorus 38, 39, 48, 49, 53, 59
Churchill, Caryl
 Fen 131
 Light Shining in Buckinghamshire
  131
 Mad Forest 131
 Serious Money 132
 Vinegar Tom 131
city state (*polis*) 33, 35, 37–8, 42, 44–5,
  188
city utopias 24, 25–6, 67, 126, 186
Civil War, English 21, 68, 75–6, 93
Claeys, Gregory 102
class 65, 72, 110, 152
classical utopianism 32–8, 51
Clifton, Glenn 118
closet drama 75–6, 85
'cloud-cuckoo-land'
  (*Nephelokokkygia*) 49, 50,
  52
Cockaigne (Cockaygne), Land of
  14–15, 24, 67, 88
cognitive estrangement 11
Coldstream, John 140
Cole, Thomas R. 107
collectives 57, 92, 94, 101, 155, 157,
  177, 184

colonialism 69–70, 80, 170–1, 172
comedy 16, 18, 19, 20; *see also* New
  Comedy; Old Comedy;
  satire
 in *The Assemblywomen* 56
 in Brenton's *Greenland* 150,
  151
 in Brenton's *Sore Throats* 142
 in critical utopias 54
 Greek etymology 31
 as language 186
 in Margaret Cavendish's plays 76
 in More's *Utopia* 16, 68
 in Shaw's *Back to Methuselah* 109,
  111–12
 slapstick 59
communism 68–9, 146, 177; *see also*
  socialism
 in Aristophanes' plays 40, 57–9,
  60, 61
 in Brenton's *Greenland* 156
 in classical utopias 33
 and George Bernard Shaw 103
Conrad, Christoph 107
conservatism, of Old Comedy 41–3
convents 86, 91
conversation *see* dialogics
Cooper, Sam 135
counterculture 10
Court Theatre, London 111
Coveney, Michael 140
COVID-19 pandemic 27–8, 174
Crates, *Wild Beasts* 45–6, 47
Cratinus 38
 Wealth Gods 45
Crawford, Julia 87
Creative Evolution 99, 101, 104, 118,
  125, 126–7
critical utopias 19, 54–5, 160, 171, 187
cross-dressing 87, 89
Curtis, Simon 148
cultural politics 160
Cyrano de Bergerac, *Comical History
  of the States and Empires of
  the Moon* 23

Dadaists 136
dancing 59, 90, 172, 178–81
Dartington utopian community, Totnes 168
Darwin, Charles 104
Darwinism 107
Davenant, William and John Dryden
  The Tempest, Or The Enchanted Island 66
Davidson, Cesi
  Articulation: Short Plays to Nourish the Mind and Soul 161, 169–73
  re-racing white narratives 170
  time travel 171–2
  use of fantasy and sf 170
  'Voice Lessons' 170–3, 187
Davis, Seven Junior 179
Day, Jessica 88
de Cervantes, Miguel 67, 106
de Guevara, Antonio, *Libro Llamado Menospecio de Corte y Alabança de Aldea* 67–8
Debord, Guy 129, 130, 142, 159; *see also* Situationists (Situationist International); Spectacle, the
  Society of the Spectacle 133–6
'Decolonise the University' movement 160
defamiliarizing 14, 57, 58
Delaney, Samuel R. 54
descriptive 11, 15, 115, 17
desire
  female 79
  hedonistic 24
  human 25, 38, 46
  libidinal 37
  new patterns of 14
  political 8, 97
  sensual 24
  queer 89
  utopian 12, 63, 77, 79, 97, 112, 130, 136, 140, 142, 152, 174, 183

détournement 135–6, 142, 149, 150, 151, 154
dialectics 28, 29, 119, 145, 148, 159, 162–3, 168–9
dialogics 40–1, 162–3, 175–6, 181–2, 187
didactic 5, 20, 43, 63
disability 118, 174
disembodiment 25, 101, 119, 120, 123
dissenting voice 29, 61, 100, 106
D'Monté, Rebecca 96
Dobrov, Gregory 54
Dolan, Jill, *Utopia in Performance: Finding Hope at the Theater* 29–30, 179
domestic violence 138–9
Donawerth, Jane L. 81
Donoghue, Emma 89
dramatic tradition, Western 19–20
dramaturgy 6, 134, 157, 178
Ducasse, Isidore 136
Duke University Press: *Theater* 27
Dutton, Danielle, *Margaret the First* 73
dystopianism 4, 13, 19, 102, 106, 142, 160–1, 184
dystopias 2, 3, 4, 19, 27–8, 106, 124

earnest 16, 18, 20, 55, 63, 77, 123, 128, 186
earnestness 21, 54
eco-communism 177
Edelman, Lee 177
Edgar, David 130, 132
Edmondson, Ricca 114
education 24, 70, 71, 79, 81, 82
Ehn, Erik 30
Elliott, Robert C. 62, 63
Elysian Fields 35–6
Enlightenment, the 102, 125
environmentalism 149, 153
equality, women's 40, 43, 77–8, 94–5, 97
Eshun, Kodwo 181, 183

estrangement 53, 11; *see also*
    cognitive estrangement
Etchells, Tim 169
etymology, of 'utopia' 13, 32
eugenics 99, 100, 104
Evans, Rhiannon 37
Evenden, Michael 113
evil 108–9
evolution, human 104, 107; *see also*
    Creative Evolution
Eyat-Confino, Irene 23

Fabian Society, the 103
fantasy 22–4, 38, 79, 83, 84, 101,
    125–7, 170, 185–8
fascism 102, 103
Faver, Cheryl 28, 161
feasting 36, 50, 59
female genital manipulation (FGM)
    174, 175
female-only spaces 65–7, 73, 81,
    83–5, 89
feminist utopias 19, 54–5, 77–80,
    84–5, 91–5, 97; *see also*
    women
Ferguson, John 34
    Utopias of the Classical World 37
fiction, narrative 14, 15–16, 53–4, 65,
    85, 185, 186, 188
Floating Point (music group) 179
Fourier, Charles 27, 37
fourth wall, breaking of 56, 59
'free love' 25, 146, 147
Friedan, Betty 114
Frow, John 22
Frye, Northrop 150
    Anatomy of Criticism 21, 22
future 3, 6, 21, 28, 30, 40, 80, 97, 101,
    130, 145, 160, 164, 166, 169,
    173, 182, 184, 186–7, 189
futurism 26, 171, 177

Gearhart, Sally Miller 54
    The Wanderground 137
gender equality 40, 43, 77–8, 94–5, 97

Genesis, book of 108, 170
genre 18–26, 38–40, 90, 97, 150
geographies, imaginative 52, 165
gerontology 107, 114, 118; *see also*
    ageing
Giesecke, Annette Lucia 35
Gilman, Charlotte Perkins, *Herland*
    16, 24, 85–6
Goddard, Lynette 174
Godwin, Francis 9
    *The Man in the Moone; or, A
    Discourse of A Voyage
    Thither* 65
Golden Age, The (classical) 14, 21, 24,
    26, 57, 67
golden ages 36–7, 44, 45, 69
Gott, Samuel
    Nova Solyma 65
grate, the (in *The Female Academy*)
    84–5
Gray, Susan 26
Greece, Ancient 14, 22
Greek Comedy *see* New Comedy;
    Old Comedy
green worlds 150–1
Griffin, Christine 180
grotesque 40, 41, 42, 56
Gutmann, David 115

Hale, Piers J. 125
Hall, Edith 41, 60
Hall, Sarah, *The Carhullan Army*
    81, 94
Halliwell, Stephen 31, 43
Harvey, David 16–17
Heddon, Deirdre 167
hedonism 5, 24–5, 187
Henrietta Maria, Queen 93
Hesiod
    Theogony 188
    Works and Days 188
Hesiod, *Works and Days* 36, 37
heteropatriarchy 148, 167, 168, 175;
    see also patriarchy
heterotopias 6, 9, 66, 80

Hiley, Jim 139
Hobby, Elaine 76
Holmesland, Oddvar 97
Homer 26, 88
   The Odyssey 34–5, 36, 38, 47
Homotopia LGBTQIA festival 174
hope 126, 166, 182
   against hope 168, 184
   as commitment 167
   as political position 5
   collective form of 7
   critical 7
   false 160
   utopian 86, 160, 169
Hopkins, Rob 5, 189
Horwood, Joel, *This Changes Everything* 161
Hulbert, Dan 125
human, superior (superhuman) 99, 109, 118, 123, 129, 187
humour *see* comedy
Hurwit, Jeffrey 37–8
Hustvedt, Siri, *The Blazing World* 73
Hutton, Sarah 76
Huxley, Aldous, *Brave New World* 106, 121, 127

Idle Women project 173
Impact Theatre Co-operative 164
individualism 155–6
individuals, importance of 99, 100, 101
innovation 97, 174
interconnectedness 181–2
island utopias 36, 84, 170, 172, 183
Isles of the Blessed 24, 36–7

Jackson, Barry 111
Jameson, Fredric 4, 17, 19, 22, 23, 116, 186
Jankowski, Theodora A. 91
Johns, Alyssa 69
Jonzun Crew (music group) 177

Kavanaugh, Philip R. 180
Kellett, Katherine R. 75
Kendall, Walter 103
Khanna, Lee Cullen 68, 79
Klaić, Dragan 12, 28, 30
Kolmerten, Carol A. 81
kômôidia 38, 42; *see also* Old Comedy
Konstan, David 40, 51–2
Korstevdt, Benjamin 179
Kumar, Krishan 14, 16, 32–3, 67
Kushner, Tony, *Angels in America* 131
Kyle, Barry 138

labour 24, 27, 35, 37, 45, 47, 149
Labour Party 104, 153,
Lamarck, Jean-Baptiste 104, 125
Langner, Lawrence 112
Lape, Susan 41
Largess, Bill 113
Laudien, Heidi 69
laughter 42, 42, 63, 77, 112, 142
Le Guin, Ursula 54
   The Dispossessed: An Ambiguous Utopia 17, 51
   The Left Hand of Darkness 137
   The Word for World is Forest 169
Lenin, Vladimir 103–4
Lenker, Lagretta Tallent 107
lesbianism 89, 91
Levitas, Ruth 17
libertarian 25, 58, 68
Life Force (*élan vital*) 100, 104, 105, 111, 119, 125
Lilley, Kate 78
liminality 66, 92, 95, 96
longevity 105, 109–10, 113–20, 125, 126, 128
Lucian of Samosata 76, 77
   Trips to the Moon 23
luxury 45, 47

MacDonald, Claire, *Utopia: Three Plays for a Postdramatic Theatre* 161, 164–9, 172

Correspondence 167
dialogics 166–7
An Imitation of Life 164, 165
performances 164–5
Storm from Paradise 167–8
male gaze 84, 87
Manuel, Frank E. and Fritzie
 P. 71
Marlow, Christopher 70
Marshall, C.W. 32
Marx, Karl, *Das Kapital* 103
Marxism 105, 134, 157
Mascetti, Yaakov A. 79
May, William F. 116
McGrath, John 132
'Me Too' movement 160
Mellor, Anne K. 77
Menander 32
 Samia 39
Metagenes 24
 Thurio-Persians 45
metatheatre 32, 56, 90
Miéville, China 23
millenarian 67, 69
Miller, Arthur, *The Creation of the*
 World and Other Business
 131
Minois, Georges 126
modernity 22
Montaigne, Michel de, 'On Cannibals'
 (essay) 69–70
Moodie, Erin K. 62
moon, voyages to 9, 23, 66
Moore, Marcus J. 179
morals, inversion of 49
Moray, Yvette 180
More, Thomas, *Utopia* 13, 14–15, 17,
 40, 130, 161
 anti-hedonism in 24
 dialogic structure 162–3
 equality in 77–8
 as essay 166
 geography of Utopia 52
 and George Bernard Shaw 100,
  109, 122, 123

humour in 16
influence on Howard Brenton
 137, 150
older people in 106–7
and Plato's *Republic* 32–3
and plays of Margaret Cavendish
 83, 88, 90
satire in 18, 63
as science fiction 22
sexuality in 58
slavery in 124, 171
'visitor to utopia' 51
Moreno, Alfonso 41
Morris, William, *News from*
 Nowhere 17, 18, 19, 24, 78,
 88, 129
 devaluing of reading in 27
 influence on Howard Brenton
  136–7, 154
 older people in 106
 sceptical voice in 53
 socialism 16, 102, 157
Mosher, Joyce Devlin 75
motherhood 24
Moulton, Carroll 51
Moylan, Tom 54, 160, 187
Muggs, Joe 181
Muldoon, Roland 132
Mumford, Lewis 24
Munk, Erika 29
Muñoz, José Estaban, *Cruising*
 Utopia: The Then and
 There of Queer Futurity 7
music 177–81
myths 24, 26

nakedness 141
narrative modes 53–4
natural world 25
naturalism, dramatic 19
nature 37, 38, 45–6, 67, 70
Nelson, Stephanie 42
neoliberalism 5, 13, 131
Neville, Henry, *The Isles of the*
 Pines 65

New Comedy 32, 39, 40; *see also* Old Comedy
'new world,' exploration of 65–6
New York Theatre Guild 111
Nichols, Peter 60
Nolan, William F. and George Clayton Johnson, *Logan's Run* 106
nomadic 30
nostalgia 35, 106
novel, the 1, 5, 19, 20, 30
nowhere 2, 12, 30, 52, 137, 178

Olbricht, Erika Mae 72
Old Comedy 11, 20–1, 24, 32–6, 40, 46–7, 62, 96; *see also* New Comedy
  animals in 45
  characteristics 38–9
  content of 44
  dramatization in 53
  nature in 37
  origin of utopias in 31
  politics of 41–3, 54
  satire in 63, 77
Old Garrick Theatre, New York 111
older people *see* ageing; Ancients; longevity
oppression, of women 87, 89–90
ordinariness 10, 149, 151, 154, 157, 158
otherness 29, 113, 115, 184
Out of the Woods collective 177, 184

Paloma, Dolores 90, 91
pandemic, COVID-19 27–8, 174
parabasis 39, 53
paradise 34, 35, 45, 66, 67, 79, 149
parados 39
parody 38, 43
Parrinder, Patrick 33
past, the 6, 17, 21, 26, 38, 40, 45, 164, 173, 186
pastoral utopias 31, 34–5, 38
Pasupathi, Vimala C. 93

patriarchy 84, 89, 90–1, 93
Patrick, J. Max 15
Payne, Linda R. 82
peace 40, 43, 45, 49, 129, 151, 180
peaceful 25, 28, 37, 38, 49, 51, 70
Peloponnesian War 47–8, 55
People's Theatre, Newcastle 121
Pepys, Samuel 70
performance 11, 29, 30, 38–9, 66, 85, 90, 159, 176, 179–80
pessimism 168–9, 183
Pherecrates 24, 44
  The Miners 45
Philmus, Robert M. 162–3
Piercy, Marge, *Woman on the Edge of Time* 17, 54, 97, 127
Plato 26, 27, 78
  Laws 37
  The Republic 11, 24, 32–4, 37, 40, 106–7
Platte, Gabriel, *A Description of the Famous Kingdom of Macaria* 65
pleasure, sensory 88–9, 91
'PLUR' (peace, love, unity and respect) 180
poetry 1, 12, 26, 36, 44, 62, 109
Pohl, Nicole 65–6, 67, 81
post-apocalyptic 10, 160, 184
post-capitalism 13, 125, 133, 151, 157, 162
power, female 94–6
Pozzi, Dora C. 50
present, the 21, 30, 40, 47, 145, 159, 161, 164, 172, 173, 179, 180, 187
primitive 35, 38, 44, 52, 153, 155, 187
private 1, 5, 75, 96, 131, 132
  family 58
  finance 103
  life 33, 60
  parts 140
  possessions 57
  property 57, 58, 114
property rights, women's 93

proto-Lacanian imagery 45–6
psycho-sexual relations 142, 144
punishment 70, 100, 101, 124
Purkiss, Diane 96

queerness 6, 7, 74, 89, 91, 174, 177, 184, 186

Ra, Sun 177–8
Rabelais, François 88
  Abbey of Thélème 68, 69
Raber, Karen L. 72, 93
rave scene 178–180
Ravens, Chal 179
realism 20, 26, 39, 54, 178, 188
  capitalist 159
  non- 170
reason 25, 26, 27, 67, 79, 83, 102, 186
Rebellato, Dan 161, 185
récupération 135
Red Ladder (theatre group) 1
Redfield, James 39
Rees, Emma 71, 73
  Margaret Cavendish: Gender, Genre and Exile 74
religion 24, 68–9
Revermann, Martin 43–4
revolution 147, 159
  Russian 102–4
Riley, Sarah 180
Romer, F.E. 52
Roselli, David Kawalko 42, 61–2
Rosen, Ralph M. 77
Rousseau, Jean-Jacques, *The Social Contract* 155
Rowbotham, Sheila 77, 80, 145, 157
Royal Court Theatre 129–30, 148, 151
Royal Shakespeare Company 138
royalism 72–3, 93
Ruffell, Ian 31, 37, 43
Russ, Joanna, *The Female Man* 17, 18, 52, 54, 79, 94, 154

Sargent, Lyman Tower 15, 24, 44, 60, 78
  'Utopian Literature in English: An annotated Bibliography from 1516 to the Present' 81
  Utopianism: A Very Short Introduction 44
Sargisson, Lucy 15, 16
satire 17, 18, 38, 43, 61, 63, 102, 109, 121, 122, 163
sceptical voice 46–7, 53, 58–9, 61
Schmidt, Paul 30
science 101, 126–7, 149
science fiction (sf) 9, 19, 22–6, 127, 170, 177, 178, 187
Scott, Sarah, *Millenium Hall* 69
Segal, Lynne, *Radical Happiness: Moments of Collective Joy* 5
Sellar, Tom 28, 29
Senni, Lorenzo 179
set-design 151
sexual activity 57–9, 61–2, 84, 91, 140–1, 148
Shakespeare, William 89, 91, 150
  A Midsummer Night's Dream 50
  The Tempest 69
Shaw, George Bernard 22, 26, 99
  attitude to the human body 118–19
  Back to Methuselah 25, 101, 104, 105, 107, 108–20, 125, 126, 131, 186
  Creative Evolution, views on 99, 101, 104
  Fabianism 103
  Farfetched Fables 101, 104, 105, 120–4, 127
  Marxism 105
  and More's *Utopia* 100, 109, 122, 123
  portrayal of old age 101, 105–10, 113–20, 125, 126–8
  The Simpleton of the Unexpected Isles 100, 105, 123
  socialism 99–104
  stage productions 112–13, 115

and the superior human
    ('superhuman') 99, 109,
    118, 119
Shaw Society 121
Shelley, Mary, *Frankenstein* 22
Shelving, Paul 115
Sherburne, Philip 179
Short, Mick 162
Sidwell, Keith 39
Sierra, Horacio 91
Simpson, Leanne Betasamosake
    181–2
sincere 18, 101, 122, 125, 126
sincerity 63, 128, 160, 163,
Situationists (Situationist
    International) 129, 130,
    133–6, 138, 147, 149; see
    also Debord, Guy
Skinner, B.F, *Walden Two* 16
Sklar, Zachary 169
Slater, Niall W. 53
slavery 46, 52, 86, 119, 124, 171,
    172–3, 187
Smith, Andy, 'Plays for the People'
    161
Smith, Anna Deavere 28
Smith, Nicholas D. 50
socialism 16, 61, 65, 68, 130, 131,
    156–7
    and eugenics 104
    in Morris' *News From Nowhere*
        102, 103
    in Shaw's plays 99–104, 123
societies, utopian 11–12, 15, 16
Socrates, *The Republic* 26–7
Socratic dialogue 122, 162
Socratic philosophy 33–4
Sommerstein, Alan 41, 42
Soper, Kate, *Post-Growth Living:
    For an Alternative
    Hedonism* 5
soviet bloc 13, 102, 104
space 5, 6, 9, 25, 66, 68, 176, 177–8,
    187
Sparks, Julia 126

Spectacle, the 139–40, 141, 142–3,
    149–50, 153, 156, 157; *see
    also* Debord, Guy
spectator 20, 29, 43, 46, 51, 53, 56, 57,
    58, 61, 90, 112, 150, 160
speculative 19, 58
Spivey, Nigel 27
St. Félix, Doreen 176
Stafford-Clark, Max 129
stage, the 2, 159
staging 85, 112
Stalin, Joseph 103–4
Stanton, Kamille Stone 75–6
state, the 33, 37, 41, 57, 131, 133
state-building 35, 68
Stauffer, Devin 50
Storey, Ian C. 20, 45
Stott, Andrew 151
subjectivity 6, 28, 79, 81, 96, 99, 115,
    116, 134, 135, 155, 156, 167,
    175, 176, 182, 183, 187
Sullivan, John 27
Sun Ra Arkestra, 'Space is the Place'
    177–8
superhumans 99, 109, 118, 119, 123,
    171, 187
supernatural 8, 23, 25, 127, 186
Suspect Culture (theatre group) 161
Suvin, Darko 11, 22
Switzky, Lawrence 119, 124

Tasso, Torquato, *Aminta* 69, 106
technology 23, 35, 113, 134, 149, 153,
    186, 187
Teleclides 44
telepathy 115, 137, 153, 171, 176, 187
temporality 6, 7, 8, 21, 54, 68
Thatcherism 10, 129, 132
theatre 11, 26–9, 132, 159, 159–60, 164
Theatre Guild 113
'Theatre in Crisis' conference 132
Theatre of the Oppressed 173
theatres, closure of (1642) 75–6
Thesleff, Holger 33
time travel 171–2

Tompkins, Joanne 66
totalitarianism 16, 54
tragedy 20, 27, 39, 40; *see also* comedy
Trans rights 160
travel writing 20, 53, 63
trilogy form 138–9
Troxel, Patricia 151, 155
Turner, Cathy 134
Turner, Paul 16

Ubersfeld, Anne 162
Uninvited Guests (theatre group), *It is Like It Ought to Be: A Pastoral* 161
'utopia,' definition and etymology 12, 13, 32, 33, 67
Utopian Studies 12, 17, 31, 81, 189
utopias 79
    anarchistic 67, 68, 79
    archistic 67, 79
    automatist 37, 44–6
    critical 54–5, 160, 171, 187–8
    feminist 19, 54–5, 77–80, 84–5, 91–5, 97
    island 36, 84, 170, 172, 183
    non-fictional 17
    origins 11, 20, 31
    pastoral 34–5, 38
    pre-modern 24
    in prose fiction 53–4, 65, 85

Vieira, Fátima 14–15, 33
violence, domestic 138–9
'visitor to utopia' trope 11, 16, 17, 21, 78, 79, 96, 110
    in Davidson's *Articulation* 171
    in More's *Utopia* 51
    in Shaw's *Back to Methuselah* 114

Wagner, Wilhelm Richard, *Ring Cycle* 112
Waidner, Isabel, *Liberating the Canon: An Anthology of Innovative Literature* 174
war 47–8, 55, 95, 102–3, 121, 123

Warehouse Theatre, London 138
warriors, female 92–4
Washington Stage Guild 113
Watergate Theatre, London 121
Webb, Darren 4, 14, 185
Weintraub, Stanley 103
Wells, H.G. 103
    A Modern Utopia 18, 19, 21–2, 24, 78, 121
    The Time Machine 22
Wesker, Arnold, *I'm Talking About Jerusalem* 131
white narratives 170, 182
will, human 9, 25, 37, 38, 40, 104, 125
Willi, Andreas 43
Williams, Gweno 76, 90
Winstanley, Gerrard 37, 68–9
    The Law of Freedom 68
Wiseman, Susan 84
Wittig, Monique, *Les Guérillères* 81, 94
Wohl, Victoria 42
women; *see also* female-only spaces; feminist utopias
    Amazonian 67, 81, 94
    authors 65, 69, 71, 78, 85–6
    in classical utopias 106
    education 71, 82
    equality of 40, 43, 77–8, 94–5, 97
    oppression of 87, 89–90
    property rights 93
Wood, Tanya 86
Woolf, Virginia 71
World War I 102–3
work 24, 37, 46, 77, 116, 131, 131, 135, 154
Wu, Duncan 145

Yde, Matthew 101, 123
young adult fiction 19
youthfulness 105–6

Zamalin, Alex, *Black Utopia* 176
Zeitlin, Froma. I. 60
Zumbrunnen, John 61

www.ingramcontent.com/pod-product-compliance
Lightning Source LLC
Chambersburg PA
CBHW062217300426
44115CB00012BA/2109